AF600603

FROM COLONIAL TO MODERN

Transnational Girlhood in Canadian, Australian, and New Zealand Children's Literature, 1840–1940

FROM COLONIAL TO MODERN

Transnational Girlhood in Canadian, Australian, and New Zealand Children's Literature, 1840–1940

MICHELLE J. SMITH
KRISTINE MORUZI
CLARE BRADFORD

UNIVERSITY OF TORONTO PRESS
Toronto Buffalo London

Toronto Buffalo London
utorontopress.com

ISBN 978-1-4875-0309-3

Library and Archives Canada Cataloguing in Publication

Smith, Michelle J., 1979–, author
From colonial to modern : transnational girlhood in Canadian, Australian, and New Zealand children's literature, 1840–1940 / Michelle J. Smith, Kristine Moruzi, Clare Bradford.

Includes bibliographical references and index.
ISBN 978-1-4875-0309-3 (hardcover)

1. Children's literature, Canadian – History and criticism. 2. Children's literature, Australian – History and criticism. 3. Children's literature, New Zealand – History and criticism. 4. Girls in literature. 5. Femininity in literature. 6. Sex role in literature. 7. Imperialism in literature. 8. National characteristics, British, in literature. 9. Australian literature – British influences. I. Moruzi, Kristine, author II. Bradford, Clare, author III. Title.

PR9080.5.S65 2018 820.9'3523 C2017-907195-5

This book has been published with the support of the School of Communication and Creative Arts, Deakin University.

University of Toronto Press acknowledges the financial assistance to its publishing program of the Canada Council for the Arts and the Ontario Arts Council, an agency of the Government of Ontario.

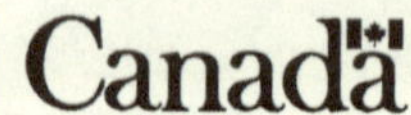

Contents

Illustrations

Acknowledgments

This project was made possible by a Discovery Grant (DP110101082) funded by the Australian Research Council, incorporating an Australian postdoctoral fellowship for Michelle Smith at the University of Melbourne. Kristine Moruzi's research was funded by a Grant Notley Memorial Postdoctoral Fellowship from the University of Alberta. We also enjoyed the support and collegiality of the staff working in literary studies in the School of Communication and Creative Arts at Deakin University.

The research for this project took us to a variety of libraries. We benefited from valuable assistance at the Toronto Public Library, the State Library of Victoria, and the National Library of New Zealand. Thanks are also due to some of the fabulous scholars who are working in the field of colonial girls' studies, including Beth Rodgers, Susan Cahill, Sarah Emily Duff, Kristine Alexander, and Laura Ishiguro. We would also like to offer special thanks to Cecily Devereux at the University of Alberta and Elizabeth Braithwaite at Deakin University.

University of Toronto Press has been incredibly supportive throughout the long gestation of this project. We would like to thank Mark Thompson for helping to bring the project through to publication.

FROM COLONIAL TO MODERN

CHAPTER ONE

Introduction

If we truly want to know what kinds of beliefs a culture holds about its women, the most insightful way to find out is to examine the expectations and ideals it conveys to the next generation. Girls who are located between childhood and womanhood are a locus for a culture's hopes and fears for the future. Since the eighteenth century, books and magazines specifically for the enjoyment and edification of girls have been published. These various kinds of print culture have sought to reinforce, negotiate, and transform notions of girlhood. They also reveal how the cultures in which they were produced imagined girls and the life stage of girlhood. Nineteenth-century literature and magazines for girls were largely ignored in feminist scholarship until the mid-1990s, when girls' print culture became the focus of, most notably, Sally Mitchell's *The New Girl: Girls' Culture in Victorian England, 1880–1915* (1995). Mitchell argues that girls' culture in the late-Victorian period around the British Empire has remained unexamined as separate and distinct from that of women, and she draws attention to the liminality of the period of girlhood, which came to occupy a transitional space between family and married life. Mitchell's foundational work has inspired a significant amount of scholarship on English girls' literature and magazines,[1] which identifies a fairly consistent set of qualities that constitute ideal femininity. Yet

1 See also Lynne Vallone's contemporaneous *Disciplines of Virtue: Girls' Culture in the Eighteenth and Nineteenth Centuries* (New Haven: Yale University Press, 1995), which compares American and British girls. More recent scholarship includes Beth Rodgers's *Adolescent Girlhood and Literary Culture at the Fin de Siècle: Daughters of Today* (Houndmills: Palgrave Macmillan, 2016) as well as our own monographs, Kristine Moruzi, *Constructing Girlhood through the Periodical Press* (Aldershot, UK: Ashgate, 2012) and Michelle J. Smith, *Empire in British Girls' Literature and Culture: Imperial Girls, 1880–1915*.

the print culture of the English girl's sisters around the British Empire has remained unexamined. As a result, the extent to which these models of girlhood were circulated to girl readers who lived in the British Empire has remained unclear.

The growth of white settler colonies throughout the British Empire corresponds with the flourishing of girls' print culture in the nineteenth and early twentieth centuries. While a large number of English books, magazines, and annuals were shipped around the globe to girls in colonial locations, countries such as Australia, Canada, and New Zealand also began to publish their own texts for girl readers as a sense of national distinctiveness developed.[2] This raises additional questions of how English models of girlhood were adopted and modified in different colonial settings and to what extent colonial girlhood exhibited common qualities driven by the transnational aspects of girls' print culture. Though several scholars have examined early children's literature in Australia, Canada, and New Zealand,[3] girls' literature, which was not necessarily restricted to "child" readers, has been overlooked. In total, this corpus of texts constitutes hundreds of books and at least a dozen magazines, such as Canada's *Snow Drop* (1847–53) and *The Canadian Girl* (1930–61) and Australia's *Parthenon* (1889–92). A small number of authors, such as L.M. Montgomery, remain well known and studied today, yet the vast majority of colonial girls' texts are rarely read and have largely been forgotten. Nevertheless, some of these authors for girls, such as Australia's Ethel Turner and Mary Grant Bruce, enjoyed phenomenal and prolific success in both their home countries and England.

---

2 We use the terms "Australia," "Canada," and "New Zealand" for ease of expression throughout this monograph. Canada did not exist as a single entity until Confederation in 1867, uniting Upper and Lower Canada, New Brunswick, and Nova Scotia. The other provinces joined between 1871 (British Columbia) and 1949 (Newfoundland). Similarly, the Commonwealth of Australia became a federation in 1901. New Zealand was part of the Colony of New South Wales until it was declared a Crown colony in 1841.

3 Much of this research has been bibliographic in nature, such as Maurice Saxby's *Offered to Children: A History of Australian Children's Literature, 1841–1941* (Sydney: Scholastic Australia, 1998), Marcie Muir's *Australian Children's Books: A Bibliography* (Carlton, VIC: Melbourne University Press, 1992), Betty Gilderdale's *A Sea Change: 145 Years of New Zealand Junior Fiction*, Sheila Egoff and Judith Saltman's *A New Republic of Childhood: A Critical Guide to Canadian Children's Literature in English* (Toronto: Oxford University Press, 1990), and Joan Weller's "Canadian English-Language Juvenile Periodicals: An Historical Overview, 1847–1990," *Canadian Children's Literature* 59 (1990): 38–69.

We focus on Australia, Canada, and New Zealand because of their similarities as British white settler colonies and because each produced a significant number of publications for girl readers by the early twentieth century. While the case could be made for also including South Africa in this study, we have excluded it because of South Africa's substantially different historical and cultural relationship with the British Empire as a former Dutch colony with a majority black African population and because of the small corpus of children's literature published in English by South African writers in the period.[4] We include some British novels, magazine articles, and girls' annuals in chapter 3, "Girlhood in the British Empire," in order to show how colonial girls were imagined from the imperial centre as both fictional characters and readers and in chapter 5, "Environment and the Natural World," because of the large number of nineteenth-century emigration novels that depicted the process of settlement in unfamiliar natural worlds. Nevertheless, the majority of this monograph is primarily concerned with texts that we define as Australian, Canadian, or New Zealand because they were written by authors who resided in these countries for a significant portion of their lives, or at the time of their authorship of the texts we discuss. This does not preclude the inclusion of texts written by authors who fall outside this definition but who nonetheless made important contributions to the ideals of colonial girlhood operating in Canada, Australia, and New Zealand. As we explain in our discussion of local publishing history that follows, not all of the novels we examine were necessarily published within the respective colonies. Britain, in particular, was the node through which many books for girl readers around the empire had to pass.

The earliest texts for Canadian, Australian, and New Zealand children that were published in the colonies began appearing in the 1840s, which marks the start of our survey. Prior to the 1840s, as we will discuss in chapter 2, "Colonial Girls' Print Culture," few books were published in the colonies, and none for children. Anything being read by children at this time was imported from Britain. The publications of the colonial book and magazine industry of the 1840s signal the gradually emerging interest in the books available to colonial children, with relatively few children's books published throughout the nineteenth century.

4 The first book-length study of nineteenth-century South African children's literature was published by Elwyn Jenkins in 2002. As Jenkins observes, "South Africa never produced girls' writers of the stature of America's Louisa May Alcott, Canada's L.M. Montgomery, and Australia's Ethel Turner and Mary Bruce" (8).

More books began to appear in the latter decades, but it was in the early twentieth century that publishers – both British and colonial – became seriously interested in producing books and magazines for children. We conclude this volume with a discussion of girls' books and magazines published in the twentieth century before 1940. Works published in the interwar period contain distinct representations of girls' education, employment, and modernity that differ significantly from those of works published after the Second World War. Moreover, the model of transnational girlhood that we explore here is predicated on a sense of imperial belonging that began to wane after 1940.

This book argues for the transnationalism of colonial girlhood and colonial girls' literature between 1840 and 1940. Girls' texts can be set within the global processes of print culture production, distribution, and reception, and during this period, the imperial framework is an important one. However, we argue that the culture of girlhood created and reinforced through girls' books and magazines published in Canada, Australia, and New Zealand transcends imperialism to become transnational. These models of girlhood were shared between the settler colonies and certainly contain many similar attitudes towards family, the natural world, education, employment, modernity, and race. Yet these texts also reflect distinct attitudes that emerged out of unique colonial experiences. Transnationalism in this case does not mean a unified model of girlhood that elides national difference. Instead, the transnational model enables difference through the circulation of girls and their literature throughout the empire and beyond. Moreover, this transnational model is inherently more fluid and flexible than an imperial model, which could only ever be based on a British ideal. Instead, as we discuss in chapter 3, we see frequent comparisons between Canadian, Australian, and New Zealand girls and the qualities that distinguish them from one another. The transnational girl who appears in these texts is situated within the local while also responding to models of girlhood that come from other colonial locations, the metropole, and beyond.

Situating the Colonial Girl within the British Empire

For as long as British imperialism was conceptualized as the enterprise of men, women were largely excluded from its history. Literary scholarship and "new imperial history" since the 1980s, however, have widely adopted the perspective that "the very idea [of empire] as well as the building of empires themselves cannot be understood without employing a gendered perspective" (Levine 1). This body of research explores the idea of empire within the frameworks of masculinity, femininity, sexuality, and the experiences of colonized women. It has also sought to identify how women both contributed to and resisted the work of British imperialism and to understand how women's experience of colonial life differed from that of men. Anne McClintock, Laura E. Donaldson, and Ann Laura Stoler, for example, have highlighted the ambiguous situation of white colonial women, who did not possess the formal power of British men but nevertheless exercised some authority over colonized women and men. McClintock influentially describes this tension: "white women were not the hapless onlookers of empire but were ambiguously complicit both as colonizers and colonized, privileged and restricted, acted upon and acting" (6). British women operated as "agents of empire in their own right" as mothers, homemakers, missionaries, nurses, and teachers and through their imagined ability to "civilize" Indigenous people (Stoler 41).

British women were often understood as "guardians of the race" in their reproductive capacity (Ware 37), but they were also configured as repositories of British morality. Jane Mackay and Pat Thane describe the way in which "notions of imperial destiny and class and racial superiority were grafted onto the traditional views of refined English motherhood," thereby "produc[ing] a concept of the Englishwoman as an invincible global civilising agent" (xx). Within imperial discourse, the treatment of British women signified British civility in comparison with "uncivilized" nations that allowed women comparatively less freedom in the areas of education, work, and marriage (Levine 6). From 1834, the Society for the Propagation of Female Education and other major missionary societies sent single women to teach in India, which, Jane Haggis suggests, "marked the beginning of the process of incorporation and professionalisation of women's work" (55). Early feminists then co-opted the ideal of British Victorian femininity as morally superior and enlightened to support arguments for women's movement beyond the home and into a wider range of employments and endeavours in the British Empire. Antoinette Burton demonstrates that, by reconfiguring the ideology of racial superiority, which suggested that the strength of the nation would dwindle if mothers were occupied outside the home, liberal feminists used "racial responsibility" as a strategy to justify their work as "imperial citizens" (*Burdens* 138). Through the civilizing mission, women's work acquired "new and permissible scope, national and imperial prestige, and a secular, world-civilizing status as well" (Burton, "Contesting" 390).

In the latter half of the nineteenth century, women's employment opportunities within Britain, while slowly expanding in scope, remained limited. Emigration to a British dominion or colony, however, provided greater opportunities for female independence and employment at the same time as it increased the population of white settlers. The problem of "surplus" women, who were statistically unlikely to find a husband in England, encouraged female emigration to the settler colonies from the 1860s to the 1880s and substantially increased the population of white women in these colonies. Young women were aided by organizations such as The Girls' Friendly Society, the Women's Emigration Society, and the Female Middle Class Emigration Society, which provided assisted passage and support on arrival to girls seeking employment in Canada, the United States, and Australia.

While colonial spaces justified greater freedoms for some British women, the figuration of women as mothers of the empire encouraged control of their sexuality. Anne McClintock argues that the exaltation of the maternal function of imperial women meant that "by the turn of the century, sexual purity emerged as a controlling metaphor for racial, economic and political power" (47). With increasing numbers of British women arriving in white settler societies, anxieties about miscegenation gave rise to the regulation of interactions between settlers and Indigenous peoples. Such anxieties were propagated in part, as Angela Woollacott demonstrates, by the international circulation of "captivity narratives," which, she argues, constituted "a cornerstone of the widespread view that the colonies were no place for a white woman" at the same time as they justified colonial rule (*Gender* 42). As colonial homemakers, women were charged with upholding the notions of racial superiority on which imperialism rested and with staving off the threat of degradation from all that was situated outside domesticated, "English" space. Jenny Sharpe suggests that racial anxieties, in the Indian context, required the colonial housewife to "guard ... against contamination from the outside" (92).

As scholars have focused on the centrality of the home and family to women's entanglement in and contribution to the British Empire, increasing critical interest has begun to focus on the place of domesticity within colonialism. Philippa Levine suggests, for instance, that "making a new home" was the task assigned to women, "whether planting roses in the withering Indian sun to emulate an English cottage, or braving the winters of the Canadian prairie in log cabins" (8). Most significantly, Janet C. Myers's *Antipodal England: Emigration and Portable Domesticity in the Victorian Imagination* (2009) explores how domesticity was assumed to be the "natural purview" of the English and could therefore be used in service of the empire (9). She outlines the concept of "portable domesticity," through which British women emigrants to Australia "played a critical role as powerful cultural mediators" in the second half of the nineteenth century (10–11). Myers's concept speaks to the broader way in which women's domestic practices in settler colonies reinforced British cultural values and enabled emigrants "to transplant their national identity" (5). While groups who failed to establish a sound domestic life in England were located outside of the nation, in colonial locations such as Australia, domesticity marked the difference between settler and indigene (Myers 8). Similarly, colonial girls' fiction, much of it domestic in theme, also functioned to reinscribe this sense of cultural identity, not through domestic objects but through the production and dissemination of texts that reproduce a British domesticity adapted for colonial settings.

Nevertheless, the co-option of domesticity into the work of imperialism did not ensure that the two ideologies coexisted without contradiction. Diana Archibald proposes that British Victorian texts about the New World demonstrate "how the ideals of womanhood and 'home' promoted by domestic ideology conflict in many ways with the argument in favour of immigration to imperial destinations" (5). British feminine ideals did not conform to masculine notions of exploration, conquest, and adventure, or even to the practicalities of the essential process of establishing a home in sometimes harsh colonial environments. As we shall suggest, such conflicts contributed to the gradual formation of new feminine ideals for young women in each settler colony. Archibald suggests that British fiction continued to insist upon "a British ideal woman" (10–11), which therefore encouraged "the formulation of revised versions of domesticity in the Neo-Europes" and led to "the ultimate formation of the national identities of Canada, Australia, and New Zealand and thus may have contributed to their ultimate rejection of British rule" (10).

While recent scholarship identifies the need for further research in the field of gender and empire, this monograph proposes to add another element of complexity to the critical debate. Colonial women may have enacted power over colonized people who were in the role of servants or employees, but girls in Britain's colonies were subordinated in power terms not only by their gender but also by their age. Levine notes that British imperial thinking commonly conceived of women as "like children, a group apart from men and a group to be defined and managed by men" (6), meaning that girls might be doubly infantilized. Though boys could expect to grow into the role of the white male settler, who Levine describes as "the brave heroic figure of nineteenth-century imperial rhetoric" (6), girls would never occupy this position. While Michelle J. Smith demonstrates how British girls' print culture formulated various roles for girl readers within the imperial project, such as those of future mother of the race, colonial settler, and nurse, girls' print culture from Australia, Canada, and New Zealand has been almost entirely neglected in studies of colonial literature and culture. This corpus of hundreds of novels and periodicals, we argue, offers up the potential to see how girls in these three settler societies were constructed as members of the British Empire, as part of a transnational network of colonial girls, and, eventually, as modern citizens of emerging independent nations.

As children's literature works to socialize young readers into the ideologies that are assumed in a given culture, these texts also document the transformations in how girls in Australia, New Zealand, and Canada were positioned to understand their gender, race, education, environment, and religion and their sense of belonging to the British Empire and a developing nation. Fiona Paisley points out that imperial and colonial race politics were especially concerned with "governing native races and improving the white race, both to be achieved through a focus on the rising generation" (240). While, as Paisley notes, the process of colonization relied upon the transformation, "civilization," or removal of Indigenous children, the girls' texts considered in this monograph pay only occasional attention to Indigenous girlhood, and none were written by Indigenous authors. The implied readers of these texts are girls of British descent, and the small number of works that make Indigenous girls their focus – such as the Australian Mrs Aeneas (Jeannie) Gunn's *The Little Black Princess of the Never-Never* (1905) or one of several fictions that feature Māori "princesses," such as Mona Tracy's *Piriki's Princess and Other Stories of New Zealand* (1925) – reinforce the ideas of the superiority of British ways and the need for Indigenous traditions and ways of life to be abandoned. While Woollacott observes that "much of the scholarship on gender and empire has privileged European women as subjects and slighted indigenous or colonized women" (*Gender* 3), our study necessarily concentrates on the "colonial girls" who occupied print culture in this period, from which Indigenous girlhoods were regularly excluded or presented in caricature.

Transnational Approach to Colonial Girls' Literature

Ideas of girlhood circulating throughout the colonies of Canada, Australia, and New Zealand are undoubtedly based on British ideals of femininity. Yet we contend that the colonial girl is a transnational figure who is made visible through a comparison of the models of femininity appearing in girls' colonial texts. This book responds to the recent "transnational turn" in Australian literary studies, and in literary studies more broadly, in which we look beyond national boundaries to explore the extent to which colonial literature is connected to the world (Jacklin 1). Studies of national literature tend to elide the commonalities that exist among different nations. In the case of colonial girls' texts, these commonalities are the basis upon which we conclude that the colonial girl is transnational in her attitudes and expectations for her future. As Ann Taylor Allen explains, "The underlying assumption of a national history is that each nation – its landscape, its cultural and political self-expression, its rise and fall – is unique and distinctive. But without comparing it to others, the historian cannot assess what is distinctive to the nation and what it shares with others" (95). Similarly, Arjun Appadurai has questioned the idea of a discrete national culture and has argued that the national imaginary is inflected by a series of transnational cultural flows (49). A transnational examination of girls' fictions can identify unifying features of girlhood that would otherwise be missed. The development of a transnational model becomes possible when narratives from different nations are placed alongside one another and examined both for their distinct depictions of colonial conditions for girls and for their similarities.

Other literary scholars have made related claims for the importance of considering national literary history beyond the boundaries of the nation. Bill Ashcroft argues that Australian literature must be considered "world literature," rather than simply an extension of English literature, because of its "institutional exclusion from the English literary canon" (35). This liberates colonial writers from the constraints of "inherited tradition" and confirms their writing within "a system of reception and distribution rather than its identity as an aesthetic production" (Ashcroft 35). The reception and distribution of girls' texts is central to our argument about the transnationality of colonial girlhood. Paradoxically, the elements of the texts that define their nationality – such as their publication, distribution, and reception – are also simultaneously part of the production of their transnationality. To be part of the "transnation," according to Ashcroft, is to be part of "an endlessly mobile cultural phenomenon, a horizontal reality – distinct from the vertical, hierarchical authority of the state" – in which culture "*exceed[s]* the boundaries of the nation-state and operat[es] beyond its political strictures through the medium of the local" (36). Katherine Bode makes a related argument that local practices were important "in shaping colonial literary culture, including the activities of British publishers in that market" (28). The flows of people and, importantly, cultural forms that characterized the British Empire during the nineteenth and early twentieth centuries form the basis of a globalized world based upon networks of language, commodities, and financial interest.

Although globalization can be narrowly defined as a late twentieth-century phenomenon enabled by economic and cultural forces that transcend the borders of the nation state, the complex relationship between the local and the global is "hardly new, and is probably a shared feature of all national literatures" (Huggan 13). The British Empire is central to the formation of a shared consciousness about gender identity, since empires "were critical sites where transnational social and cultural movements took place. These movements took the shape of a triadic relationship, in which flows between colonies were as important as those between metropole and colony" (Grant, Levine, and Trentmann 2). Recent scholars argue that transnationalism is a phenomenon that has been operating for centuries, in which "complex back-and-forth flows of people and cultural forms" complicate the centre–periphery model, which sees "power, commodities, and influence flowing from urban centres to a peripheral developing world" (Jay 3).

The transnational girl subject emerges from white settler colonies such as Canada, Australia, and New Zealand that demonstrated, while also redefining, their imperial connections to England. The model of colonial girlhood envisioned in girls' print culture presents an "imagined community" of girls (B. Anderson 46), based on age, race, class, and gender, who are brought together through a shared understanding of the imperial connection and their determination to situate themselves as both part of young nations and part of the burgeoning empire. As Elsbeth Locher-Scholten notes, the focus of recent studies of women's role in the empire has shifted "from an emphasis on the victimisation of colonised women to an interest in their agency; from blaming western women for the fall of empires to recognising them as supporters of empire or critical-colonial actors; from separating gender issues in metropole and periphery to interactions, contacts and contests between both" (449). These interactions – of texts, people, and ideas – are central to our exploration of colonial girlhood, since transnational girlhood is enabled through the circulation of ideas, people, and commodities such as books and magazines. By including gender as a category for analysis, we propose a model of transnationalism in which the production, distribution, and consumption of girls' texts is situated within global processes of print culture and book history. This model allows us to demonstrate the extent to which girls were able to consume texts written in countries other than their own and the degree to which the ideologies found in those texts were consistent with one another. The models of femininity advocated in girls' fiction suggest how ideologies of girlhood transcend national boundaries.

The female figure is often presented as an iconic representation of empire, "as in Britannia, Lady Liberty, Mother India, and so forth," yet these figures can obscure or even embody "the inequities of gender relations within the nation where political power largely resides in the hands of certain types of men" (Friedman 26). By focusing on children's literature, we will show how girls' print culture offers a more nuanced representation of gender that addresses issues of colonialism, imperialism, nationalism, and transnationalism.

Crucial to the construction of this transnational girlhood is the reiteration of transnational models of femininity. Gender theorist Judith Butler examines the repeatability of gender acts, drawing on Derrida's notion of iterability to assert that gender performativity "must be understood not as a singular or deliberate 'act,' but, rather, as the reiterative and citational practice by which discourse produces the effects that it names" (2). By reiterating the norms associated with femininity in colonial spaces, girls' print culture produces and reinforces a transnational model of girlhood in its pages. Yet, as Clare Bradford warns, "universalising readings that forget the local and the particular in their desire for order and consistency" can produce inaccuracies (*Unsettling* 5). The challenge in this study is to attend to the macro level of girls' print culture while also accounting for the local social, cultural, political, and economic conditions of girls and women and the specificities of girls' print culture production.

Understanding the globalized production, dissemination, and reception of girls' texts is crucial to the development of a model of transnational girlhood. Graham Huggan notes that Australian literature "has always been shaped as much by external market forces as by internal producers and commentators" owing to its "small domestic market with offshore titles that made up the bulk of book sellers' lists" (6). At the same time, the status of English as a global language "presented the possibilities of a market that spanned the world" (Huggan 6). Peter Morton investigates what he terms "the hemorrhage of [Australia's] literary brainpower" between 1870 and 1950 (1), a phenomenon made possible by the colonial networks, shared language, and common customs of Australia and England. Nick Mount makes a similar argument about the Canadian literary landscape, writing that "traffic in literary goods and influences moved more freely across Canada's borders" in the 1880s and 1890s and "like other forms of economic and intellectual traffic was especially fluid across the country's only land border" (13). Luke Trainor points out with respect to major Antipodean publishers (who were also booksellers) of the period that "Robertson and Angus & Robertson of Sydney ... operated in New Zealand, just as Whitcombe & Tombs [based in New Zealand] established a Melbourne office ... reminding us that neither British publishers, nor colonial editions, had a total predominance" (114). In Australia and New Zealand, affordable colonial editions of titles by British and colonial authors distributed by British publishers had a significant market share, but books also travelled between the colonies.

Not only were girls' texts already travelling throughout the British Empire and America but the market for (and marketing of) children's books was increasing. Australian, Canadian, and New Zealand periodicals of the time contain advertisements for girls' books and periodicals published in London and exported to the colonies. Girls were clearly encouraged to purchase, and read, texts from other countries. The shared experience of reading the same texts and the transnational elements of the texts to which girls had access between 1840 and 1940 are important aspects of these works' meanings. The transnationalism of authors and their novels was further reinforced through a book-reviewing culture that promoted at least some books that were produced elsewhere. An examination of the publication, advertisement, and review of girls' fiction and annuals demonstrates the porous nature of national boundaries. Girls' novels were often published by companies with extensive international networks, thereby enabling wide distribution throughout English-speaking countries. In addition, a book was not always first published in the author's home country. The economics of book publication meant that colonial writers, in particular, often made arrangements to have their books published in larger metropolitan cities, such as London, New York, and Boston. L.M. Montgomery's *Anne of*

Green Gables first appeared under the Boston imprint L.C. Page in 1908 and was published later that same year by British publisher Isaac Pitman.[5]

Given the porous nature of the Canadian border, and the significant role played by American publishers and novelists within the Canadian literary market, a book need not have been published in Canada first (or at all) to be discussed here as a Canadian girls' text. Leslie McGrath notes that "several notable British authors of juvenile fiction who travelled to British North America used it as a setting for adventure stories that were read in the colonies" (404). These authors include Captain Frederick Marryat, Robert Michael Ballantyne, Juliana Horatia Ewing, and James De Mille. As Gail Edwards and Judith Saltman explain, the definition of "Canadian" is

> bound up in the particular histories of authorship, publishing, and book distribution [in Canada]. As a robust, indigenous publishing industry for children was slow to develop, children's Canadiana, prior to the mid-twentieth century, necessarily refers not only to Canadian-authored and Canadian-published materials, but also to those titles created for children by expatriates, by non-Canadians who briefly visited Canada, by arm-chair travellers, by foreign illustrators who researched Canadian visual images, and by foreign publishers, all reflecting views of the Canadian hinterland from a distant metropole. Few of these books were directly intended for Canadian audiences. They were written for British or American readers, who gained their first textual and visual images of the perceived Canadian reality through a filtered sensibility. (6)

In Canada, and to a lesser extent in Australia and New Zealand, we encounter girls' texts that were written by authors, often women, who had only limited experience with the countries in which their novels are set. The fact that they would use colonial settings for their novels despite little or no lived experience there speaks both to the attractiveness of these exotic locations for British readers and to the extent to which the ideals of girlhood transcended national frameworks. One reason for this universal ideal was the shared experience of language. This study is limited to Canadian texts published in English, since the shared language is a crucial commonality between texts written for and published in Canada, Australia, and New Zealand.

---

5 See Cecily Devereux's "A Note on the Text" for a detailed discussion of the publishing history of *Anne of Green Gables*.

As the histories of the nascent Australian, Canadian, and New Zealand publishing industries show, all lacked the capacity to produce a large number of titles for young readers until the twentieth century. All three were reliant on the importation of books for young people from Britain, other colonies, and the United States to supplement locally published books and magazines, and most colonial authors depended on international publication and distribution in order to achieve sufficient royalties to earn a living. Yet the movement of girls' print culture around the British Empire was not only because of practical market issues in the colonies. At the core of what made the international circulation of girls' books possible was a belief in the commonalities of white girlhood and a shared world view.

Organization of This Book

The ways in which both literature and feminine ideals travelled across the globe form the basis of this monograph's first section, "Empire and Transnational Flows." In chapter 2, "Colonial Girls' Print Culture," we examine the histories of children's literature to foreground the transnational circulation and distribution of British, American, and colonial girls' texts and to demonstrate the extent to which girls in Canada, Australia, and New Zealand were encouraged to – and actually did – read texts from other countries. Reading surveys in the late nineteenth and early twentieth centuries reflect how girls' reading patterns shifted radically over a period of about twenty years. Between the 1880s and the early twentieth century, with the emergence of a more robust juvenile publishing market, the reading of British and colonial girls changed significantly. Girls in their teens consumed very different books and magazines during this period than their predecessors did. Moreover, by drawing on newspaper advertisements, book reviews, and correspondence columns, we show that colonial girls had access to a wide range of books and magazines from England, and, to a lesser extent, from other colonies and America.

In chapter 3, "Girlhood in the British Empire," we examine British depictions of colonial girls in novels and annuals to show how texts produced in the imperial centre imagined girls who lived in, or emigrated to, Australia, Canada, and New Zealand. We demonstrate how these British projections of colonial girls were freed from some of the traditional constraints of femininity, making them appealing fantasy figures for British girl readers. Yet even as they were positioned as somewhat exotic exhibits of colonial girlhood, these girls remained constrained by traditional expectations of duty and morality. Furthermore, British imperial, racial, and class norms were upheld and valorized by girl protagonists in these texts. In this chapter, we situate these British examples alongside ones produced and published in the colonies to show how local writers were often more concerned with the colonial girl's future role within the nation. These representations of colonial girls depict ideas of empire and imperial belonging in tension with emerging national ideals.

In the second section, "National and Transnational Dynamics," we focus on how these tensions and, in some cases, synergies operate with respect to formulations of family, the natural environment, and race. Across the three colonial locations, girls' fiction most commonly has a domestic setting, with the girl protagonist's contribution to her family – through which she rehearses her future role as wife and mother – at the heart of the narrative. In chapter 4, "The Colonial and Imperial Family," we consider how family is entwined with a transnational sense of belonging in narratives about orphaned or abandoned girls. We examine how unconventional or "transnormative families" enable colonial girls in England to forge new, loving relationships and how British girls can similarly be embraced by adoptive families in Canada and New Zealand. Moreover, these novels charge colonial girls with a key role in fashioning unconventional families and demonstrate how new nations might be adopted as readily as new families.

To white British settlers, the colonies constituted unfamiliar environments that were almost inevitably depicted as threatening, especially to children. Chapter 5, "Environment and the Natural World," considers how colonial girls were situated within radically different environments, and how changing representations of their relationship with the natural world are interrelated with the gradual movement from imperial to nation-based formulations of belonging. From the late nineteenth century, in contrast with the fiction of British authors and early settlers, colonial-born authors begin to find a place for girls within natural environments that were once imagined as hostile and unattractive but came to be strongly associated with unique national characteristics.

In chapter 6, "Race and Texts for Girls," we move from the specificities of colonial environments to the distinct depictions of race in girls' fiction to examine the ways in which race complicates literary attempts to fashion transnational and national femininities. We analyse the somewhat rare and typically problematic Aboriginal, Māori, and First Nations femininities that were incorporated into girls' print culture. There are commonalities in the representations of Indigenous girls, which reinforce Terry Goldie's finding in *Fear and Temptation* (1989) that the literatures of Australia, Canada, and New Zealand demonstrate "uniformity" in their depictions of Indigenous people (6). Nevertheless, this chapter also shows how different colonial histories, and typologies that located "black races" differentially within hierarchies of race, contributed to the variations in how Indigenous girls were incorporated within or excluded from emerging conceptions of national identity within girls' print culture.

Most colonial girls' texts situate Indigenous girls in the past, rather than as part of the futures of young nations. In the third section, "Modernity and Transnational Femininities," we shift our focus to the ways in which these futures were imagined through girls. Chapter 7, "Work and Education," first explores how girls' education was situated within the British Empire before turning to a wide range of fictional texts from the 1860s through to the 1920s in Canada, Australia, and New Zealand to show that while colonial education systems were established locally, they nonetheless reflected common ideas about girls' education and future employment. This fiction typically considers the contribution that girls could make through their education and labour, and the range of texts, from colonial settler fiction of the 1860s and 1870s to school stories of the 1920s and 1930s, demonstrate the changing nature of girls' education and employment. This chapter contrasts settler labour with the educational labour of the school story, which was popularized in England but also inspired colonial authors to adopt the genre for local settings. The movement of the genre around the empire enables us to demonstrate the generic conventions and girlhood ideals that circulated transnationally.

In chapter 8, "Girlhood and Coming of Age during the First World War," we examine girls' fiction published in Canada, New Zealand, and Australia during and immediately after the Great War, which produced a transnational subject that transcended domestic roles and national boundaries. This literature reflects a patriotic fervour that extols imperialist greatness and transnational allegiances alongside a strong national pride, and girls in these texts are encouraged to understand and accept their responsibilities to family, community, and nation in their support of the war effort. Heroic models of femininity encompass both the courage and patience required to keep the home fires burning and the bravery associated with active participation at the front. Texts such as Grant Bruce's Billabong series, Ethel Turner's war-time trilogy, and

Montgomery's *Rilla of Ingleside* contain models of female support for the war that encourage girls to think of themselves as active war-time participants as they also consider their "sisters" in other countries who were similarly supporting the war. Because girls' war-time texts were published, advertised, and distributed throughout the British Empire, girl readers found representations of war-time girlhood that encouraged a global sisterhood, promoted allegiances across borders, and encouraged their participation in national, transnational, imperial, and gender-based communities.

Chapter 9, "Modernity and the Nation," focuses on texts reflecting the changed conditions for women and the ways in which anxieties about modernity appear in fictional representations as well as in the periodical press. We examine the phenomenon of the "modern girl" as she appears in newspapers and magazines and concerns surrounding this figure in Canada, Australia, and New Zealand. We then turn to predominantly post-war fiction, including Isabel Maud Peacocke's *Robin of the Round House* (1918), Grant Bruce's *Golden Fiddles* (1928), and Nellie McClung's Pearl Watson trilogy (1908–21), to demonstrate the transnational similarities among these texts in an era when femininity seemed to be under threat from the new opportunities available to women in terms of work and employment.

Through this comparison of Canadian, Australian, and New Zealand texts published between 1840 and 1940, we develop a new history of colonial girlhoods that shows how girlhood in each of these emerging nations reflects the unique political, social, and cultural contexts of each country, and their differing relationships to the imperial centre and Indigenous peoples, but we also read girls' print culture across national boundaries to identify and interrogate transnational commonalities and differences. This print culture was central to the definition, and redefinition, of colonial girlhood during this period of rapid change. Examining these novels and magazines shines a light into neglected corners of the literary histories of these three nations. More importantly, their analysis in the chapters that follow also strengthens our knowledge of femininity in white settler colonies, which has typically been theorized and explained with little attention to the next generation of women – girls – and their socialization through print culture.

SECTION ONE

Empire and Transnational Flows

CHAPTER TWO

Colonial Girls' Print Culture

It is curious to compare the taste of the modern girl with that of the girl of twenty years ago; fashion in reading has changed as greatly as fashion in dress, and it must be confessed for the worse.

–Florence B. Low, "The Reading of the Modern Girl" (1906)

In Florence B. Low's 1906 *Nineteenth Century and After* article, "The Reading of the Modern Girl," about the change in girls' reading habits, she reflects a contemporary anxiety about the books and magazines available to girls, and how the emergence of popular girls' culture has produced materials that look remarkably different from those of the mid to late nineteenth century. She laments the absence of Charles Dickens and Elizabeth Gaskell and bemoans novels written by "second-rate" authors (Low 278). These comments, by someone who nostalgically recalls the literature of her youth, demonstrate the extent to which the production and distribution of girls' fiction had changed by the beginning of the twentieth century. Although her comments pertain specifically to British book production, the colonial girls' reading experience is remarkably similar, reflecting the emergence of British and colonial girls as a market for new books and magazines. Understanding the types of reading materials available to colonial girls, and the degree to which British and colonial texts travelled across time and space, is central to the model of transnational girlhood that we develop in this book. This chapter examines how, when, and where books from British, American, and colonial writers were referenced – particularly in advertisements, book reviews, and correspondence columns – to show that colonial girls were encouraged to purchase and read texts from other countries as well as those written by local authors, even if they were originally published abroad.

Literary histories in Canada, New Zealand, and Australia tend to be critical of the necessity of colonial authors' publishing with London publishers, arguing that this meant writers had to adapt to British expectations. Yet "writers often preferred to seek foreign publication because it was advantageous to do so" (Bones 867). The first novel published by a woman writer in Australia was Anna Maria Bunn's *The Guardian* in 1838, and the first locally produced Australian children's book, Charlotte Barton's *A Mother's Offering to Her Children*, soon followed in 1841. These pioneering books, as Patricia Clarke notes, were printed in the offices of newspaper publishers (Bunn's by *The Colonist* and Barton's by the *Sydney Gazette*), and the costs were most likely borne by the authors themselves (11). It became typical for novels to be published in England, however, even in this early period, as evidenced by Mary Theresa Vidal's *Tales for the Bush* (1845), Catherine Spence's *Tender and True: A Colonial Tale* (1856), and Maud Jean Franc's Sunday-school books in the 1860s. It was not until the 1880s that local newspapers and periodicals started to feature women's and children's columns and pages that afforded Australian women writers the opportunity to earn a living by their writing locally. Women also began to establish their own publications, such as Louisa Lawson's successful *Dawn* (1888–1905) and Maybanke Susannah Anderson's *Woman's Voice* (1894–5).

Yet book publication for Australian writers rested largely in the hands of British publishers throughout the colonial period. The Publishers Association of Great Britain, formed in 1896, which functioned as a cartel, regulated book prices in settler societies including Canada, New Zealand, South Africa, and Australia. Richard Nile and David Walker argue that, as a result, it was more efficient for the local book trade in Australia to act as importers and retailers rather than as publishers who sought out local literary talent (8). Australians primarily bought books produced in Britain until well into the twentieth century and, despite the country's small population, were the greatest single overseas market for British books (Nile and Walker 10). At the close of World War I, increases in the price of materials required to produce books, such as paper and metals, and the popularity of expensive hard-covered books "had the effect of reasserting British hegemony in the Australian trade" (Nile and Walker 7). Even by the end of World War II, less than fifteen per cent of books sold in Australia were published in Australia (Lyons xviii).

While the dominance of British publishers discouraged the emergence of local firms, the first major Australian publishing house, Angus & Robertson of Sydney, was founded in 1888. Louise Mack's *Teens: A*

Story of Australian Schoolgirls (1897), the first Australian girls' school story, was also the publishing house's first novel to be published in Australia. It went on to publish children's classics such as Norman Lindsay's *The Magic Pudding* (1918) and the illustrated works of May Gibbs. Brenda Niall argues that locally produced children's literature "does not properly begin until the 1890s, when Australian writers displaced the hastily-scribbling travellers and the stay-at-home romancers" (1). From this decade, as Heather Scutter observes, there was also "a remarkable and culturally specific flourishing of girls' romances and domestic tales" (298). The establishment of a Melbourne branch of the English publisher Ward, Lock & Co. in 1884 encouraged the development of local writers for the youth market. The publisher went on to offer contracts to both Ethel Turner and Mary Grant Bruce, who became the leading writers of Australian girls' fiction, and later added other writers for girls to its juvenile list, including Lilian Turner, Lillian Pyke, Vera G. Dwyer, and Jean Curlewis (Ethel Turner's daughter).

Nevertheless, though many Australian writers for young people, and for girls specifically, found an avenue for their fiction through Ward, Lock & Co., the publication of the books in London ensured that they had to cater to a dual readership. Niall explains that, "for much of the twentieth century and all of the nineteenth century, the British child had to be taken into account" by Australian writers (2). In practice, the most popular of these Australian authors were also writing for girls in other parts of the empire. The Canadian *Bookseller and Stationer* includes an advertisement for Ethel Turner's *Three Little Maids*, for example ("The Publishers' Syndicate" 9). A December 1900 reviewer in that same magazine comments that Turner's novel "will undoubtedly prove the most popular girl's story published in this country in recent years. Miss Turner has made an excellent name in England and is now recognized as the literary successor of Louisa M. Alcott" ("Books and Periodicals" 13). The most fascinating element of this description is that it elides Turner's Australian heritage and instead connects her to British and American traditions. Monthly school magazines were a unique Antipodean publishing phenomenon that answered a perceived need for nation-based educational reading, and one of the few types of print culture that did not consider secondary audiences in Britain. These included South Australia's *Children's Hour*, which began publication in 1889, and Victoria's *School Paper*, in 1896 – whose articles were often reproduced in the New Zealand *School Journal* (we discuss both publications in chapter 8) – though they often contained substantial British content.

New Zealand also imported most of its books from Britain, as well as from its colonial neighbour, Australia. By the turn of the century, Australia's population had reached approximately 4 million people, compared with 1 million in New Zealand (Dunlap 48). A much smaller market made the logistics of a local book trade more difficult and less profitable, and as a result, the total number of New Zealand children's books published prior to 1940 is likely fewer than 150 books in total.[1] Betty Gilderdale, who has compiled the only comprehensive account of New Zealand children's books in this period, notes that the first children's title to be published was Edward Tregear's *Fairy Tales and Folklore of New Zealand and the South Seas* by Lyon & Blair in 1891 ("Children's Literature" 529). Whitcombe & Tombs released its first children's book, *Maori Fairy Tales*, by Johannes Carl Andersen, in 1908. Like Australia's Angus & Robertson, Whitcombe & Tombs was able to compete against British publishers because it was also a printer and bookseller, and it went on to become the dominant New Zealand children's book publisher in the 1920s. The majority of texts published for young readers in New Zealand prior to 1950 were actually educational books, which Whitcombe & Tombs specialized in producing (Price 144). Given the ready flow of British children's periodicals across the empire, the only examples of magazines published for young readers in New Zealand were related to school readerships, such as the New Zealand Department of Education's *School Journal*, first published in 1907.

While Ward, Lock & Co. brought the stories of a large number of Australian writers for girls to British readers, the only New Zealand author for girls who was contracted to its list was Auckland's Isabel Maud Peacocke, whose first book, *My Friend Phil*, was published in 1915. In addition to Peacocke's twenty-two books, Phillis Garrard's three Hilda books (published between 1929 and 1938) and some of Edith Howes's fairy books for younger readers are among the only girls' books by New Zealand authors to be published internationally.[2] As Gilderdale points out, international publication was an important source of royalties for New Zealand authors ("Children's Literature" 531). Yet, as in the case of Peacocke, publishing in Britain could mean that titles were "sold out" before copies even reached their home country (Gilderdale, "Children's

1 Gilderdale's *A Sea Change* lists around 150 titles, but a number of these were written by British authors and published in Britain.

2 The Hilda books were published by Blackie & Son, and Edith Howes published a number of titles with Cassell & Co. and Ward, Lock & Co.

Literature" 532), and the authors were, consequently, little known in New Zealand. Peacocke was widely championed and reviewed in Australian newspapers throughout her career. On the publication of her first novel, in an article syndicated in dozens of regional newspapers, she is favourably compared with Ethel Turner (*My Friend Phil* 6). Her association with Ward, Lock & Co. is seen as part of the publisher's work in bringing "Australasian authors" "to the world of book readers," indicating a willingness to see New Zealand fiction as intimately tied to Australian fiction (*My Friend Phil* 6). The slippage between the literature of the two nations is evident in a South Australian newspaper's list of forthcoming books for the Christmas of 1913, entitled "Books by Australian Authors," which includes titles by Mary Grant Bruce, Lilian Turner, Vera G. Dwyer, and Edith Howes, who has "of New Zealand" inserted in brackets after her listing for *Maori Land Fairy Tales* (4).

As in New Zealand, the production of books and periodicals in Canada was limited. In the years prior to Confederation in 1867, book publishing in Canada was, as Carole Gerson explains, "seldom financially viable" (*Canadian Women* xv). This literary history is complicated by the presence of both French and English authors. As Coral Ann Howells and Eva-Marie Kröller point out, "one striking feature of Canada's literary history is that it has always been a fractured discourse, notoriously difficult to define along chronological or national lines" (2). Claude Potvin notes that only fifty-one French-Canadian children's titles were published before 1920. Similarly, historian Neil Sutherland observes that "in the early years of the [twentieth] century, many youngsters found reading materials very hard to come by. Many families, even amongst those who could afford them, had no books other than a bible, a catechism, and other religious material" (11). Children's pages of newspapers and magazines would, as a consequence, have been eagerly consumed.

With few Canadian publishers, English-Canadian authors sought publishing venues in London, New York, or Boston. Foreign publications – American, British, and French – "satisfied much of the market for books and magazines, leaving domestic publishers at a disadvantage" (Distad 293). The literary culture in nineteenth-century Canada was not sufficiently substantial to materially support domestic authorship on a large scale, especially since the Canadian publishing industry found it less expensive to reprint familiar English or American books than to support new Canadian authors. Moreover, the inadequate protection for books published in Canada meant it was smarter to first publish in New York or London, since "Americans preferred to pirate Canadian-authored work than to pay for it" (Gerson, "Literature" 100). As a consequence, "few authors of children's literature, born or resident in what is now Canada, found domestic publishers for their work" (McGrath 404). Even by the turn of the twentieth century, "most Canadian authors ... still had to find publishers abroad" (McGrath 407).

Although the majority of texts read by Canadian girls between 1840 and 1940 would have come from elsewhere, Canadian texts were published. Susanna Moodie and her sister Catharine Parr Traill were among the earliest Canadian writers for children. Traill is best known for *Canadian Crusoes: A Tale of the Rice Lake Plains* (1852), the first Canadian novel for children.[3] Two children's magazines published in Montréal, the *Snow Drop* (1847–53) and the *Maple Leaf* (1852–4), were the first Canadian periodicals for children, but they were not commercially successful, and the majority of their content came from British and American sources (Gerson, *Canadian Women* 77). Mid-Victorian novels, such as Margaret Murray Robertson's *Shenac's Work at Home: A Story of Canadian Life* (1866) and Agnes Maule Machar's *Katie Johnstone's Cross: A Canadian Tale* (1870), contain common plots where the girl protagonist bravely withstands periods of hardship (Waterston, *Children's* 113).

The domestic market for children's books in Canada remained relatively small prior to the First World War, with most Canadian publishers acting as distributors for American and British firms (Edwards and Saltman 32). Two of the most popular books around the turn of the century, Margaret Marshall Saunders's *Beautiful Joe* (1893) and Montgomery's *Anne of Green Gables* (1908), were first published in the United States. During this period, a number of British and American publishing houses opened branches in Toronto. They distributed books for their parent companies and for other foreign publishers, as well as publishing original Canadian content. As a consequence, "many Canadian-authored and illustrated books published in Canada had a smaller market and reached a more limited audience than their British and American counterparts, while Canadian authors who sought publication outside Canada faced obstacles in articulating nationalist

3 Although some writers, like Traill and Moodie, were able to make some money, their limited Canadian success was largely owing to their popularity as English authors who were able to capitalize on their renown to obtain further contracts in Canada and in London. Gerson notes, however, that although Traill's juvenile fictionalized survival guide, *Canadian Crusoes: A Tale of the Rice Lake Plains* (1852), was successful in both Britain and the United States, "its author's earnings were paltry" ("Literature" 97).

themes and images" (Edwards and Saltman 33). The children's periodicals market proved to be a more lucrative venue for Canadian children's authors, many of whom wrote for the major British and American juvenile periodicals (particularly *St Nicholas Magazine* and *The Youth's Companion* – both American) from 1870 onwards. As Carole Gerson observes, "In the pages of these international magazines, English-speaking children around the world read stories and poems" authored by Canadians (*Canadian Women* 80).

The importance of empire to discussions of colonial girls' print culture cannot be overstated. From about 1880 onwards, and as the market for children's literature became increasingly gendered, publishers took advantage of imperial networks to develop their global reach and attract buyers. Simon J. Potter explains that "diverse connections bound 'core' to 'periphery', but also forged links between each of the settler colonies, creating more complex webs of communication than has previously been acknowledged" ("Communication" 191). While Potter sees the "sharing of news" as crucial to the development of these communication networks, Alison Rukavina develops a different trajectory related to the book trade. British publishing houses, which had financial and cultural capital but lacked knowledge of the overseas markets, initially co-operated with colonial and foreign firms, but as they gradually entered these new markets and gained more experience, they were "increasingly more likely to compete for a share of the international market rather than work with colonial and foreign businesses" (Rukavina 6–7). As a consequence, major children's publishing houses, such as Cassell & Co., Ward, Lock & Co., and Blackie & Son, established offices in colonial cities like Toronto and Melbourne.

By the early twentieth century, publishing houses increasingly sought to capitalize on the wide readership found in the colonies. Richard White and Hsu-Ming Teo argue that British publishers had come to think of the Australian market as their own, since it was their largest colonial market at this time: "British book publishers fostered a view of the Australian market as a dumping ground for remaindered British books sold at vastly discounted prices, knowing they spoke to an Australian audience that shared the same imaginative geography and social or imperial values" (345–6). In contrast, British publishers in Canada encountered much more competition from American publishers.

In the 1906 Ontario Library Association's *Catalogue of Children's Books Recommended for Public Libraries,* for example, fiction from British, Canadian, and American publishers is listed, with the majority of publications being from non-Canadian sources. Although Australian books were occasionally reviewed in the Canadian press, no Australian writers appear on the list. Instead, it focuses on British, American, and Canadian texts. Notable books for girls on the list include three Susan Coolidge novels (*Eyebright*, *The Barberry Bush*, and *A Little Country Girl*), several of Frances Hodgson Burnett's novels (including *Little Lord Fauntleroy*, *Sara Crewe*, and *A Little Princess*), and Louisa May Alcott's *Little Men*, *Little Women*, *Eight Cousins*, and *Under the Lilacs*. The list's major British writers for girls include Evelyn Everett-Green, Juliana Ewing, Mary Molesworth, Evelyn Sharp, Annie S. Swan, and Charlotte Yonge. The Canadian market was inevitably more multifaceted because it had access to both British and American publications, even though this meant it could be difficult for Canadian writers to get published in Canada.

The Ontario Public Library's recommendations include few genre writers for girls. L.T. Meade is not listed, for instance, and neither is Bessie Marchant, despite the growing popularity of girls' adventure fiction. As Jeffrey Richards writes of Britain, "From the middle of the nineteenth century to the middle of the twentieth imperialism was the dominant national ideology, transcending class and party divisions" (2). Adventure fiction for boys emerged much earlier, with Ballantyne and others publishing in the 1850s and 1860s, but girls' adventure fiction began to appear only around the turn of the twentieth century. While the boys' adventure fiction of the time was typically linked to popular ideas of imperialism, in which "empire, crown, 'race', armed forces and nation became synonymous," it also came to define a particular model of masculinity based on sportsmanship, chivalry, and patriotism (J. Richards 2). The later appearance of girls' adventure fiction "speaks not only about the development of literary genres for the girl reader, but also about the place constructed for girls within the Empire in response to British imperial anxieties" (Smith 85). J.S. Bratton observes that the writers of fiction for girls were being asked not only to "maintain the old values" of the nineteenth century but also to "offer a more modern standard of activity for girls" that included "the sterner face of pioneering and imperialist motherhood" demanded by the new models of femininity required by the imperial project (197).

One such example is Marchant's *A Heroine of the Sea* (1903), set on the west coast of Canada, in which the female protagonist, Maudie, is an active, adventurous girl who lacks basic domestic skills and feels that such proficiencies are less important than her ability to contribute to the household income through fishing. As the narrator explains,

> If anyone had been so bold as to suggest that [Maudie's] time would be more profitably spent in looking after the affairs of home, she would probably have laughed them to scorn, declaring that any stupid could run a house and cook food, but that it took a person with brains to tempt the wily otter to its doom, or secure a good haul of halibut and herring. (Marchant, *Heroine* 9–10)

Maudie works as hard as any of her brothers and is content to perform this labour, but the reader understands this is because she "had never known any other kind of life than her present hard-working existence" and has no female role model to emulate (Marchant, *Heroine* 10). Only her older brother Jim recognizes that Maudie, in her "almost uncivilized condition," will never be able to marry an appropriate man if she fails to develop some suitable feminine graces (Marchant, *Heroine* 19). He hires a woman, Ella Neal, to guide Maudie in her transformation. Although her fishing skills are more than suitable for her role as a contributing member of the family, they are unsatisfactory for her future roles as a wife and, eventually, as a mother.

Initially disdainful of Ella's feminine skills, Maudie eventually comes to appreciate her ability to make a house into a home. Domestic skills may not be especially difficult, but, as Ella explains, "It requires a lot of patience, though, to keep on doing humdrum work of that sort for the good of other people when one would so much rather be pleasing one's self in some other way" (Marchant, *Heroine* 35). The idea of sacrifice is central to definitions of girlhood in girls' texts throughout this period, in which female protagonists are often asked to forgo their desires for the benefit of the family. Anne of Green Gables, for instance, gives up her education in order to help Marilla after Matthew dies. In Isabel Maud Peacocke's *Brenda and the Babes* (1927), Brenda's mother must give up writing when it causes her to neglect her family duties, as we discuss in chapter 7. In *A Heroine of the Sea*, Maudie is transformed after her brother is injured and Ella's feminine skills prove vital in saving her brother's life. Maudie yearns to become "a womanly woman, a graceful, gentle creature, as wise as Solomon on all matters connected with domestic comfort and the making and wearing of dainty array" (Marchant, *Heroine* 147). With a new wardrobe and enhanced domestic skills, she develops "into a gracious and noble woman" who willingly takes on the responsibility of keeping the home together and means to do it "to the very best of her ability" (Marchant, *Heroine* 220, 254). The ability and the willingness to transform a house into a home is a key facet of colonial life. While the girls in adventure fiction have exciting escapades, they must also demonstrate their commitment to settling an untamed land and transforming the colonial location into a model home in which future generations of colonial children could be raised as healthy, happy, and prosperous citizens.

The success of adventure fiction like Marchant's throughout the British Empire was based on the assumption that readers from England and from white settler colonies were homogenous, a point to which we return in more detail in the next chapter. This implicit assumption is based on the reality that British publishers made minimal, if any, attempts to customize the contents of their publications, with the result that a British girls' periodical could be easily sold throughout the empire. Similarly, fiction for British girls would appeal to girls from Australia, Canada, and New Zealand. Although girls' magazines occasionally made explicit reference to their colonial readerships, the majority of the content was aimed at British girl readers. This is not to say that these texts failed to include colonial content. The *Girl's Own Paper*, for example, actively encouraged healthy working-class girls to emigrate by including stories and informational articles about life in the colonies. The Girls' Friendly Society, an organization designed to provide training and support to working-class girls, produced a quarterly publication, *Friendly Leaves*, about emigration opportunities. At the turn of the twentieth century, adventure fiction featuring colonial girls began appearing more frequently in girls' magazines such as *The Girl's Realm*. British texts for girls were highly interested in the colonies, with timing that coincided with the height of imperial expansion from about 1880 until the advent of the First World War.

Colonial Girls' Reading

Relatively few British or colonial texts were written and published explicitly for girls in the middle decades of the nineteenth century. Only as the children's book publishing market became increasingly gendered in the 1880s and 1890s were more books and magazines being published especially for girls. As a consequence, estimating the extent and range of British girls' reading, much less that of colonial girls, can be difficult. One of the few nineteenth-century explorations of British girls' reading was published by Edward Salmon, who examined the books available to girls in the 1886 "What Girls Read." He explains that "girls ... in recent years have been remarkably favoured in the matter of their reading. They cannot complain, with any justice, that they are ignored in the piles of juvenile literature laid annually upon the booksellers' shelves" (515).

Salmon's comments refer to additions to the girls' book and magazine markets of the 1870s and early 1880s, with recommendations including *Every Girl's Magazine* (1878–87) and the *Girl's Own Paper* (1880–1954) as well as British and American authors including Louisa May Alcott, Mary Mapes Dodge, Anne Beale, Anna Sewell, Elizabeth Wetherell, L.T. Meade, and Charlotte Yonge (Salmon 515).[4]

Salmon's review signals the shift by publishers to produce more texts written specifically for girls. The results of a survey of girls' reading choices conducted by Charles Welsh in 1884 suggest that, while girls were still reading some classic texts, such as those by Charles Dickens and Sir Walter Scott, they were also reading more girls' fiction. In the responses of over a thousand British schoolgirls ranging in age from eleven to nineteen, girls identified their favourite authors, writers of fiction, and magazines. The most popular authors, by a large margin, were not traditional girls' authors. Instead, Charles Dickens placed first (with 355 votes) and Sir Walter Scott placed second (with 248). The first domestic fiction novelist on the list is Charlotte Yonge (with one hundred votes), and she would not primarily have been considered a girls' novelist, although girls would have read her fiction. The girls may have been listing authors that they felt would receive teacher approval, rather than those that they were actually reading. As Salmon notes, the absence of any of the "recognised writers for girls" is somewhat surprising (528). Although Elizabeth Wetherell (fifty-six votes), Hesba Stretton (twenty-seven), Grace Aguilar (twenty-three), and Louisa May Alcott (fourteen) do appear on the list, they receive relatively low rankings.

Perhaps a more genuine indication of girls' reading habits appears in the list of favourite books, with Alcott's *Little Women* (1868) appearing in seventh place (twenty-one votes), after *Westward Ho!* (1832) (thirty-four votes) and Wetherell's *The Wide, Wide World* (1852) (twenty-nine votes) in first and second positions respectively. Other notable children's books, which were more likely to have been read by girls, include Yonge's *The Daisy Chain* (1856), Stretton's *Little Meg's Children* (1868), Alcott's *Good Wives* (1869), and Mrs O.F. Walton's *Christie's Old Organ* (1874). With the exception of four Americans – Alcott, Wetherell, Mark Twain, and Harriet Beecher Stowe – the list is otherwise entirely British. Unsurprisingly,

4 Susan Warner published under the pseudonym of "Elizabeth Wetherell," which is the name by which she generally appears in the press during this period. We refer to her as Wetherell throughout.

given the limited scope of colonial children's publications in the 1880s, no colonial texts appear on this list of favourites.

Just as Salmon was interested in girls' reading choices, so too were writers in the Australian press, although no equivalent survey exists. Instead, in the 1870s, articles concerning girls' reading begin to appear. For example, "The Books Girls Read," reprinted from the British *World* newspaper, was published in the *Sydney Morning Herald* on 7 January 1878. In this article, the author laments the "melancholy" sight of girls, "mere children in years," who are "devouring debasing novels" that feature unfaithful and irreligious women and men ("Books Girls Read" 3). This piece was reprinted frequently over the following months in various Australian newspapers, suggesting that editors felt their readers would find the sensational article of interest.[5] This anxiety about British women's reading habits was a common phenomenon in the nineteenth century, as Kate Flint explains, because, while reading was essentially a "private activity," it had "social implications" caused by the experiences of reading aloud and "sharing tastes, values, interests, [and] narratives" (4). The breadth of the article's reprinting throughout Victoria, Tasmania, New South Wales, and Queensland suggests the potentially widespread concern about girls' reading choices during this period and helps to explain the belief that there was a need for more books targeted directly at girls.

The rise in girls' book publishing in the 1880s prompted an 1885 article in *The Australasian*, in which "Humming Bee" discusses "A Parcel of Girls' Books" that she has recently borrowed.[6] In this "great pile of juvenile literature," she can find only one "old friend," the American Louisa May Alcott with her latest novel *Rose in Bloom* (1876). This novel, "Humming Bee" says, is "flanked on all sides with a crowd of strangers, hardly one of whom I know, excepting in the most casual way" (343). She reviews a somewhat eclectic bunch of girls' books from a range of publishers and authors, including Mary Molesworth's *Rosy* (Macmillan, 1882), Mrs Willoughby Luxton's *The New House That Jack Built* (Routledge, 1883), Sarah

5 *The Mercury* (Hobart, Tasmania, 15 January), *The Burrowa News* (New South Wales, 19 January), *Ovens & Murray Advertiser* (Beechworth, Victoria, 19 January), the *Gippsland Times* (Victoria, 21 January), the *Daily Northern Argus* (Rockhampton, Queensland, 23 January), the Melbourne *Weekly Times* (26 January), the *Mount Alexander Mail* (Victoria, 28 January), the *Geelong Advertiser* (6 February), the *Warwick Argues and Tenterfield Chronicle* (Queensland, 14 February), and the *Launceston Examiner* (Tasmania, 22 February).

6 Lucy Gullett, married to the paper's editor, Henry Gullett, headed "The Lady's Column" under the name of "Humming Bee" (Lemon).

Doudney's *A Long Lane with a Turning* (Hodder & Stoughton, 1884), Esmé Stuart's *Miss Fenwick's Failures* (Blackie & Son, 1884), L.T. Meade's *A Band of Three* (W. Isbister, 1884), Johanna Spyri's *Heidi's Early Experiences* (W. Swan Sonnenschein, 1882), and Emily Holt's *Lady Sybil's Choice* (J.F. Shaw, 1879).[7] Most of these authors are relatively well-known girls' writers, but the publishers vary significantly, further suggesting the range of British publishers who were distributing to Australia as well as the absence of local publications for girls. "Humming Bee" understands the market for these books, explaining that *Rosy* is "essentially a girl's book" that "will be enjoyed by girls all through their teens" and that *Lady Sybil's Choice* is "a very interesting story for thoughtful girls, by whom the religious tone of the book will be appreciated" (7). "Humming Bee" does not need to define the girl, Australian or otherwise, who will enjoy these books. Instead, the girl is understood as a clearly defined and knowable subject who is created through and in girls' books.

The Canadian *Bookseller and Stationer* also promoted the international appeal of British novels as it reviewed the "handsome catalogue, printed in colors" of Blackie & Son of London. Blackie's books were "sure to command readers in Canada," since Canadian readers were assumed to be interested in both English and colonial stories ("Announcements" 14). The catalogue includes adventure fiction, such as three new G.A. Henty novels, Bessie Marchant's South African tale *Held at Ransom*, and *With Rifle and Bayonet*, a tale of the Boer War by Capt Brereton.[8] It also includes a "number of attractive books for lads and girls," such as *Cynthia's Bonnet Shop*, a story of an Irish girl's London shop by Rosa Mulholland, and *A Newnham Friendship*, a story of women's higher education by Alice Stronach ("Announcements" 14).[9]

---

7 *Heidi's Early Experiences* is the only novel in translation in this list. In the nineteenth and early twentieth centuries, the translation of children's stories into English was relatively uncommon, with the exception of fairy tales, as Kristine J. Anderson explains.

8 Henty was, of course, a wildly popular writer of adventure fiction for boys. He wrote three or four books each year for Blackie & Son after 1883, writing altogether over 120 books, "and contributed stories and articles to nearly as many more, apart from prolific work in newspapers and periodicals" (Newbolt). Frederick Sadleir Brereton served with the Royal Army Medical Corps as a medical officer (Dacorum). He began publishing adventure fiction with Blackie & Son in 1900 and published over fifty novels.

9 Rosa Mulholland is an Irish novelist who wrote over forty novels for adults and children. Little is known about Alice Stronach. In addition to *A Newnham Friendship*, she co-authored *The Champion* with Mary Lucy Pendered in 1902 and translated *Professor Hieronimus* from the Danish with G.B. Jacobi in 1899.

In the *Victoria Daily Colonist*, based in Victoria, British Columbia, girls' books are advertised, but little attention is paid to reviewing the books themselves. One exception is the *Anne of Avonlea* review in September 1909. The presence of this review, a reprint from the *Boston Transcript*, further emphasizes the transnational nature of girls' print culture as well as the potentially earlier publication of Montgomery's novel in the United States ("Here and There" 8). In December, reflecting the interest in Christmas book sales, book advertisements were common in the newspaper. Advertisements for British annuals such as *The Boys' Own* ($1.75), *The Girls' Own* ($1.75), *The Girl's Realm* ($1.75), *Little Folks* ($1.00), *Chums* ($2.00), *Our Darlings* ($1.00), *Blackie's Boys' Annual* and *Blackie's Girls' Annual* ($1.00 each), and *Chatterbox* ($0.75) appear above a section entitled "New Copyright Fiction," which includes both *Anne of Green Gables* and *Anne of Avonlea* ("New Items" 18). Both priced at $1.50, these two novels are as affordable as the larger annuals such as *The Girls' Own* and *The Girl's Realm*, which are aimed at older girl readers, although the novels would have been significantly shorter ("New Items" 18).

In the Canadian press, British books were marketed to girls and boys separately. Unlike Canadian novels, which tended to be marketed as "Canadian," British books were divided into categories based on the implied readership. In Eaton's 9 December 1911 department store advertisement in Toronto's *The Globe*, for example, the category "Books for Girls" includes novels by well-known girls' novelists such as Marchant, Rosa Mulholland, Ethel Turner, Mrs De Horne Vaizey, Annie S. Swan, L.T. Meade, and Louisa May Alcott ("Eaton's" 32). This list includes notable Australian, American, and British authors, but no Canadian women. Given the popularity of *Anne of Green Gables* at this time, Montgomery is an obvious omission in this category. In other sections of the advertisement, Burnett's *The Secret Garden* and *A Little Princess* are listed, as is McClung's *Sowing Seeds in Danny*. In a section devoted to annuals, most of those listed in the *Victoria Daily Colonist* advertisement discussed above are also mentioned here. In this example of Canadian advertising, Canadian books are not separated from American and other international ones. Instead, the books are grouped together based on their similarities in terms of readership (girls, boys, men, and women) or in terms of the type of book (modern fiction, gift books, annuals, and religious texts). While most of the books are British, the ad includes American and Australian books as well, suggesting the extent to which Eaton's understood and encouraged its readers' transnational book buying interests.[10]

New Zealand girls were also encouraged to read British books, which were implicitly understood to appeal to them. A "London Correspondent" provides a review of the latest books suitable for Christmas presents for New Zealand girls and boys. Written in London on 12 November, the review only appeared in the *Evening Star* on 8 January 1887 and missed the Christmas book-buying rush. The correspondent writes that "Xmas is once more approaching, and that if my annual budget of information relative to the literary 'good things' of the season is to reach the Antipodes in time to be of use to buyers of New Year's gifts, the task of investigation and review must be set about without delay" ("Christmas Presents" 1). The correspondent writes, since some of the new books "may not have reached the colonies yet I will affix the publisher's name, so that your booksellers may know exactly to whose agents to apply for them" ("Christmas Presents" 1). The writer is aware of the exigencies of the New Zealand bookselling market, with significant delays between a book's publication and its arrival in New Zealand, and is trying to accommodate the demands of the colonial newspaper reader who wishes to purchase any of the recommended books. Like many reviews published during this period, the recommendations are split into books for boys and those for girls. The writer observes that "girls used not to be so well off for books as boys, but latterly *nous avons changé tout cela* [we have changed all that]" ("Christmas Presents" 1). At this time, girls in Britain and in the colonies had access to a range of books, including the latest volume of *The Girl's Own Annual* and *Joan Wentworth*, a story of continental life by Katherine Sarah Macquoid. Another novel for girls included on the list is *Astray*, a novel written by Charlotte Yonge, Esmé Stuart, Christabel Coleridge, and Mary Bramston, which is "a readable but not especially successful

10 A similar advertisement in 1918 has some of the same authors for girls, including Marchant, Mulholland, and Swan, but it also includes some new entrants, such as Angela Brazil and E.E. Cowper. The rise of American series fiction is also evident in this ad, with Ruth Fielding (fourteen titles), Moving Picture Girls (seven titles), and Motor Maid (six titles) books all available for 35¢ each. Other series had different pricing, with the Camp Fire Girls books (seven titles) at 45¢ each and books from the Mary Louise (three titles) and Aunt Jane's Nieces (ten titles) series at 65¢ each.

attempt at collaboration" ("Christmas Presents" 1).[11] The reviewer more enthusiastically recommends *Philippa* by Mary Hullah, *Dorothy's Dilemma* by Caroline Austin, and *The Eversley Secrets* by Evelyn Everett-Green. These British books are understood to appeal to Antipodean girls despite being written by British women and primarily for British girls, implying that girls everywhere are united by a set of shared interests and concerns, a point to which we return in further detail in the next chapter.

These locally authored stories are shared across Canada, Australia, and New Zealand such that the importance of all of the nations forged from the British Empire was asserted. Advertisements indicate that *Anne of Green Gables* was widely promoted and read in Australia and in New Zealand, where a local edition was published by Dunedin's J. Braithwaite by early 1909. Mary Grant Bruce's Billabong books were also advertised and reviewed in New Zealand.[12] The lasting association between these books for girls in these new nations forged out of the British Empire is visible in several of the correspondence columns in *The Australasian*'s "The Young Folk" section. In 1918, correspondent Nancy Welsh, who writes that she enjoys Ethel Turner's novels, is informed by the editor "Patience" that she would likely be "very fond" of both *Anne of Green Gables* and *Six Little New Zealanders* as well ("The Young Folk: Answers and Letters" 688). Similarly, in 1923, Mollie Leslie, who enjoyed *A Little Bush Maid* and other titles in Grant Bruce's Billabong series, is encouraged by "Patience" to read *Six Little New Zealanders* and several titles by New Zealand author Isabel Maud Peacocke ("The Young Folk: Answers and Letters" 512).

In the early twentieth century, and with the rapid increase in popular fiction for girls, girls' reading again came under scrutiny. In Britain, Florence B. Low examined the question of British girls' reading, describing how the majority of fifteen- and sixteen-year-old girls chose "simple, inoffensive tales by second-rate authors and authoresses (especially the latter)" when asked to identify their favourite novels (Low 278). Others selected novels that were "popular at the circulating libraries" and

---

11 This brief review concurs with Oscar Wilde's opinion, published in the 28 October 1886 *Pall Mall Gazette*, in which he describes the novel as "tedious from the noblest motives and wearisome through its good intentions" (4).

12 Although Ethel Turner's latest novels were occasionally reviewed in the *Toronto Star* and *The Globe*, the only mention of Mary Grant Bruce occurs in a "Just Off the Press" column briefly mentioning the 1938 publication of *Told by Peter*.

"hardly suitable to juvenile tastes" (Low 278). Since high-quality literature is being pushed to the side in favour of what Low sees as inferior texts, girls are unable to "digest food of a superior nature" (Low 278). Low's survey questions reflect her bias towards canonical, and somewhat dated, English fiction, such as Scott, Thackeray, Dickens, Austen, and Gaskell, rather than more contemporary popular fiction.[13] She laments that Dickens and Scott, "although still read by the younger generation, are no longer loved with that absorbing passion which so often took possession of their parents and grandparents" (Low 279), suggesting the changing nature of girls' reading throughout the nineteenth century as well as the emergence of a distinct genre of literature for children. Popular fiction was replacing serious literature of the past, which Low believed would likely result in the destruction of "all taste for serious and continuous reading" (Low 280). The quality of girls' fiction was a significant concern for Low as girls increasingly read books written specifically for them and of an ephemeral nature, which meant they rapidly fell in and out of fashion.

Low's concern about the quality of books read by girls and the importance of providing them with higher-quality literature is echoed in the colonies during this period. In November 1919, the Canadian *Charlottetown Guardian* included on its front page a detailed summary of an address on "Literature for Young People" at the Women's Institutes Convention. In this address, Bona Mills, secretary of the Y.W.C.A., explains that "the awakening of the girl in her teens to new phases of mental activity reveals itself in her passion for reading. The books which they have read have a tremendous influence on their mental life" ("Close" 1). Like Low, Mills is concerned about the quality of girls' reading and claims modern writers produce few suitably wholesome books. Consequently, she argues, "The books that girls read should be carefully chosen and adapted to real life" to provide "a concrete ideal of womanhood ... in which the girls and women are sound, reasonable and good, have lived and enjoyed life to the end ("Close" 1). In Britain and its colonies, the feeling was that girls should be reading appropriate materials to help

13 The following questions were asked in Low's survey: Which are your favourite novels?; Which of Scott's novels have you read?; Which of Thackeray's novels have you read?; Which of Dickens's novels have you read?; Which of Jane Austen's novels have you read?; Which of Mrs Gaskell's novels have you read?; Do you like C. Yonge's stories?; Do you like Miss Muloch's stories?; Do you like Miss Thackeray's stories?; Do you read magazines? If so, which?; Which are your favourite poets?; Name six poems you are very fond of (Low 279).

transform them into women who can contribute to the nation and the empire.

Yet the specific question of colonial girls' reading required a separate survey, which Constance Barnicoat undertook in response to Low's article. Barnicoat was herself a colonial girl, born and raised in New Zealand before moving to England, where she found employment working for W.T. Stead, founder-editor of the *Review of Reviews* (McCallum). After Low criticized modern girls' reading, Barnicoat set out to "find out what the girls in as many as possible of our Colonies and dependencies really do read, and in what direction their tastes lie" (939). Drawing upon the connections already established by the League of the Empire, a new list of survey questions was drawn up and distributed to different schools throughout the empire.[14] British and colonial high school girls between the ages of fifteen and eighteen were asked to complete the questionnaire, which included a series of twelve questions designed to discover what fiction, poetry, newspapers, and magazines were read by girls.[15]

These questions are intended to "draw out a girl's general intelligence" by allowing her to explain any special hobbies or areas of study as well as her more general reading preferences (Barnicoat 940). They privilege certain male authors by explicitly naming them (Sir Walter Scott, William Thackeray, Charles Dickens, Charles Kingsley, George Meredith, Rudyard Kipling, Rider Haggard, Gilbert Parker, Arthur Conan Doyle, and J.M. Barrie), and those named authors are understood to be writers of quality. Only one question is specifically about women writers (George Eliot, Jane Austen, and Charlotte Brontë), although girls are encouraged

14 The League of the Empire "was founded in 1901 ... to help spread a greater sense of imperial loyalty and unity by correspondence between children throughout the Empire" (Hendley 67). A letter of support from Colonial Secretary Joseph Chamberlain in 1903 to the education departments of the empire requested that "they give the scheme favourable consideration" (Hendley 78).

15 The questions were as follows: What books do you read for recreation?; Which novels have you read of the following writers: Scott, Thackeray, Dickens, Kingsley?; Of the following living novelists: Meredith, Kipling, Rider Haggard, Gilbert Parker, Conan Doyle, Barrie?; Name any novels you have read by the following women writers: George Eliot, Jane Austen, Charlotte Brontë; Name any novels that interest you by other writers than these; Which English classics do you like best?; Which poets?; What are your favourite poems?; What is your favourite study? What books do you read in connection with it?; What is your favourite hobby? What books do you read in connection with it?; Do the daily or weekly newspapers interest you? If so, what parts?; Which of the monthly magazines do you read? (Barnicoat 939–40).

to identify novels they read for recreation as well as novels that "interest" them beyond those by the authors listed.

In Barnicoat's review of the responses, she "conveys an impression of alert, usually discriminating and intelligent young women readers proliferating at home and abroad" (Flint 161). She finds that "colonial girls whose opportunities may fairly be compared with those of their British sisters, are usually quite as well read for their ages, and they generally read far fewer 'girls" books" (Barnicoat 941). This suggests either that colonial girls were more mature than British ones, in that they had moved beyond juvenile reading, or that their access to girls' books was more restricted. Although numerous reviews of children's books and annuals appeared in colonial newspapers, which indicates their presence in the colonial marketplace, girls in these countries may have been more likely to read adult fiction because of its wider availability in home and public libraries.

Attitudes towards colonial girls' work are reflected in some of Barnicoat's observations about the differences of colonial life. She observes that "the bright climates and open-air life of many Colonies, and the fact that most Colonial girls have to take a turn in domestic work of one kind or another, often militate against their spending very much of their leisure over books" (941). Girls' reading is not seen as part of their education. Instead, it represents entertainment and leisure, which can only be appropriate when a girl's domestic duties are complete. This attitude may explain why colonial girls preferred boys' stories, and particularly boys' school stories. Barnicoat observes that the colonial girl is "devoted to adventure books, often of the hair-breadth escape, somewhat bloodcurdling order" (943). The publication of this study in 1906 predates much of the adventure fiction for girls that would begin to flood the market in the 1910s.

Moreover, and likely as a consequence of the increased domestic responsibilities for colonial girls, the results also "revealed certain general differences between the British and the Colonial girl" (Barnicoat 943). For instance, the colonial girl is "usually the older for her years. When sixteen or seventeen, she tends to put away such girlish things as Mrs. L.T. Meade, for instance, and long before this age of discretion she usually scorns girls' magazines" (Barnicoat 943). Barnicoat's own attitude towards girls' fiction and magazines is somewhat dismissive, potentially suggesting that the British models of femininity found in British girls' fiction were not as attractive or appropriate. These texts are best replaced by grown-up works more suitable for young women who have an important role in the development of the empire and the nation.

Unsurprisingly, colonial girls often supported local novelists, "especially such as deal with their own Colony. With the Australian girls, for instance, Ethel Turner is immensely popular" (Barnicoat 943). Barnicoat also finds evidence of the dominance of American publishing in the reading choices of Canadian girls: "Among the writers mentioned by Canadian girls, it is hardly surprising to find a still larger proportion of Americans ... preponderating," including Nathaniel Hawthorne, Mark Twain, Louisa May Alcott, Frank Norris, and Kate Douglas Wiggin (Barnicoat 943–4). In contrast, New Zealand girls were stronger readers, with papers that "were equal to the very best English or Scotch, and the varied nature of their reading was astonishing. No girls, perhaps, showed quite so much variety in their choice of authors" (Barnicoat 944). Unfortunately, Barnicoat includes no further detail about New Zealand girls' reading choices, although their breadth was likely a result of the small New Zealand book trade, in which most of the books available for purchase came from either Australia or Britain.

Barnicoat includes two lists of favourite novels: one for British girls, the other for colonial and Indian girls. The consolidation of all non-British girls' reading into a single list is intriguing since it suggests that these girls can be viewed as a coherent group, despite Barnicoat's attempts to identify differences between the reading patterns of girls from different countries.[16] This consolidation implies colonial girls could be interpellated as a homogenous group to which ideals of girlhood could be applied. Only three names appear on both lists: Edna Lyall, Stanley Weyman, and Marie Corelli.[17] Because of Barnicoat's consolidation process, authors that might have been popular in one colony fail to appear on the list because they were not sufficiently popular in other colonies as well. As a consequence, this list emphasizes the supremacy of British texts for

16 Favourite novelists of British girls: 1. Edna Lyall; 2. Henry Seton Merriman; 3. R.L. Stevenson; 4. Stanley Weyman; 5. Anthony Hope; 6. F. Marion Crawford; 7. Elizabeth Gaskell (nearly always *Cranford*); 8. Edward Bulwer-Lytton; 9. Marie Corelli; 10. Allen Raine.

Favourite novelists of colonial and Indian girls: 1. Edna Lyall; 2. Louisa May Alcott; 3. Mrs Henry Wood; 4. Rosa Nouchette Carey; 5. L.T. Meade; 6. Charlotte M. Yonge; 7. Marie Corelli; 8. Stanley Weyman; 9. Frederic W. Farrar; 10. Edward Bulwer-Lytton and G.A. Henty (Barnicoat 950).

17 Lyall published only a few novels during her lifetime, but received considerable acclaim. Weyman was a popular historical romance novelist who published extensively after 1890. Corelli was a popular novelist between 1890 and the beginning of the First World War.

colonial girls, regardless of where they lived. Women writers dominate the colonial girls' list, with the top seven writers being women. In contrast, only three women appear on the British list.

That colonial readers engaged with the question of girls' reading habits is reflected in responses to both Low and Barnicoat in colonial newspapers. The Wellington *Evening Post*, for example, presents a robust summary of both articles, while also providing some additional analysis. One possible explanation for Barnicoat's assertion that colonial girls read more widely is "the existence of the invaluable 'colonial editions,' by which colonial readers may buy for half-a-crown a copyright book that in England would cost six shillings" ("What Colonial Girls Read" 4). *The Otago Witness* also remarks that there are "more signs of intellectual culture than might have been expected among girls in some of our colonies" even as it laments "faults in orthography" for misspelled names and book titles ("What Colonial Girls Read" 74).[18] In Australia, the discussion of colonial girls' reading was equally interesting, with reviews appearing in a variety of papers.[19] The definition of "colonial" troubled some Australian reviewers. Since it included Canada, South Africa, and the East Indies, as well as the whole of Australasia, "comparatively little with respect to the favorite reading of girls in that part of the Empire is to be learned from the answers to inquiries covering so very wide an area" ("What Colonial Girls Read" 18). The merging of responses from a range of colonial locations meant that commentators could not ascertain the characteristics of any one nation's colonial girls' reading habits.

Colonial girls clearly read magazines and books written both by British and by colonial authors, reflecting the transnational print culture available to them. On "The Young Folk" page of *The Australasian* on 2 August 1919, Elsie Chrisp of Sydney writes that she has "read all Mary Grant Bruce's books, and almost all of Ethel Turner's" and asks for "the names of some more nice books" (248). Elsie references two of Australia's most popular girls' authors of the time, yet "Patience" responds by suggesting British authors. She writes that Elsie would "like any of Bessie Marchant's books ... as they are full of adventure. 'The Loyalty of Hester Hope'

18 Other New Zealand papers to pick up versions of the *Evening Post* article include the *Manawatu Standard* and the *Wanganui Chronicle*.

19 Reviews appeared in the Sydney *Australian Star* (10 Jan. 1907), the Perth *Daily News* (16 Feb. 1907), the Hobart *Mercury* (23 Jan. 1907), the *Launceston Examiner* (27 Oct. 1906), *The Queenslander* (3 Nov. 1906), the *Maryborough Chronicle* (22 Dec. 1906), and *The Maitland Daily Mercury* (5 Nov. 1906).

and 'The Adventures of Phyllis' are two of them. Other good stories are 'Captain Nancy' and 'Septima-Schoolgirl,' by Dorothy [*sic*] Moore, and 'The Girls' Eton,' by May Baldwin" (248). This list of recommendations is interesting for its lack of currency: two books, *The Loyalty of Hester Hope* and *Captain Nancy,* were published in 1914; the others were published in 1910. "Patience" may not have been especially up to date with the latest girls' fiction. Alternatively, she may have assumed that Elsie had not read these books because they are British, or perhaps the books had been reprinted for colonial distribution around that time. It may also potentially suggest the relative scarcity of Australian girls' fiction in contrast to the ubiquity of British girls' fiction, although the years immediately prior to this article included publications by Lilian Turner, Lillian Pyke, and Louise Mack.

These answers are somewhat puzzling given that Australian magazines regularly mentioned British and Australian girls' books in their "Literature" or "Books Received" columns. For example, in *The Queenslander*'s 12 December 1903 column on "Literature: Publications Received," Marchant's *A Heroine of the Sea* is listed along with *What Katy Did* (1872) by American girls' author Susan Coolidge. According to the column's author, the Marchant novel "gives something that will be popular with girls" ("Literature: Publications" 59). The summary of the plot that is provided in *The Queenslander* is identical to that which appeared in *The Mercury,* a Tasmanian publication, on 30 November 1903 in its "Reviews: Christmas Prize Books" column, suggesting that it may have been provided by the publisher. It explains that, although Maudie is beautiful, she "heartily despis[es] all merely feminine occupations" ("Literature: Publications" 59). The arrival of a "sweet refined woman ... awakens her to the charm of domestic life," but Maudie understands that "her duty to her family will not allow her to forsake the hard drudgery of a fisher life" ("Literature: Publications" 59). In *The Mercury,* however, the summary concludes that it is a "healthy book for girls" ("Reviews" 2). The *Otago Daily Times* perhaps more appropriately calls it a "lively, pleasant story for girls" ("Book Notices" 8).

The significance of the colonial location varied depending on where the book was being reviewed. For example, the *New Zealand Herald* makes little of the setting of Bessie Marchant's *A Girl of the Fortunate Isles,* merely noting that the "scene of this story is laid in New Zealand" ("Books and Publications" 5). In contrast, the Canterbury *Press* reviewer felt that Canada was a much more exotic setting that made a "delightful" addition to Marchant's *A Heroine of the Sea,* particularly "the fishermen, Klondyke miners, and, above all, the Red Indians" ("New Books and Publications" 7). This comment demonstrates how some content, especially that depicting the familiar settings of England (and particularly London) or New Zealand, received very little attention. In contrast, foreign environments like Canada were seemingly more interesting and thus remarkable. The colonies became an exotic setting, especially for readers who had not visited that location. An adventure novel set in one's own country, even when the author herself had not visited there, was not especially notable unless the depiction seemed unfaithful. A novel set elsewhere, however, deserved special mention and might be specifically sought out for its foreign setting.

Colonial girls' reading can be understood as remarkably similar, regardless of where the books originated. Girls in Canada, Australia, and New Zealand had access to a wide variety of predominantly British books. Local books, where available, were also eagerly consumed, and some of the most popular made it into other colonial markets, although primarily when they were published by a British or American publisher with international connections. Where distribution networks were available, these books were circulated to other regional areas as well. The library records from the Lambton (New South Wales) Mechanics' and Miners' Institute indicate that *Anne of Green Gables* was borrowed thirty-four times between 1908 and 1912.[20] The fact that the institute held a copy of *Anne of Green Gables* demonstrates that the novel travelled beyond metropolitan locations like Melbourne and Sydney to regional towns. As Julieanne Lamond observes in her analysis of these library records, "the reading of periodicals and recent fiction from the United States and Britain marked its patrons' participation in global networks of print culture" (357). Similarly, Canadians had access to fiction by Australians and Americans alongside British and Canadian texts. These transnational networks extended to New Zealand, as well, with advertisements for *Anne of Green Gables* appearing as early as February 1909 and a book review appearing that same month in the *Otago Daily Times.* Colonial girls' transnational print culture is especially evident in a review of four

20 The Lambton Mechanics' and Miners' Institute was a small library in a mining town in New South Wales. Its borrowing records from 1903 to 1912 are digitized in the Australian Common Reader database (www.australiancommonreader.com). The Lambton Institute "was one of the some thousand such institutes established in Australian towns and cities during the nineteenth century" to provide "access to reading material for many Australians living outside of metropolitan cities" (Lamond 355).

books – Montgomery's *Kilmeny of the Orchard*, Ethel Turner's *The Raft in the Bush*, Lilian Turner's *Three New Chum Girls*, and Mary Grant Bruce's *A Little Bush Maid* – in the same periodical in November 1910. Presumably, the *Otago Daily Times* received review copies from local Dunedin publisher R.J. Stark & Co, which is identified as the publisher and printer of each book. In this sense, colonial girls' print culture was undeniably a function of the book production and distribution networks that were expanded in the 1890s and became increasingly sophisticated in the twentieth century.

Given the global production, dissemination, and reception of girls' texts, the emergence of a universalized model of girlhood based on shared understandings of girls and their responsibilities is unsurprising. In the next chapter, we will examine this model of girlhood to undercover the ways in which girls were introduced to certain behaviours designed to guide them towards their future roles as wives and mothers.

CHAPTER THREE

Girlhood in the British Empire

Oh, the Empire girl
Is a perfect pearl,
With Australian gold in her hair,
And the sunny skies of New Zealand
Have made her yet more fair;
Her eyes are the diamonds from Africa,
Her skin the Canadian snows,
While the colour that dwells
In her cheek only tells,
Of the beautiful English rose.
So no more let us sing about the English lass,
Such distinctions have had their day,
We are birds of all one feather,
So we bunch them all together,
Irish shamrock, Scottish heather,
In a big bouquet;
With flow'rs from all fair countries
Which the Union Jack unfurl,
And these we all together call,
The British Empire girl.

–Lawrence Hanray, "The British Empire Girl" (1907), published sheet music

In the lyrics from "The British Empire Girl" (1907), Lawrence Hanray suggests a homogenous empire girl made up of the best qualities of each of the colonies. She is a "perfect pearl" of imperial girlhood. Her whiteness, symbolized by the pearl, is emphasized in the description of her fair blonde hair and her white skin, with the only colour coming from her rosy pink cheeks. The rhetoric of whiteness is accentuated by the empire girl's presence in all the "fair countries" in which the Union Jack flies. At the same time, the empire girl overcomes distinctions based on regional differences. The English girl is no longer distinct from the Irish or the Scottish girl; instead, these girls are represented as birds of a feather, and they can be brought together as part of a big bouquet, united by the Union Jack flying over the British Empire. This song foregrounds the complementary nature of the empire girl's component parts and their mingling into a perfect whole.

A similar shared Canadian imperial identity is depicted in Canadian Mary Bourchier Sanford's *The Young Gordons in Canada* (1913). In this novel, published by the Religious Tract Society, a financial down-turn forces the Gordon family to sell their English home and emigrate to Canada.[1] The novel follows the family as they adapt to their new circumstances. Amidst a variety of adventures and numerous attempts to make enough money to cover the family's expenses, seventeen-year-old Joyce is whisked away by some nearby friends to take part in a tableau organized by the Imperial Order Daughters of the Empire (IODE) for a local charity.[2] The conclusion of Joyce's tableau is entitled "The Lay of the Emblems" and features Canadian girls performing speaking parts as England, Scotland, Ireland, and Canada. Each girl quotes from a different section of "The Maple Leaf," a song written by the Rev John McCaul and originally published in 1852, before coming together to wave maple leaves and sing the chorus: "Then hurrah for the leaf, the maple leaf, / Up, Canadians, heart and hand! / High in heaven's free air waves your emblem fair, / The pride of our forest land" (Sanford 205).[3]

---

1 A financial set-back was a common plot device in emigrant narratives. In *The Redfords: An Emigrant Story* (1886), Ann Jane Cupples uses a bank failure to explain the Redfords' loss of fortune and subsequent decision to emigrate to New Zealand.

2 The IODE was a Canadian organization of "female imperialists" founded in 1900 to help "in the construction of an Anglo-Canadian identity that celebrated all things British and advanced Canada's destiny as a part of the British Empire" (Pickles 2).

3 The song was first published in *The United Empire Minstrel* in 1852, a volume dedicated to "the loyal Orangemen of the United Empire." Author-editor William Shannon explains that the publication "is now presented to all those who earnestly desire to maintain the existing connexion between Great Britain, Ireland, and the Colonies" (v). The volume was reprinted in 1876 as *The Dominion Orange Harmonist: A Collection of the Best National, Constitutional, and Loyal Orange Songs and Poems.*

The tableau and the accompanying song suggest the complex interconnections between empire and nation that can be found in colonial girls' fiction. The girls in this story simultaneously represent both the British Empire and the Dominion of Canada. It is possible, and desirable, for them to symbolize the beauty of the English rose, the "free and fair" Scotch thistle, and the "love, valour, [and] wit" of the Irish shamrock before being transformed into the Canadian girl embodied by the "free hearths" of the "fair forest land" (Sanford 205). Although Canadian girls are here identified as especially free in comparison to other colonial girls, in general, colonial girlhood was seen by British authors as less constrained than that of Britain, an idea that we explore further in chapter 4. As the audience rises up to join in the singing of the chorus, they too perform their roles as Canadian and imperial subjects who support the empire while also embracing the colonial nationalism that emerged from it. The conclusion of the evening with the singing of "God Save the King" reinforces, for the audience and the readers, the supremacy of the British monarchy.

British and colonial writers depicted appealing heroines throughout the colonies and promoted the ties of imperialism to develop a universalized colonial girl who was interchangeable throughout the empire. These colonial girls could be, and were, commonly defined in relation to domesticity, femininity, family, empire, and work ethic, and the traits embodied by these girls, particularly in girls' fiction, were remarkably similar regardless of the author's or the protagonist's nationality. Although these girls strongly identified as national subjects, they also saw themselves simultaneously as British. This chapter will demonstrate how British girls' fiction generated imagined pictures of colonial girlhood and the ways in which those representations were both national and imperial. It will then contrast these ideas of girlhood with those produced and published in the colonies to explore the differences between local writers' depictions of the colonial girl's future role within the nation.

The favourable portrayal of the colonies is a characteristic of British girls' books and magazines in the late nineteenth and early twentieth centuries. In a slightly earlier novel, *The Redfords: An Emigrant Story* (1886), for example, the narrator invites readers to skip over the difficult months of early settlement: "We must ask our readers to suppose some months to have passed over our friends the Redfords, so that when next we visit them they are beginning to look upon themselves as established colonists, and to get over the first difficulties which settlers feel in a country like New Zealand" (Cupples 85).[4] As we discuss in more detail in chapters 5 and 7, earlier settler fiction and travel narratives emphasize the challenges of establishing a foothold in the colonial world. By the turn of the twentieth century, however, British girls' fiction depicted the colonies as offering opportunities for improved health, employment, and marriage prospects, while also presenting a natural, less constrained world for girls.

J.S. Bratton explains that the didactic function of some juvenile literature promoted the dissemination of imperial ideologies in the nineteenth and early twentieth centuries: "in the fiction for the young over many decades [there exists] a powerful and multi-faceted presentation of Englishness, as a moral and ethical baseline, and therefore a starting point for the justification of the Empire" (78). Many writers praised "English or British national characteristics, and the land itself, in order to establish a sense of what is good and to be valued. For the imperialist writer, the extension of this Englishness overseas is a cogent reason for colonial expansion" (Bratton 78). British girls' fiction reflects this idea of Englishness to a certain extent, but it also presents colonial girls as adapting to the challenges of the colonial location. Thus British and colonial representations increasingly reflect different attitudes towards and expectations of the colonies and colonial girlhood. In British girls' print culture, colonial girlhood is typically characterized by health, freedom, and heroism. Novels such as those by Bessie Marchant depict colonial girls who are offered freedoms that would have been unacceptable in England, thereby presenting a fantasy of colonial girlhood to English readers. These colonial characters are actively involved in establishing and maintaining the home as a place of safety, security, and domestic happiness. British girls' periodicals were similarly interested in promoting the colonies as suitable emigration destinations for girls who were ready and able to work.

In contrast, colonial depictions of girls often display a concern with their future roles, which are typically expected to be maternal. In newspaper and magazine articles published for a wider audience, but which discuss girls' roles in furthering national development, childbearing is emphasized. As Cecily Devereux has noted, in the face of Darwinian fears about degeneration, racial "regeneration could only happen

4 Ann Jane Cupples emigrated to New Zealand in 1894, although her mother and five sisters emigrated there in 1858 (White).

in the settler colonies, and it could only happen if sufficient numbers of white women went to the colonies to 'breed' this improved race in what were represented as inherently purer spaces" ("New Woman" 179). The imperial girl is encouraged to consider the possibilities of colonial locations such as Canada, New Zealand, or Australia as places where she would reasonably be expected to conform to many British middle-class beliefs, but where she "could discover more about [herself] and the ways in which [she] could serve her country" (Rowbotham 220). Thus girl readers could – and were expected to – simultaneously identify as both British and colonial.

This attitude was consistent – although not precisely identical – across white settler colonies, in which "colonists saw no tension in being nationalists and imperialists" (Eddy and Schreuder 6). As Joan Beaumont explains, Australians "saw no contradiction in having dual loyalties or multiple allegiances" to Britain and the British Empire and to Australia (172). In fact, being a member of the empire "ultimately transcended and was superior to [being a part] of the nation" (Beaumont 172). Phillip Buckner similarly writes that, in Canada, "the true Canadian was British ethnically, and depending on the context English Canadians tended to define themselves as either British or Canadian without much distinction" (3). Helen Bones likewise explains that "New Zealanders, as members of a British world system ... were interested in what made them nationally distinctive, but this meant distinctive *within* British culture and the empire rather than distinct *from* it" (865). Given this shared sense of both imperial and national identity, girl readers were unsurprisingly encouraged to see themselves as part of both communities.

This shared imperial identity was developed and promoted in colonial girls' print culture of the second half of the nineteenth century and into the twentieth century. This identity is, as Stuart Ward explains,

> a notoriously slippery field of study because it is so subjective and multifaceted. No group identity is ever truly stable or coherent, and even the most homogenous communities are prone to fragmentation due to the countless distinctions of age, class, gender, occupation, religion, political persuasion, and so on. Yet ... all social groupings share certain assumptions about their distinctive characteristics. (220)

Girl readers throughout the empire could be both British and colonial, with distinct identities based on national and imperial frameworks. These frameworks were based on identities that were not essential or fixed. Catherine Hall discusses the British and colonial "desire to mark boundaries of social and political authority, who had power and of what kinds" (203). This means, according to Hall, that a "girl is not born English, or feminine, or working class. Rather, those identities are brought into being through discursive or symbolic work that demarcates the self from the other" (203). The books and magazines consumed by colonial girls produced identities based on shared understandings of what it meant to be British in diverse colonial settings. Yet colonial girls' print culture negotiated and reworked some of the limitations of authority that were based on outdated or irrelevant conceptions of class, femininity, and, to a certain extent, race. This does not refer to non-white racial difference, which had important implications for girls' texts, as we discuss in chapter 6. Instead, at least some racial difference, such as that associated with the Irish, is at times elided in fiction for girls. In part, the relaxation of some of these social hierarchies contributes to the Redford family's decision to remain in New Zealand after their fortune is restored because they "like [it] ... ever so much better ... Far better than the stiff old country" (Cupples 91). Much of the discussion that follows in subsequent chapters seeks to understand the kinds of freedoms enjoyed by colonial girls and the circumstances under which they could take advantage of such freedom.

This shared imperial identity among girls from Canada, Australia, and New Zealand forms the basis of the transnational girlhood that developed throughout this period, enabled by the print culture consumed by colonial girls. Graham Huggan explains that "the 'postcoloniality' of national literatures such as Australia's is always effectively *transnational*, either derived from an apprehension of internal fracture ... or from a multiplied awareness of the nation's various engagements with other nations, and with the wider world" (Huggan viii). British and colonial girls' texts shared a "transnational consciousness that embodies a tension between dual identification as British and colonial" while promoting a "shared vision of femininity in colonial settings" (Bradford, "Children's Literature" 21). British and colonial middle-class girls' fiction and periodicals include a variety of different perspectives about the types of behaviours that were appropriate for girls, but they show remarkable consistency regarding the importance of duty, family, work, femininity, and purity. Although the girls who are depicted in the turn-of-the-century periodicals were demonstrably more modern in their social and economic attitudes, they nonetheless remained concerned about fulfilling their responsibilities to their families, being engaged in useful work, and maintaining their health, beauty, and reputation. This feminine ideal was not defined as explicitly imperial, but it formed the basis of the transnational ideal that emerged in girls' literature and magazines in the nineteenth and early twentieth centuries.

These girls' texts travelled to and between the colonies and were important components of the "paper empire" that Jeffrey Richards describes as being "built on a series of flimsy pretexts that were always becoming texts" (3). The girls who appear in the pages of novels and magazines are always in the process of "becoming" (30). As Devereux explains,

> In fiction and across cultural representations, the Anglo-colonial girl was fashioned as a figure for young women to embody, her image and the ideology she staged in the things she did and the things she wore circulating in and through the paper that carried her around the empire. 'Made in Britain', the colonial girl is an agent of empire, an advertisement for and consumer of its products and technologies, and an imperial commodity in circulation in and through the mobilising of her representation in print. ("Fashioning" 30)

The British model of girlhood employed throughout girls' print culture was a standard against which all girls, whether colonial or not, were measured. This British identity was constantly circulating throughout the empire and was inevitably being modified as a consequence of time and geography, yet colonial contributors and colonial girls themselves frequently framed their discussions of girlhood in relation to the British model.

Colonial girls regularly encountered British models of femininity that simultaneously defined ideals about girls and girlhood, whether they were living in England or the colonies. Lyn Pykett writes that Victorian periodicals are not "transparent records which give access to, and provide the means of recovering, the culture which they 'mirror'" (102). Instead, periodicals are a "central component" of culture and society that "can only be read and understood" within that context (Pykett 102). Colonial girls inevitably encountered British models of girlhood alongside British conceptions of colonial girlhood that did not always, or fully, represent colonial girls' experiences. The model of femininity, whether it was colonial or British, was always, as Margaret Beetham explains, "represented ... as fractured, not least because it is simultaneously assumed as given and as still to be achieved" (1). While Beetham is referring to women's magazines targeted at an older readership, her comments are even more relevant to the field of girls' magazines, in which the implied readership is still understood to live in the liminal space between childhood and womanhood. The models of femininity frequently include girls who are in the process of becoming women but who also already have the feminine skills they will need as adults. What we see from examples of colonial girls' reading choices and contributions to the periodical press is that they were equally engaged as British girls with refining and contesting these definitions of girlhood.

Colonial Girlhood in British Fiction and Annuals

British girls' fiction and periodicals typically depict the colonies and the girls who inhabit them quite favourably. This contrasts with Diana Archibald's conclusion that the colonies appearing in adult fiction are often characterized as "savage, rough, wicked, vulgar, indecent, violent, and/or hypocritical," while England is depicted as "virtuous, noble, moral, respectable, comfortable, pretty, and/or trustworthy" (4). While adult novels were more preoccupied with women's struggles in unfamiliar and often harsh locales, girls' books were oriented towards a fantasy of colonial life in which girls had more freedom and opportunity. Undoubtedly, some uncivilized elements can be found in the colonies, but in girls' adventure fiction, colonial girls are independent and courageous, and they persevere in the face of significant adversity. These qualities are crucial to the maturation of the female protagonists and are intended to appeal to girl readers throughout the empire while also reflecting perceived norms in white settler colonies. Colonial girls existed in a liminal space between civilization and the natural world; they were typically freer, healthier, and more capable as they fulfilled their nations' need for independence and freedom while also maintaining British ideals of civilization and culture.

This liminal space is evident in Bessie Marchant's *A Countess from Canada: A Story of Life in the Backwoods*, an adventure fiction novel published by Blackie & Son in 1911. The novel follows Katherine Radford as she runs the family general store at Roaring Water Portage while educating her brothers and teaching night school to the male workers in the area. Although she has been educated in the civilized environs of Montréal and is trained to be a teacher, Katherine's skills and abilities are more suited to the outdoors. As she explains after spending the morning teaching, "I have been wishing all the morning that I were a man; then I could go off hunting, trapping, or even lumbering, and so breathe fresh air all day long" (*Countess* 12). Although she is capable of managing the domestic space, her father's lingering illness means that she is more often called upon to work outdoors. Carrying supplies over long distances provides her with multiple opportunities to perform heroic feats, although these adventures sometimes come at the expense of her femininity. Her capability nevertheless enhances her physical attractiveness, as, for example, when she helps her father with the dog sled: "Katherine was sparkling, glowing, and rosy, with a life and animation which she never showed indoors" (14). Although her father believes such physical activity "isn't work for a girl" (21), Katherine models a steadfast willingness to do whatever work is required: "It is work for a girl, if a girl has got it to do" (21). Marchant reminds readers that girls must respond and adapt to the challenges presented by the colonial environment, an idea that we expand upon in chapter 5.

The isolated spaces that define the Canadian landscape offer possibilities for success, and even love, for those girls who are resourceful and determined. Katherine, "under her girlish softness and pretty winning manner, had hidden a firm will and purpose, a sound judgment, and a resourcefulness which would stand her in good stead in the emergencies of life" (22). Even though the colonies are depicted as poor and uncivilized, they also offer opportunities. As the narrator remarks, "Life would have seemed dreary and monotonous enough if it had not been for the hard and constant work ... She did not mind the work. Young, strong, and with plenty of energy, the daily toil seemed rather pleasant than otherwise" (67). The colonies are designed for the young, the healthy, and the energetic, and girls with these qualities will be successful.

Colonial girlhood in adventure fiction represents a freedom from traditional feminine conventions, particularly in relation to bravery and heroism. As Richard Phillips explains, adventure in girls' fiction is a "rite of passage and test of strength" that enables the heroine to be transformed from a girl into a (marriageable) woman (103). Katherine does not require as great a transformation as some of Marchant's other heroines do, such as Maudie Belloc of *A Heroine of the Sea*, who, as we discussed in the previous chapter, requires the civilizing influence of a governess to accept her domestic and caregiving responsibilities. Instead, Katherine marries and learns only after the wedding that her new husband has inherited a title. She worries that she is "not fit to be a great lady" because of the menial work that she had to do while living in the backwoods of Canada (358). People "had seen her staggering along the portage paths laden with heavy burdens; they had seen her struggling to row a boat up river against a strong current; they had met her dripping with wet or covered with frost" (353–4). Yet her husband reminds her that "work is no degradation" and says, "Perhaps it is better for us that we have had to toil so hard; we shall be able to sympathize with other workers, and to help them" (358). The Canadian environment will enable them to better perform their aristocratic roles when they move to England. Moreover, Katherine is unable to resist the ties of love and of empire. The newly married couple never considers rejecting the title. Their responsibility as English subjects is clearly understood, and they begin imagining their life back in England, far removed from Roaring Waters Portage. Katherine, for example, wonders whether she will be able to manage a house full of servants. She is simultaneously colonial and English, bringing together the hardy elements of her Canadian character with the feminine refinement associated with the English aristocracy. Her national identity is subsumed within an imperial identity that requires girls to fulfil a variety of demands that shift between the colonies and the British Empire.

Similar evidence of this shared colonial identity is found in other Marchant novels. In *The Ferry House Girls* (1912), for example, two Australian girls take on additional responsibilities when their father is away. The younger daughter, Lucinda, is described as a "good all-round worker" in "the manner of colonial girls" (Marchant, *Ferry* 148–9). She can "wash and bake, and sew, as well as a grown woman," and she is "a very great comfort in the household," helping keep everyone cheerful (Marchant, *Ferry* 149). Marchant's use of "colonial girls" implies that girls throughout the white settler colonies can be viewed as homogenous. A review in the Adelaide *Register* reinforces this interpretation: "This is an Australian story, or, rather, a colonial one, for the author is writing from book knowledge" ("A Book List" 4). Because Marchant lacks lived experience in Australia, *The Ferry House Girls* represents a generalized, British understanding of Australian geography, culture, and femininity in which colonial girls have no unique national qualities. Instead, Lucinda, as a colonial girl, has the domestic skills required to establish and maintain a household.

Lucinda and her older sister Vic resemble the protagonists of Marchant's earlier *A Girl of the Fortunate Isles* (1906), which is also set at a ferry crossing, this time in New Zealand. Like the girls in *The Ferry House Girls*, this book's heroines, Margaret and her younger sister Judy, spend a lot of time in domestic work, although Judy pursues her education, eventually causing her eyesight to fail. Colonial girls, like their British sisters, must not "overstudy" beyond what their health can sustain (Marchant, *Girl* 194). Margaret's steady work, both domestic labour and paid employment operating the ferry for her uncle, are positioned as ideal. Indeed, Margaret wonders what it would be like to have an entire day of rest, without any responsibilities, but then remarks, "I dare say I should be heartily tired of it long before sunset came" (Marchant, *Girl* 197). The "promise of gracious, glorious womanhood" that others can see in her is produced by and enabled through her work ethic and her duty to her family (Marchant, *Girl* 157). These ideals are reproduced in many of Marchant's novels, regardless of where the stories are set. Marchant depicts colonial girlhood as an identity that extends beyond the borders of the nation and that is shared among girls with British heritage.

In Marchant's 1920 novel, *Sally Makes Good*, the colonial girl succeeds because of her attitude, her adaptability, and her work ethic, not because of where she was born. In this novel, the Willet family moves from England to Tasmania after Major Willet is granted a plot of land following his First World War service in the British army. Accompanying him are his wife, two sons, and three daughters. Everyone, according to the protagonist, Sally, had done his or her bit during war time. Her older sister Veronica worked in a munition factory, while her other sister Dora joined the Women's Army Auxiliary Corps and drove a motor lorry in France. Sally, however, "had no budding genius for anything. The only thing for which she was noted was a cheerful way of looking at life" (Marchant, *Sally* 23). Sally's attitude is central to her success in Tasmania, especially in contrast to her sisters. Sally is an "ordinary" girl, except that she "worship[s] babies," is steadfastly cheerful, and would "rather do things for [her]self" (Marchant, *Sally* 91, 12, 35). These qualities prove essential to adapting to her new life. A positive attitude to the many and varied challenges of colonial living, a love for children that identifies her as a suitable future mother, and a strong work ethic all signify her suitability for colonial life.

Not all girls are as likely to succeed in the colonial world. The war-time opportunities taken up by Sally's sisters, for example, were insufficient to prepare them for this colonial environment. They are, as Mrs Willet observes, "rather out of place in the Tasmanian wilds" (Marchant, *Sally* 141). Only those girls who are capable and unselfish thrive in the bush:

> Veronica and Dora are smart-looking, up-to-date girls, but they are chiefly intent on having a good time and doing well for themselves. Sally is warm-hearted, sweet, and good. She can't wear her clothes with the air of

> distinction that comes like second nature to the other two, but she would give those same clothes to meet another's need, if occasion called for it, even though the giving meant that she had to go cold herself. (Marchant, *Sally* 251)

Sally's unselfish nature means that she is a genuine boon to others around her, able to care for the sick and the young. In this way, she makes "a mark for herself" and is engaged by the end of the novel to a well-educated local man whose bravery is demonstrated by his war service (Marchant, *Sally* 91). He is, in every way, a suitable match for Sally as they make their way together in the new world of Tasmania. Importantly, the qualities that contribute to Sally's success are not based on specific national attributes. Instead, Sally's strengths are similar to those found in characters from other Marchant novels. The shared experience of colonial girlhood is based on attitude, health, and a willingness to work.

The girls' periodicals and annuals published in London similarly depicted this shared colonial identity. These publications were one of the main sources of reading materials for girls in Canada, New Zealand, and Australia, although Canadian girls also had access to American publications such as *St Nicholas Magazine.* In the 1900s, British publishers of annuals, in particular, began to pursue the colonial market more aggressively. By adapting British girls' annuals, publishers such as Blackie & Son, Cassell & Co., and the Religious Tract Society (RTS) sought to attract colonial girl readers. Each publisher adapted its British annuals, targeted at boys and girls separately, for colonial audiences. The RTS's *The Empire Annual for Girls* (1909–30) produced and distributed the same content to girls in white settler colonies but targeted colonial girls specifically, by changing the title to *The Empire Annual for Australian Girls,* for example. Cassell & Co. similarly published *The British Girl's Annual* (1910–13?) as *The Australian Girl's Annual, The Canadian Girl's Annual,* and *The New Zealand Girl's Annual.* By comparing the RTS's *Empire Annual* to Cassell's *Girl's Annual,* we can see how transnational girlhood was developed based on a shared imperial identity.

Although these annuals targeted specific readerships of colonial girls, imperialism – and, of course, profit – rests at the core of these print publications. With no variation of the content and only minimal customization of the title and cover, they present a common model of imperial girlhood and assume a homogenous readership of girls throughout the empire to whom their materials could be marketed and sold at a low cost. These annuals were responding to two changes in the publishing industry. The first of these changes was the emergence of colonial editions that we discussed in the previous chapter. With the colonies, especially Australia, established as an important market for colonial editions of major British novels, publishers hoped they could attract juvenile readers to the colonial editions of major British annuals as well. At the same time, changes in the market for girls' periodicals, such as declining readership of the RTS's *Girl's Own Paper*, which it had launched in 1880, meant that new forms of publication were needed to attract colonial readers. These annuals, composed of new material and not dependent on weekly or monthly subscriptions, offered a new model in which to present fiction, poetry, and illustrations to girl readers throughout the empire while also providing content somewhat similar to the bound annual volumes of well-known girls' periodicals like *The Girl's Realm* and the *Girl's Own Paper*.

To attract readers, the content in these annuals needed to depict a coherent model of girlhood that was based on shared British ideals of femininity, including duty, family, and sacrifice. This shared imperial identity is reinforced through articles such as "The Most Beautiful City in the Empire: Which Is It?" Appearing in the 1910 volume of *The Empire Annual*, this article presents an overview of, and argument for, the "chief cities of our Empire" (H. Williams 195). The rhetoric of empire is pervasive throughout the article with comments such as "our vast and ever-growing Empire" and the depiction of Québec as "that bright gem in the Imperial crown" (195). Other cities under consideration include Edinburgh, Dublin, and London. The speaker for Sydney wins the debate when he concludes, "When you have taken in all these charming details [of the surroundings of Sydney Harbour], I think you will agree with me that no city of any importance in the whole Empire can compare with Beautiful Sydney, the gem of the Southern Seas" (H. Williams 201). Girl readers of the annual are expected to adopt two simultaneous positions, in which they are devoted to a particular city based on their national affiliation while also being interested in, and receptive to, arguments about other locations based on their shared imperial connections.

This dual address works because these annuals developed a common ideal of girlhood within their pages. In the opening article of *The Empire Annual*, "To My Friends the Readers" by the Bishop of Durham (Dr Handley C.G. Moule), girlhood is explicitly defined based on an idea of one's duty to God, a belief that womanhood "must be its own true self" and not be "a mere imitation of man," and an understanding of the "unspeakable and supreme importance of the power of true womanhood upon the whole life of humanity" (Moule 10–11). This obviously reflected *The Empire Annual*'s RTS origins, since the other annuals are less explicitly committed to a Christian ethic. The role of the girl in modern life is seen as so important that it transcends any national or imperial borders.

The girls in these annuals are expected to share an identity that demonstrates an interest in, and awareness of, girls from everywhere within the empire. The contents of the 1910 *Empire Annual* reflect this diversity. They include "My Canadian Christmas," "A Day of My Life at Girton," "Wild Life in India," "School-Girl Life in South Africa," and "The British Ambassador," among many others, thereby bringing together experiences of girlhood in England, at the Cambridge women's college Girton, alongside those in colonial locations including Canada, India, and South Africa. The contents of the annual appear to be a deliberate attempt to appeal to girls from throughout the empire while also promoting a shared understanding of what it means to be an imperial girl. By explicitly including content from Canada, Australia, South Africa, India, and England, the editor promotes an imperial framework based on a shared understanding of British culture. As "A Wandering Briton" explains in "In Praise of Canada," the "Empire spirit" abounds – that "spirit that takes our people quite contentedly to all parts of the world, civilised and uncivilised, almost as a matter of course. To us it is not exile. Our kin are everywhere and no land seems utterly strange" ("Wandering" 333). The reader is positioned within the empire through the use of "us" and "our" and invited to support imperial objectives when the author notes, "Perhaps that is why we so soon get proud of the new lands, and ready to defend the claim … against all opposition" ("Wandering" 333). Despite the exoticism of the foreign, the girl is not expected to engage with it in any substantive way, as is evident in the coloured frontispiece, "A Critical Moment." This image depicts snarling tigers attacking elephants, on top of which ride Indian guides and male British hunters. The colonial girls who read these annuals might imagine themselves in this setting, but they will not typically see images of themselves fighting off wild tigers. Even the relatively staid photos of students' rooms at Girton are curiously devoid of girls.

Importantly, however, girl readers are supposed to encounter these diverse elements of the empire through reading, as is illustrated by the girl on the cover (see Figure 3.1), who is reading rather than engaging in more active pursuits. In this image, a girl with long hair sits reading a book. Wearing an old-fashioned gown or possibly a nightdress, she is

3.1 Cover. *The Empire Annual for Australian Girls*, 1910.

enclosed within a heart-shaped figure. Two crowns, signifying British rule, appear at the left and right of "Australian" in the title. Underneath the crowns are two pruned trees, one with flowers and the other with apples, framed within hearts. Positioned beneath the girl is a flower, and ribbons connect the images on each side with the girl in the centre. The reader's focus is drawn to the reading girl, who is positioned as a feminine object subject to the reader's gaze. The book she holds is a striking red, signifying the importance of reading, while she is depicted in more muted blue and brown tones. This cover contrasts with later volumes of the annual, in which the modernity of girlhood is more evident and girls are depicted riding horses (1915), boating (1916), and playing golf (1918).

The model of girlhood is explicitly defined in the pages of *The Empire Annual*. In Mrs Creighton's 1911 article "To the Girls of the Empire: The Call to Service," she encourages girls to respond to the

> special call ... to share in the work that we believe the British Empire is bidden to do for the good of the whole world. If we British people fail to rise to the great opportunity that lies before us, it will be because we love easy ways, and material comfort, and all the pleasant things that come to us so readily, because we have lost the spirit of enterprise, the capacity to do hard things, and are content with trying to get the best out of life for ourselves. (n.p.)

Creighton intertwines service to God and service to empire for her girl readers. The "opportunity" of empire is achievable only if the British people – and the readers themselves, who are explicitly understood as British, even if they reside in the colonies – rise to the occasion and eschew material comfort to do the "hard things" that make life better for all. She also reminds girls that they should be religious role models: "Women who follow their husbands into the distant parts of the earth, and are called to be home-makers in new lands, may find themselves not only compelled to stand alone, but called upon to help maintain the religious life in others" (Creighton n.p.). The women to whom Creighton refers are presumably not the colonial readers of the annual, since the target readers, based on the contents, are likely unmarried girls under twenty years of age. Yet she invites girls to imagine a future in which they follow their husbands to the far reaches of the empire to be homemakers and help instill a religious life in others. While girls, both British and colonial, might have different perspectives on the empire – colonial girls

3.2 Masthead from *The Girls' Empire*, 1902.

are less likely to follow husbands elsewhere, for example – Creighton nonetheless appeals to all when she remarks that

> [m]any girls have dreams of the great things they would like to do. But they do not know how to begin, and so they are restless and discontented. The first thing to do is to train themselves, to do every little thing that comes along as well as they can, so as to fit themselves for the higher work that may come. It is worth while for them to go on with their studies, to train their minds to habits of accurate thought, to gain knowledge of all kinds, for all this may not only prove useful in the future, but will make them themselves better instruments for any work that may come to them to do. (n.p.)

She emphasizes the need for service. Girls must train themselves so they will be ready to help wherever they are required, in England or in one of her colonies, for "there is some service wanted from you; to give that service will be your greatest blessing, your deepest joy" (Creighton n.p.).

Other annuals produced at the turn of the twentieth century were less overtly concerned with the female role of service, instead focusing on the new opportunities available to girls. The earlier, and short-lived, *The Girls' Empire: An Annual for English-Speaking Girls All over the World* (1902–4) catered to a wider range of interests, including athletics, exercise, and sport; health; cooking; pets; and employment. Yet empire remained a central concern. Unlike *The Empire Annual*, which targeted specific girls with its customized cover and title pages, *The Girls' Empire* was aimed at imperial girls and made no effort to target specific girls based on nationality. In the masthead (see Figure 3.2), a girl stands in the middle of the image with a globe in front of her. The rays of a setting sun extend over her head. To her left are golf clubs and a ball, while a music stand, a violin, and an open book appear on her right. These objects represent the range of an imperial girl's activities, including sport, music, and learning. The implication is that any girl living within the borders of the British Empire understands her duty to the empire.

In *The Girls' Empire*, this ideal of girlhood is articulated in articles such as "A Maori Princess: Te Rangi Pai," in which the author writes that "thoughtful girls cannot fail to feel an interest in the possible development of those races which constitute Greater Britain. This interest ... is naturally greatest in the direction of the women of those lands which have been absorbed by us in different parts of the world" (L.S.B. 89). The author asserts a shared imperial identity based on gender (where girls will be interested in other girls), empire (where girls are united by their connection to Great Britain), and race (where non-white girls are presumed not to be part of the empire). Belonging to this wider imperial community of girls carries responsibilities as well: "Many wise and beautiful things about the Maoris [*sic*] are to be found in several well-known books, which if you have never read, as girls of the Empire, and presuming you wish to be well-informed, it will be your duty to get" (L.S.B. 89). The books recommended by L.S.B. are not children's literature. Instead, they include *The Long White Cloud* (1898), a history of New Zealand by the Hon W.P. Reeves; *Maori Superstitions* by Sir George Grey; and *The Defenders of New Zealand: Being a Short Biography of Colonists Who Distinguished Themselves in Upholding Her Majesty's Supremacy in These Islands* (1887) by Walter Edward Gudgeon. These texts are clearly aimed at adult readers, yet their inclusion in a girls' booklist implies that girls were interested in and expected to be capable of this level of reading and had access to these texts. To be knowledgeable about the empire is defined as an essential duty of all imperial girls.

Colonial Girlhood in Colonial Newspapers and Magazines

In colonial newspapers and magazines, the colonial girl is described using different language from that used by British publications. Instead of a providing a model of girlhood that depended on a shared imperial identity, colonial periodicals highlighted aspects of girlhood that could be considered national rather than imperial. A variety of newspapers and magazines throughout Canada, Australia, and New Zealand attempted to define their respective countries' girls in ways that privileged national qualities, often as part of the nascent nationalism that characterized all three countries from the 1880s to the early 1900s. In 1887, an

"Englishman" writes to the *Otago Witness* to inquire whether charges that New Zealand girls are "forward and fast" are well founded ("Girls of New Zealand" 33). An unnamed correspondent responds that the "above letter cannot fail to astonish the colonials who read it": New Zealand girls "will join me in laughing" at this depiction of girlhood because these girls "have a truehearted smile for every worthy man or woman" ("Girls of New Zealand" 33). Rejecting classist British society, the correspondent explains that life in New Zealand "encourages individuality and freedom of thought," and yet these girls "all marry unless they choose to remain single – marry and make good wives, and in due time rear a race of fine sons" ("Girls of New Zealand" 33). Girls' future roles as wives and mothers are foregrounded in this response, and the writer asserts that girls are not less womanly "because [their] bodies have grown to maturity under this sunny sky" ("Girls of New Zealand" 33). Girlhood in a colonial location produces women who are as feminine as those in Britain.

An article on "The Antipodean Girl" (originally by "Dog Toby" in *The New Zealand Graphic*) in 1909 describes the Australasian girl as "one of the finest types of womanhood in the world," a compliment that fills one "with hope for the future ... [for] the girls and women of our country are of a type fitted to train and to rear children who shall be equal to the very best that our British stock has produced" ("Dog" 11). This girl is situated within both racial and imperial frameworks with the reference to "British stock," and she is highly valued for the ways in which her reproductive and civilizing abilities can further the needs of the nation. This national–colonial framework is emphasized when "Dog Toby" explores the "many varied qualities" of the New Zealand girl, who will

> ride ten or fifteen miles to a dance, dance all night, ride home in the morning, and turn up to her work as fresh as ever. She has the glow of health and the natural charm of those who live in intimate contact with Nature. She makes a dutiful and devoted daughter, she makes a true and loving wife. The country girl in New Zealand represents the highest and best type of womanhood to be found the world over. ("Dog" 11)

Hard-working, fun-loving, healthy, natural, dutiful, and devoted, the New Zealand girl is the ideal daughter and wife, and she is superior to girls from elsewhere in the colonies and beyond.

Similar assertions are made about "The Canadian Girl" in *The Canadian Magazine* in 1896. Reginald Gourlay writes that this girl "presents the promise ... of developing into one of the highest types of womanhood" (506).

Like the Antipodean girl of the bush, the Canadian girl of the backwoods has the "superb vitality of the healthy vigorous race [of Canadians] from which she springs, [which] enables [her] to triumph over hardships and toils that would crush ... the daughter of a less vigorous stock" (Gourlay 507). This girl possesses physical beauty as well as a "frank kindliness of manner, an innocent self respect, and the remarkable equipoise and common sense which is to be found in her as well as in her more cultured sister" (Gourlay 507). As in "The Antipodean Girl," an attempt is made to distinguish between classes of girls, yet the Canadian girl of the upper "and generally more favoured classes" fares better than the potentially "snobbish" New Zealand city girl ("Dog" 11). The Canadian "society girl is both charming and ... genuine" (Gourlay 508). Her beauty "will stand the open air and a strong light" for she is "the flower of this strong, beautiful northern land, and a full share of its vigour and the best of its beauty is concentrated in her" (Gourlay 508). Moreover, "unlike the tropical evanescent loveliness of her Australian sister," her beauty "is not a mere gift for her youth, to be lost before she is thirty, but is, like her other qualities, meant to last" (Gourlay 508).

The comparison with Australian girlhood is natural given the connection of empire. A similar comparison is made in "The Antipodean Girl," in which the New Zealand girl is inevitably compared to the English girl: she is "more natural, less tied to conventions, more able to turn her hand to a variety of different things" ("Dog" 11). She is, however, lacking that "subtle, indefinable charm" of the "highly-bred English gentlewoman" ("Dog" 11). Although nationalism is surely a factor in these discussions, Gourlay claims he is not influenced by "any feeling of pseudo-patriotism" but is "stating a simple fact" (508). He asserts the universalism of Anglo-Saxon femininity: "It has been said with a good deal of truth, that in physical type, manner, tone of voice, culture, and even prejudices, there is the strongest possible resemblance between the women and girls of the upper classes, in all those countries inhabited by the great Anglo-Saxon race" (Gourlay 508). This assertion reflects middle-class ideologies of girlhood in which girls are presumed to resemble one another because of their racial background and their economic status. Yet a girl's future is important because of her connection to the nation: the girl "is the hope of her land, and has duties, aspirations, and a great future before her, and there is every sign that she will prove equal to her destinies" (Gourlay 508).

A similar discussion of the Australian girl was prompted by the publication of an article by Australian writer Rosa Campbell Praed in the girls' periodical *The Girl's Realm* in January 1899. *The Girl's Realm* is a British periodical that was intended primarily for British girls, although the editor acknowledges readers throughout the British colonies. In her article, Praed signals the connection to Australia's English heritage: "It is not that the Australian girl is cleverer, or prettier, or physically or mentally superior to girls of other countries. It is not that she differs in marked degree from her cousins in Great Britain – it is hardly expected that she should – but she differs enough to show that she is Australian, and not English; that she has individuality of her own" (249). Praed suggests a uniqueness to Australian girlhood that is related to the Australian setting, for she "appears to best advantage in her particular environment," especially "the girl of the bush" (250). The "bush girl" is a "natural product of the peculiar features which make Australia unlike all other countries" (Praed 250). Although the distinct Australian setting is fundamental to definitions of the Australian girl, she nonetheless "has a knack of refinement" regardless of the fact that she may "be poorly educated" or may "run almost wild, hobnob with blacks, ride after cattle, and scrub, cook, and clean" (Praed 250).

This pride in Australian girls echoes the sentiments about New Zealand and Canadian girls. What is surprising about the Praed article is the extent to which it was reprinted in Australian daily and weekly newspapers. After its appearance in the January 1899 issue, ten newspapers around Australia reprinted it between 4 February and 1 April.[5] Although Australian newspapers regularly reprinted materials originally appearing elsewhere, Praed's article was obviously expected to be of interest to Australian readers. Simon J. Potter explains that "one newspaper would pirate an item from an overseas journal, and others would then reprint the reprint" ("Webs" 629). This reflects the complex reality that the "commercialized mass media in the British Empire could sometimes link its fortunes with global identities but, at other times, seek to tap a national sense of community" (S. Potter, "Webs" 644). In this instance, an article written by an Australian author and published in a British periodical that travelled to the British colonies was reprinted in local Australian newspapers. The imperial network of media circulation is the basis

5 The article was reprinted in the *Launceston Examiner* on 11 February, *The Maitland Daily Mercury* on 11 February, *The Maitland Weekly Mercury* on 18 February, the *Daily News* on 4 February, the *Kalgoorlie Western Argus* on 16 February, the *Kalgoorlie Miner* on 7 February, the *Western Mail* on 3 March, *The Queenslander* on 25 February, the *Albury Banner and Wodonga Express* on 10 February, and the *West Australian* on 1 April.

for this transaction, yet the article also addresses national identity and belonging.

Readers were motivated to respond to Praed's article, particularly in Melbourne's *Argus.* In a letter appearing on 8 February 1899, "Aunt Tabitha" takes issue with Praed's rosy tone and finds Australian girls to be "weak and colourless" (8). Another "terrible defect" is a "want of originality" combined with a lack of intellectual endeavour ("Aunt" 8). She critiques their reading habits, which include immensely popular British novels such as Marie Corelli's *The Sorrows of Satan* (1895) and Mrs Humphry Ward's *Robert Elsmere* (1888). These adult novels were not intended to be read by girls, thereby suggesting the precociousness of the colonial girl. Although she acknowledges that Australian girls are adaptable, she feels that "it would be better for the future wives and mothers of Australia" if they began remedying their faults rather than "listening complacently to columns of gushing praise" ("Aunt" 8).

A response in *The Australasian* on 11 February 1899 signals that the discussion of Praed's article transcends the boundaries of any one periodical. The author rejects "Aunt Tabitha's" claims, asserting that the "Australian girl of to-day ... is industrious, original, energetic, thrifty, cheerful, affectionate, and neat in dress" ("Boyet" 44). A.F.M. responds in the *Argus* on 11 February 1899, similarly rejecting "Aunt Tabitha's" "very disagreeable remarks," declaring, "I feel that I must say a word in our defence" (10). Her use of "our" is significant because it indicates that girls (rather than the presumably adult contributors) are reading and responding to the discussion about Australian girlhood. She argues that the "Australian girl is possessed of energy and life enough to face any difficulties or troubles that come to her, and she invariably proves herself to be capable and competent in any work she may be called upon ... to undertake" (A.F.M. 10). "Aunt Tabitha" wrote in again on 15 February 1899, remarking, "My criticism of the Australian girl has drawn out many able and willing champions" (5).

The discussion of the Australian girl also moved beyond the pages of the periodical press, as "Tasma" writes in the *Clarence and Richmond Examiner* on 18 March 1899. She explains that the Rev George Walters lectured on the idea of the Australian girl at the Independent Order of Odd Fellows (a Friendly Society) temple in Sydney, making reference to both Praed's article and correspondence appearing in the Melbourne *Argus.* The discussion of the Australian girl is imperial, national, and local, in print and in conversation, and it illuminates the complexities of the "webs" (to use Simon Potter's term) of interconnection embedded in ideologies of colonial girlhood.

In the late nineteenth and early twentieth century, and with the emergence of a strong network of publishers alongside the burgeoning market for children's literature, a homogenous model of girlhood was produced through British fiction, periodicals, and annuals for girls. Novels written by Bessie Marchant demonstrate that the colonial girl was an ideal figure who understood the need for a strong work ethic, a positive attitude, and a willingness to care for others. The colonial girl depicted in British texts rarely includes any distinct national qualities of girlhood. Instead, the colonial girl has similar qualities based on her pluck, her willingness to work, and her commitment to her family. The ubiquity of this model of girlhood in British periodicals and annuals likewise contributed to its spread throughout both British and colonial girls' texts, since girls were expected to – and did – read undifferentiated material that depicted girlhood as universal.

Only discussions of girlhood in colonial newspapers depict a heightened anxiety about girlhood and the ways in which colonial girls might lack specific feminine qualities. At the turn of the twentieth century, journalists and commentators in Canada, Australia, and New Zealand were keenly interested in the definitions of colonial girlhood and the ways that those definitions were oriented towards girls' future capabilities as wives and mothers. Although attempts were made to identify specific attributes of Canadian, Australian, and New Zealand girls, these qualities were often quite similar. Like the qualities of girlhood appearing in Marchant's novels, each national type was natural, adaptable, capable, and healthy. Yet the fiction and annuals that were written and published in London produced a homogenous model of girlhood based on shared assumptions about femininity and focused on girls as courageous heroines who understood their responsibilities to family, nation, and empire.

What remains consistent in these two different approaches is the attitude towards empire. Colonial girls could, and did, see themselves as part of the imperial project while also being firmly located within the confines of the nation. As we will see in subsequent chapters, the nation is a constant concern, but transnational ideas and ideals of girlhood transcend the nation to produce models that are more similar than they are different. In the next section, "National and Transnational Dynamics," we examine how ideas about family, environment, and race serve to complicate the imperial ideal of girlhood and produce a transnational model that incorporates national distinctiveness within a shared network based on imperial belonging.

SECTION TWO

National and Transnational Dynamics

CHAPTER FOUR

The Colonial and Imperial Family

We little thought when Trixie, the little barbarian, as we called her, came to us from Canada, that we should all eventually be thankful to her for much solid comfort and happiness.

–Edith C. Kenyon, *A Girl from Canada* (1911)

Most of the classics of British and American girls' literature that are still read today are stories of family life, such as Louisa May Alcott's *Little Women* (1868), or of child protagonists finding family, as in Frances Hodgson Burnett's *The Secret Garden* (1911). Colonial girls' fiction is similarly preoccupied with family. There are many shared tropes and conventions in girls' domestic fiction across the English-speaking world, most obviously in its marking out the home and family as the future spheres of a girl's influence. Nevertheless, there are also unique aspects to the depiction of families in young nations emerging from their colonial past in the late nineteenth and early twentieth century. Novels about unconventional family groupings, in which orphaned or abandoned children go on to forge new relationships and establish a sense of belonging, are common in British, Canadian, Australian, and New Zealand girls' fiction published in the first decades of the twentieth century. The most enduring of these is L.M. Montgomery's *Anne of Green Gables*, which we consider in the following chapter in relation to the environment. Elizabeth Galway observes, however, that the narrative arc of orphan Anne Shirley, "as she gradually finds a place of belonging in her new community and develops a strong sense of self, mirrors Canada's own journey towards claiming an identity for itself" (37). While *Anne of Green Gables* is the most prominent example, dozens of novels depict colonial girls finding their place within new families that are also embedded within new attitudes about nation and empire.

In this chapter, we explain how these unconventional and makeshift families, usually with orphaned girls at their cores, reflect shifting imperial and national contexts. There are two distinct plot types we consider, involving the movement of girls' bodies – and their sense of belonging – to and from the imperial centre. In a number of British girls' novels, the stories of orphaned colonial girls who must return to their remaining relatives in England simultaneously grapple with ideas about familial and imperial forms of belonging. In contrast, Canadian, Australian, and New Zealand girls' novels about orphaned or abandoned children test how fluid the concept of family – and by extension national belonging – might be, often eschewing the biological family as the only rightful place for children. In Isabel Maud Peacocke's *The Adopted Family* (1923), for instance, an Irish girl prefers to live in New Zealand with a man and a Māori boy, both unrelated to her, rather than living with her biological family, yoking together a new colonial identity with a new definition of family. We contrast these two conceptions of colonial girls' travel within the British Empire to demonstrate how ideas of belonging within nation and empire were represented through the metaphor of family. These novels represent girls as easily incorporated within their new families and homelands, readily transforming colonial girls into British girls, and British girls into colonial girls, eliding the differences between the two through their suggestion of a transnational sense of girlhood.

The concept of family is always shifting and politically contentious. The ideal family is not simply a fantasy, Annette Alston suggests, but "an ideological system in which issues of power and control are embedded" (9). Both mythical and fictional idealized families model how adults should parent, and how children should behave, but also act as indicators of national strength, morality, and imperial ties. The facts surrounding the historical organization and function of families are continually debated and revised, yet the importance of valorized constructions of family in Victorian England are well established. As Elizabeth Thiel notes, the supportive family existed well before the nineteenth century, "but it was the Victorians who sought to elevate its status to that of an icon and, in so doing, to create a sense of permanence and stability in a country beset by social anxieties" (2). Indeed, when contemporary critics lament a perceived decline in the "traditional" family, as George Behlmer suggests, they often look to the past, particularly to the middle-class family "in that most famously domestic of cultures, Victorian England" (2). In the age of empire and emigration, family ties were often stretched, and expected to endure, across geographical bounds. Families in England functioned as "a beacon welcoming those back from foreign travels and the work of empire" (Peters 3), signalling the belief in an enduring connection to the mother country.

Part of the ideological work of the family is to embody the qualities seen as constitutive of nations. Behlmer describes the idealized family as "a well-armored 'little commonwealth'" (2), drawing attention to the role of families – "the most basic of imagined communities" (1) – as the building blocks of the imagined community of nation. Alston observes that the Victorian family "acted as an analogy for the health and strength of the nation" (19). Within the context of children's literature, as Kimberley Reynolds suggests, the fact that family is "central to the work of nation" is evident in novels from various time periods and national origins ("Changing" 199), such as *The Swiss Family Robinson* (1814) and Laura Ingalls Wilder's Little House books (1932–43). However, in her study of orphans, Laura Peters argues that the family and what it represented, namely "legitimacy, race and national belonging" (1), was in crisis in the nineteenth century in response to the effects of capitalism, industrialization, modernity, and empire, and was "at best an unsustainable ideal" (143). With the family understood as the foundation of a mighty and morally superior England that rightfully extended its influence throughout the British Empire, representations of families carried great ideological weight. Though there were various understandings of family and diverse realities in terms of the constitution of households, the Victorian family ideal was "patrilineal and nuclear" (Behlmer 3). The Census of England and Wales of 1871 made this plain in its description of the complete, "natural" family: "The natural family is founded in marriage, and consists, in its complete state, of husband, wife, and children" (Census). Yet many families were incomplete by these standards, and in children's literature, "unnatural" families were perhaps more commonly represented.

Girls' fiction often focuses extensively on how protagonists might prepare for their future work as wives and mothers, as we discuss elsewhere with respect to maternal feminism in Canadian and Australian fiction,[1] yet biological mothers are frequently absent from narratives about

1 See Kristine Moruzi and Michelle J. Smith, "Education and Work in Service of the Nation: Canadian and Australian Girls' Fiction, 1908–1921," *Colonial Girlhood in Literature, Culture and History, 1840–1950*, ed. Kristine Moruzi and Michelle J. Smith (Houndmills, UK: Palgrave Macmillan, 2014), 180–94.

colonial girls. In one sense, motherless colonial girls are free to temporarily eschew conventional expectations of femininity, as in the adventure fiction of Bessie Marchant. Nevertheless, a significant number of British narratives use the absent or deceased mother (and eventually the absent or deceased father) to enable colonial identity to be subsumed through the protagonist's reincorporation into England. In the following section, we consider two British novels in which orphaned Canadian and Australian girl protagonists find or create loving family connections in England, showing the ease with which colonial girls can find multiple layers of belonging in the mother country. In another British example, movement by extended family members between England and Australia reinforces the intertwined primacy of familial belonging and England as home. In the final section, we examine novels by Canadian and New Zealand authors that enable colonial girls to fashion new, adoptive families around themselves. In these two novels, unconventional or "transnormative" families are shaped just as easily as new homes in the colonies are for their English and Irish-born protagonists, contributing to what Peters describes as the "familial nature of empire by settling the colonies with British children" (79). The ease with which both colonial and British girl protagonists embrace their new homes is another example of the transnational ideal of girlhood.

Colonial Girls Return to England

English books about colonial girls, like girls' adventure fiction more generally, appear quite late in the nineteenth century and are most visible in the first decades of the twentieth century, corresponding with the height of empire. Esmé Stuart's *Harum Scarum: A Poor Relation* (1896), which was published in London, is unusual for a girls' novel of the period in that it was exceedingly successful and continued to be read for decades after its initial publication.[2] It is described in a review for *Hearth and Home* as "specially suited for girls from sixteen to twenty" ("Paperknife" 30). The novel went into at least eighteen British editions, an American edition, and a French translation and was sufficiently popular to inspire

2 Stuart was the pseudonym of Amélie Claire Leroy, a prolific novelist and contributor to periodicals. In the US edition of the novel, the subtitle "A Poor Relation" is replaced by "The Story of a Wild Girl." This is one indication of the way in which family connections between Britain and its colonies were important to readers across the British Empire but of less significance to American readers.

two sequels more than a decade later, *Harum Scarum's Fortune* in 1909 and *The Two Troubadours* (later titled *Harum Scarum Married*) in 1912. Typical of a number of English novels published between the 1890s and the first decades of the twentieth century, the book tells the story of a colonial girl who is orphaned and subsequently sent to England, a reversal of historical practice, from the mid nineteenth century into the twentieth century, in which the orphaned children of the English poor were conveniently dispatched to the colonies (Peters 17–18).[3] This subgenre of English girls' fiction includes two novels by E.L. Haverfield, *Dauntless Patty* (1909) and *The Girl from the Bush* (1912), and Ethel Talbot's *That Wild Australian School-Girl* (1925). In these novels, an Australian or Canadian girl typically causes significant discord upon arrival in England because of her colonial ways but is represented as endearing and morally superior to most English people because of her good-hearted actions and blindness to class-based conventions. Nevertheless, these novels find a range of ways to incorporate colonial girls into new families, and thereby into England, at their conclusions. In both *Harum Scarum* and Edith C. Kenyon's *A Girl from Canada* (1911), also published in England, Australian and Canadian girls are eventually accommodated within the mother country, and their desire to return to their homelands is easily discarded, even if some of the quirks that mark them out as colonial are not wholly erased. The paucity of newspaper reviews and library holdings for these particular novels suggests that they did not have significant circulation in the colonies. In this British fiction, likely aimed at British readers, it is critical to return colonial girls to the fold. In discourses about empire, the relationship between the imperial centre and its colonies was often constructed as that of a mother and child. An 1868 *Punch* cartoon, for example, represents Australia as a young girl holding a leashed kangaroo. The accompanying article, presented as if authored by "Mother Country Britannia," describes her as "a fine, handsome lass, with a bush of golden hair, blooming and buxom, who has not yet done growing – figure rather fuller than mine, but features much the same" ("Our Australian Cousin" 44). In the same way that individual family ties were stretched across the globe by emigration with expectations that they would endure, so too was England understood as a benevolent mother who would always welcome her daughters home.

3 See, in particular, Peters's chapter on "The Emigration of Orphan Children" (79–121). Peters points out that the emigration of orphans also represented "a concerted effort to ensure the familial nature of empire by settling the colonies with British children" (79).

Harum Scarum's Antonia "Toney" Whitburn is a sixteen-year-old Australian girl who is left penniless living in a "shed in the Bush" when her doctor father dies (Stuart 239). Toney's English uncle, Sir Evas, is sympathetic to the plight of his half-sister's orphaned child, but must engage in a "conflict of wills" to convince his wife, Lady Dove, to agree to offer her a home (21). With no children of her own, Aunt Dove fails to be a caring maternal substitute for Toney, and is continually aghast at her lack of knowledge about appropriate English behaviours and customs. Stuart reproduces the trope Thiel identifies in orphan fiction, in which (usually unmarried) "aunts are shown to have little or no skill in establishing a domestic idyll, [and] are frequently insensitive to children," while uncles of all descriptions are "likely to represent an exemplary family bond" (102). What is important in these novels is the familial connection between girls and uncles across the empire, which trumps the expected maternal connection between a woman and a child. As is typical in English depictions of colonial girls, such as *Dauntless Patty* and *That Wild Australian School-Girl*, Toney is closely associated with animals to connote her wild nature: her dog, Trick, which she brought with her to England, bites people on the ankle, and she has an affinity with horses and can "tame ... any animal who [comes] within reach of her magnetic influence" (62–3). She is physically active, enjoys running, does not wear stays, and has a strong concern for other people, regardless of the consequences. Aunt Dove deems that her niece is "decidedly vulgar," to which Toney replies, "Colonial, Aunt Dove; there's a shade of difference" (127), indicative of her failure to comprehend English feminine expectations. After resolving to "tame" Toney (41), Aunt Dove generates a daily timetable for her, which includes education at the vicar's home, but Toney's inherent colonial nature cannot be altered. She especially violates English class expectations and explains that Australians care more about industriousness than the kind of inherited privilege that has benefitted her relatives: "'We don't care about birth, you know, Uncle Dove, out there! It's low to ask what people were. You take a man just as he stands, that is with his boots on,' added Toney, laughing, 'because we do draw the line at beggars who won't work'" (28). Only shoeless idlers are beneath her notice.

Toney's troubling attitudes to work given the social standing of her relatives are evident when she assists the household servants and develops a much-frowned-upon affinity with Miss Crump, Lady Dove's companion. Toney performs several kind acts for the servant and ultimately reunites her with a former sweetheart with whom she has been out of contact for fifteen years. As a sign of her own tenuous position within the household, Toney resolves that she will assume Miss Crump's place as Lady Dove's companion to both enable Crump to marry and leave service and spare her resentful aunt the money required for her upkeep. Toney also shows kindness by nursing a young girl who contracts, and eventually dies from, scarlet fever, despite the risk of contracting the illness. Her selflessness and genuine nature impress a local man, General Stone, who rewards her with a substantial inheritance when he dies, removing her financial dependence upon her relations and ameliorating some of the attendant class issues through her new-found wealth. Toney's kindly uncle is made her sole guardian, while, according to the terms of the General's will, her aunt will receive a generous annual allowance for as long as Toney remains in their home, shifting the power balance between aunt and niece.

Despite her new-found wealth, Toney fails to measure up to an ideal of English womanhood, as Aunt Dove's critiques elucidate. Nevertheless, the reader is positioned to dislike Aunt Dove's selfishness throughout the series – *The Times*'s review of *Harum Scarum* describes her as "objectionable" ("Recent Novels" 5) – and thereby dismiss her rejection of Toney's incorporation within England. Toney imagines that she will eventually build houses for the needy with her fortune, and she will always remain true to "the principles she had imbibed from her father" (283). The qualities that signify Toney's Australianness, including her sense of fairness, remain unchanged, but her acceptance into England and the omission of any mention of a desire to return to Australia minimize the distinctions between identification with the colonies and connection to the imperial centre. The novel's resolution suggests that Australians are effectively "British" at heart. Nevertheless, some aspects of the colonial egalitarianism retained by Toney constitute an improvement on local traditions, thereby suggesting that some new ways of being that are fostered in white settler colonies could, in turn, be embraced in Britain.

Toney's transition to English life is completed in subsequent novels, in which she is able to shape the family to which she will belong. In *Harum Scarum's Fortune*, Toney turns twenty-one and is no longer required to live under her aunt and uncle's supervision. Though she retains some characteristics that are marked as Australian, Toney is content with life in England, comes together with her future husband at the conclusion of *Harum Scarum's Fortune*, and is depicted raising her two English-born sons in the final title in the series. In Stuart's series, as in several of these novels of colonial returnees, there is not a hybrid sense of belonging but rather a simple reincorporation into English life, which is easily enacted but which leaves some of the characteristics of the colonial type unchanged. This representation is distinct from that of the nationalist figure of the "Australian Girl" in Australian print culture, a uniquely local manifestation of modern, independent femininity that Angela Woollacott suggests served as "a vehicle for combatting English condescension to colonials" (*To Try* 159). Instead, this English novel somewhat unrealistically severs Toney from her Australian life and identity, thereby suggesting a homogenous model of colonial girlhood that is, at its core, comparable to British girlhood.

Published just a year before *Harum Scarum Married*, Kenyon's *A Girl from Canada* is a remarkably similar narrative about an orphaned colonial girl who must live with relatives in England. Thirteen-year-old Beatrice "Trixie" Parker from Winnipeg is also unwanted by her aunt, Mary Anderson, but her uncle, Robert, insists that his sister's daughter must come to live with the family. His family connection with Trixie and his late sister, which stands regardless of distance across the empire, is foregrounded in one of the novel's illustrations (Figure 4.1), with the caption "Mother said, 'Tell your Uncle Robert that I have always loved him.'" The image shows the family connection being restored as Trixie sits on her uncle's knee in a highly domestic setting. In chapter 3, we demonstrated that girls' fiction frequently expressed a sense of community or connection across the British Empire. Trixie, however, feels no real connection or affinity with England, and her sense of "home" is understood as distinctly Canadian (63). Rather than viewing her as a daughter of the empire, her "hypercritical relations" form a negative opinion of her "slight American accent" (16). As in a number of other stories of returned colonial girls,[4] Trixie has no awareness of or concern with upholding English class distinctions, and she initially clings to the family's maid, Lucy Smith, just as Toney aligns herself with the servant Miss Crump. At the outset of this narrative, and in other similar stories, the colonial girl is implicitly aligned with the lower classes, disrupting conventional ideas about familial relationships and class. Trixie's "wild" temperament is also emphasized through her affinity with animals, especially horses, and when she escapes from her locked bedroom through a window, she is hyperbolically described as "a little barbarian from the wilds of Canada" (31).

4 See Michelle J. Smith, "Wild Australian Girls?" *Girls, Texts, Cultures*, ed. Clare Bradford and Mavis Reimer (Waterloo, ON: Wilfrid Laurier University Press, 2015), 237–60.

MOTHER SAID, "TELL YOUR UNCLE ROBERT THAT I HAVE ALWAYS LOVED HIM."

4.1 "Mother said, 'Tell your Uncle Robert that I have always loved him.'" Illust. Victor Prout. Edith C. Kenyon, *A Girl from Canada* (London: Religious Tract Society, 1911).

The narrative nevertheless depicts a greater change in Trixie's demeanour and dress than Toney undergoes, as she gradually bends to English feminine ideals in an attempt to find her place within her new family. She is initially mystified by expectations about fine clothing, preferring to ride a horse to a visit and wait outside the home rather than wear her best clothing. Trixie exclaims, "But I cannot be everything" (52), when concerns are expressed about her shabby dress. "Everything" represents the clash of English convention with youthful Canadian femininity borne of isolation as well as greater freedoms and dangers. She explains her running abilities, which she learned from her father: "on our lonely farm, if any evil-disposed person came when the men were away, it might be that a girl could only find safety in flight, or if there was a big forest-fire near, coming our way, we might have to run from that" (69). We examine in further detail in the next chapter the transition, in the early twentieth century, to girl protagonists who are capable and hardy in colonial natural environments. As Trixie cannot be "everything," she learns to discard those aspects of her colonial femininity that are not valued in England. In a modified version of the civilizing narrative typical of an Indigenous character, Trixie begins to dress in "pretty clothing," and as her "English education" progresses, she begins to feel "a new timidity about thrusting her opinions on others," as English people "have to fall into ranks and observe restrictions of which we knew nothing in Canada" (139). These are superficial attributes, however, and the most admirable of Trixie's heroic and selfless qualities, which are common to heroines across British girls' school stories and adventure fiction, remain intact. For instance, when a boat capsizes, Trixie removes her clothes, swims out to the boat, and saves her cousin, Elsie, from drowning. Twenty-one-year-old Elsie serves as the point of comparison with Trixie. Not only is she unable to swim, she is also unable to relate to people outside of her social sphere, like the nearby Tomkins family, who are farmers. While Elsie manages to offend the Tomkins family, Trixie is always welcome in their home, and when the Andersons fall on hard times, she runs away to become the Tomkinses' "servant," showing her desire not to be a financial burden upon her relatives.

As Trixie is eminently likeable, several homes are available to her at the novel's conclusion, including that of Mr Atkinson, an "elderly colonial" who made his money from the Californian gold-fields (249). Mr Atkinson takes a shine to Trixie and wishes to adopt her, thereby making her an heiress. The millionaire is actually Uncle Robert's estranged brother, John, who has assumed a different name, and Trixie is confronted with the dilemma of wanting both uncles in her life. Trixie inspires the brothers to forgive each other for their past dispute, and John, the millionaire, helps his brother re-establish himself, as well as providing money for Robert's daughters. As Trixie and Uncle John "have won each other's love," she chooses to live with him, with Uncle Robert's blessing (283). After a brief trip to Canada to visit her childhood home, the uncle and niece establish a home on an estate in England. The novel closes with cousin Elsie remarking to her sister, Hilda, that they had not considered when "the little barbarian" arrived they "should all eventually be thankful to her for much solid comfort and happiness" (284). The shame and financial dependency that English family members imagine that the colonial girl will bring never eventuate; instead, she improves the lot of her relatives, much as the colonies themselves generated wealth for Britain through trade and natural resources.

In both novels, colonial girls inspire love through their genuine natures, heroism, and concern for others. These qualities enable the orphaned girls to shape new family bonds that are not based solely on blood or class lines. The formation of Trixie's new loving family with Uncle John, which is at the core of *A Girl from Canada*'s happy ending, very clearly includes the servant Lucy, who will live with Trixie, and the Tomkins family. Her connection with her Aunt and cousins is minimized and is entirely absent from the description of the new family structure with which Trixie is rewarded. While Trixie is able to improve the situation of Aunt Mary, Uncle Robert, and her cousins, heredity alone is not enough to provide Trixie with an ideal home. The narratives of both Trixie and Toney demonize aunts and valorize uncles in ways that Thiel suggests commonly work in children's literature to reinforce patriarchy and "the concept of male supremacy" (102). Nevertheless, the colonial girl protagonists in these novels do play a crucial part in shaping new families from the unwelcoming English ones they are initially forced to inhabit. Toney achieves this by banding together with other like-minded individuals to perform charity work until she is emancipated and then builds a new English family of her own, while Trixie remodels the concept of family through bonds based on love, which transcend heredity and class boundaries.

In both novels, the shared qualities of the imagined colonial girl are evident: there is very little to distinguish the returned Canadian girl from the returned Australian girl. Likewise, both colonial girls, after initial hurdles largely erected by disagreeable aunts, are easily reincorporated into England at the centre of their own, newly constituted families. Toney and Trixie are transnational figures in their similarities and because of the way in which their colonial identities are largely erased as they settle into England. As daughters of the empire, they are welcomed into the metaphorical English family even if immediate family blood ties are weak or compromised.

E.L. Haverfield's *Dauntless Patty* (1909) and *The Girl from the Bush* (1912) fit a similar model of orphaned Australian girls returning to England. Her *Queensland Cousins* (1908), however, provides a slightly different manifestation of this transportable model of girlhood in its representation of the ultimate Englishness of the colonial girl who still belongs to a traditional family. The novel denies the possibility of colonial identity among colonial-born children and emphasizes the danger and undesirability of Australian life. The story's Orban children, who live on a north Queensland sugar plantation, feel no attachment to Australia and describe England as their "real 'home'" and "our country" because of the sense of belonging engendered by their mother's stories of her life there (191, 98). The narrator repeatedly uses the word "our" to connote English beliefs and notions of superiority, for example, in the remark that "the common things of our everyday existence were marvels to [the Australian children]" (16). The eldest girl of the family, Nesta, is enamoured with the idea of England, remarking, "English stories always make me ache to go there" (17), which, predictably, is exactly the effect conveyed by the novel, with persistent emphasis on the hardships and dangers of Australia as contrasted with the desirable qualities of England. Mrs Orban finds life on the plantation distressing but must remain because work for her husband is not as readily found in England. Nesta's brother, Eustace, on whom most of the Australian section of the narrative rests, is assigned the protective role over their mother in their father's absence on business travel. His protection is required because of the threats of wild Indigenous neighbours and a thief who has been stealing from the property, who turns out to be the stablehand, Manuel. Manuel's acts, which throw the family into a panic in the absence of Mr Orban, also highlight the Orbans' experience of the unsettling presence of Chinese and Malay field hands with no "white neighbours" nearby (22).

In addition to positioning implied British readers to understand the Australian landscape and fauna as unnatural, the novel encourages the reader to share the perspective of the Orbans' English relatives, such as their class-inflected judgment of how the Orbans appear in photographs as "pasty-faced, spiritless beings. The prints that the girls were dressed in were rather washed out; Peter had outgrown his suit. They were ill-clad, shy and awkward" (95). *Queensland Cousins* works against the mythology present in other British and Australian texts of Australian life as provoking health and vigour, such as in the pro-emigration propaganda in the *Girl's Own Paper*, where these benefits are emphasized for working-class girls. The negative perception of Australian life in *Queensland Cousins* rests largely on the middle-class English family's viewing their relatives as having fallen below their station because of the threats to domesticity and to firm class boundaries encouraged by colonial labour. Unlike the first two novels discussed above, which use colonial girls to critique class norms, however, *Queensland Cousins* upholds these class values and positions the Australian girl as desiring acceptance into that system.

Andrew Hassam suggests that when colonial Australians visited Britain, the "desire for recognition and incorporation" prevailed (4). The remainder of the narrative of *Queensland Cousins* shows the Orban children's struggle to be welcomed "home" to England by their cousins, Herbert and Brenda Dixon, who are horrified by Australian customs and act as gatekeepers of the incorporation that was eagerly desired by colonial returnees. The Orbans' failure to adhere to class or age distinctions through work on their sugar plantation is of particular offence to Brenda: "The thought of her uncle going daily to his work in shirt-sleeves; of her aunt helping in housework; her cousins brought up just anyhow, without a governess or any schooling, shocked her sensibilities" (189). The real debate that occurs between the cousins relates to the domestic space of Maze Court, the Dixons' home. The British cousins suggest that the Australian children eat with their servants, drawing attention to their lack of knowledge about the class divisions within the middle-class English home, and snobbishly remind the Orban children that people dress for dinner in England, unlike "savages" (189). These sleights and the resulting arguments provoke the children to engage in a battle of domestic knowledge on a tour of the house.

Where Eustace was pre-eminent as the protector of the Australian homestead in the narrative segment set in Australia, in the portion of the novel set in England, his sister Nesta comes to the fore in the domestic realm. As Herbert shows the Orban children around the family home and introduces each room, Nesta repeatedly interrupts, demonstrating her knowledge of this English family domicile and taking up the challenge to demonstrate Australian civility and domestic knowledge. Nesta wins out over her English cousin Brenda when she demonstrates her fuller knowledge of family history in correctly identifying the portrait of an ancestor. Nesta is annoyed by her brother's failure to join in the task of showing the refinement of the Australians and solidifying their place within their extended English family.

The initial conflict between the cousins and the reluctance shown by the Australians to remain in England is largely due to the mistaken belief that their Aunt Dorothy – who briefly visits the Orbans in Queensland – has drowned on the ship journey back to England. When she miraculously returns, the unease dissolves: "The change was something like a fairy tale to the Bush children; every one seemed suddenly 'magiked' into different beings. This, then, was home as mother had known it" (235). The transformation to contented British children is achieved instantaneously, with any sense that the children might wish to return to Queensland neatly quashed and Australian identity instantly erased. Furthermore, the novel suggests that ties to Australian identity are easily broken, particularly in light of the obvious superiority of British life, again reinforcing the primacy of a transnational identity. The novels discussed in the preceding section reinforce that colonial girls are at once British girls and project the myth that colonial girls will always have a home in the mother country. As we will show in the following section, the transnational qualities of the colonial girl are similarly evident in novels in which girls born in Britain or Ireland are equally able to find new families, new homes, and a new sense of belonging in the colonies. These novels emphasize the ease with which colonial girls, colonial identities, and colonial homes can be made, demonstrating that the slippage between British and colonial girlhood was imagined to operate in both directions.

Adoptive Families and Adopted Lands

Children's fiction at the turn of the century most commonly emphasizes a girl's rightful place with her mother, father, and siblings, if they exist. This tendency is evident in Ethel Turner's *Mother's Little Girl* (1904), in which a suburban Sydney family who falls on hard times eventually, and reluctantly, agrees to allow their youngest daughter to be sent to live with her childless aunt in Queensland. In return for a sum of money that helps the large Waller family out of straitened times, and the provision of the best care and fineries for the infant girl, Aunt Alice is permitted to raise Sylvia as her own. Nevertheless, as Sylvia grows, she controls the adults who seek to indulge her. When Sylvia eventually has the opportunity to interact with her biological siblings, whom she believes to be cousins, she is innately drawn to them and wants to behave as they do.

When Alice finally realizes that Sylvia rightfully belongs with her birth family, her husband, Wilf, agrees that "she would have grown to far better womanhood in the rough-and-tumble of the nest she belonged to" (241). This novel asserts the primacy of family ties, which remain unbroken even through the separation of a child from her closest blood relations. The title of the serialized version of the story in the *Kalgoorlie Western Argus* (1904–5), "The Gift Impossible," makes it clear that a loving mother can never willingly relinquish a child, no matter how much it might benefit a lonely relative.

Nevertheless, despite stories such as *Mother's Little Girl*, which are fixated on the unbreakable bonds of biological family, in a sizeable number of novels, particularly those set in the colonies, child protagonists have either been wholly orphaned or have at least lost their mothers. This is particularly the case in relation to those stories in which girls have been raised by their fathers, who later also pass away, as is the situation in both *A Girl from Canada* and *Harum Scarum*, as well as in L.M. Montgomery's *Emily of New Moon* (1923). Mortality rates of the period meant that widows were twice as common as widowers in England. However, men outnumbered women overall in the colonies, and colonial girls in fiction are far more likely to have lost their mothers. In 1963, Rosemary Wighton observed that "the list of no-mothers in Ethel Turner far outweighs the list of mothers," noting the way in which the author popularized "the freedom and pathos of the motherless Australian child" (19). With the sacred bond of mother and child dissolved in so many stories of colonial girls, different kinds of family constructions become possible and desirable, much the same way that bonds with the mother country can be subordinated to an embrace of colonial and national identifications.

Adopted families, in particular, suggest that unconventional, makeshift kinds of families can provide an equally loving home as and sense of belonging equivalent to the traditional family. It is worth briefly turning here to scholarship on the orphan in American literature, which repeatedly describes the parentless child as a distinctly American preoccupation tied to the nation's historical origins. Carol J. Singley, for instance, describes "disrupted biological families and elective family units" as "a defining feature of American literature, in a way that is strikingly absent in other national literatures" (3). Singley proposes a connection between the representation of orphans and American independence in her suggestion that "as the colonies came of age, won political independence from England, and flourished as a new nation, writers embraced a mythology of fresh starts afforded by the genealogical break with the birth country" (7). In her history of the "rhetorical uses" of adopted and foster children from 1850 to 1929 (2), Claudia Nelson suggests that a significant number of works in which adopted or foster children "change society or adapt triumphantly to its demands" contribute to the ongoing characterization of the United States itself as a "self-made orphan" (4). Noting that American childhood stories are most often about orphans, Jerry Griswold similarly sees the fictional orphan as a reflection of the country's picture of itself: "as a young country, always making itself anew, rebelling against authority, coming into its own, and establishing its own identity" (242). Nevertheless, as Singley perceptively explains, popular stories about orphans do more than "celebrate the child as emblematic of youthful American nationhood" (99). In addition, fiction about adoption mediates "tensions between inherited and constructed forms of identity [and] expresses white, middle-class hopes and misgivings about changing definitions of family, faith, and nationhood" (Singley 99).

The emergence of Canada, Australia, and New Zealand as independent nations was substantially different from the revolutionary beginnings of the United States. Ideas of rebellion and the rejection of British authority were not central to their progress towards self-government and nationhood, although acts of resistance were certainly present in their histories, particularly from First Nations, Aboriginal, and Māori people. Formal connection with Britain remained, however, regardless of independence and the removal of the hierarchical relationship between the imperial centre and its former colonies. In 1926, in the *Balfour Declaration*, all three dominions formally agreed that they were "united by common allegiance to the Crown, and freely associated as members of the British Commonwealth of Nations" (2). While the three nations were substantially different in numerous respects, they did share a common and lingering bond with Britain that coexisted with strengthening ideas about a unique national identity. With such different narratives of their own emergence in comparison with the United States, it is unsurprising to find that colonial children's fiction about orphans does not take the same shape as the triumphal, individualist American narratives Nelson considers.

In novels about colonial girls or set in the colonies, family ties are disrupted by immense distances from England as a matter of course. The importance of bloodlines is diminished, even to the point where several colonial girl protagonists who return to England receive substantial inheritances from unrelated benefactors, ensuring that they do not have to remain dependent on begrudging distant relatives. In contrast with American children's literature, fiction about colonial girl orphans focuses on the importance of new kinds of family constructions enabled by financial independence rather than the individualist successes of the child against all odds. In her study of family mythology in nineteenth-century British children's literature, Thiel uses the term "transnormative family" to describe familial units "outside of the established order," such as those headed by single parents, step-parents, other relatives, siblings, or the state in the absence of one or both natural parents (8). Most Victorian children's novels about transnormative families attempt to portray these alternative groupings as "akin to the 'natural', idealized family mode" (Thiel 9–10). Yet, Thiel argues, despite attempts to restore the security of the patriarchal family unit, there are moments in most of these novels about the middle classes that suggest that "the successful transnormative family can rarely be anything more than a myth" (71). She suggests that the situation is different, however, in British novels about children of the pauper or "degenerate" classes, who often find a place within successful transnormative families. In their positive and convincing representation of adoptive families, novels about colonial girls who find a place in such families, as we show below, are closer to the pauper narratives that Thiel describes. Yet they differ in one important respect, as colonial girl protagonists themselves play a key role in choosing and creating the new, transnormative families in which they will belong.

A striking example of a colonial girl forming the core of an unconventional family structure is Isabel Maud Peacocke's *The Adopted Family* (1923), which, like *Harum Scarum*, places greater faith in family bonds created through love than in those formed through heredity. The novel is set in Peacocke's homeland of New Zealand and begins with an Irish girl being effectively abandoned by her father. Nine-year-old Deirdre O'Neill's mother, Zilda, is a professional singer, and her father, Terence, is consumed with managing Zilda's career, which prompts him to seek out someone to care for the girl while he and his wife embark on a tour. He contacts an old friend, Michael Rivers, who agrees to care for Deirdre for a few months with the aid of his sister, Ellen Meade, who will keep house. Terence departs without telling his daughter that he is leaving, and she is devastated to be separated from her beloved father. She has largely been raised by servants and expresses little emotion about her mother, who has been preoccupied with her performances. As a bachelor who runs a country station, Riversdale, near Auckland, Michael is ill-equipped to raise a girl, especially after the acrimonious departure of Ellen. Nevertheless, the two soon strike up a loving bond, which is enhanced by the presence of other children who visit throughout the year, including Michael's nephew Bill Wellsford, Sefton (Ellen's son), neighbour Tom Somers, and eventually, an orphaned Māori boy, Rewa. Deirdre's life on the farm without a maternal influence is crucial to her transition from a "little bundle of skin and bone and nerves" to unconventional, colonial femininity (313). Much like Norah in Mary Grant Bruce's Australian Billabong series and foreshadowing Hilda in *Hilda at School*, Deirdre soon learns to ride astride on her horse with a stock-whip "in a boyish riding costume of bloomers and linen shirt like Bill's" without breaking a sweat and can outrun most boys and withstand rough-and-tumble games without crying (67).

The adoptive family in this novel is formed not for the simple purpose of creating a colonial home for the "brown little maid" from Ireland but in order to fashion a functional, extended family composed of the Old World, New World, and Indigenous people (283). Deirdre becomes the centre of the adoptive family, especially with respect to Rewa, a boy of approximately ten years of age, whom the children encounter when visiting a Māori village. Rewa was already an orphan, and after the death of his grandfather, he had "lain down to die" (160). Deirdre connects with the distraught Rewa and takes him into the bush for a picnic, but he refuses to return to his village afterwards and follows the children home to Riversdale. In a chapter entitled "A New Addition to the Family," Deirdre convinces Michael to allow Rewa to stay. Her Irishness, as distinct from Englishness, is likely crucial to the ease with which she is able to develop a familial relationship with an Indigenous boy. Nevertheless, Deirdre emphasizes that Rewa is "not black" (163), which is significant because of racial categorizations of the period that regarded Māori as "closer" to white people than Indigenous Australians were. Deirdre assumes responsibility for him, a seemingly conventional enactment of the feminine civilizing mission, which is nevertheless rare in girls' literature given the frequent elision of Indigenous child characters. As Michael explains of Deirdre's pivotal role in drawing their diverse family group together, "She's adopted us all ... and manages us all too" (172). Deirdre's mother is neglectful, but the space of New Zealand allows Deirdre to rehearse an idealized maternal role.

Rewa's place at Riversdale, in which he contributes to work on the farm, is complicated when his sister, Aroha, comes to claim him. A Māori clergyman explains to Michael, who worries about Rewa's "degenerating" under the influence of his sister (259), that Aroha has a legal right to Rewa, and that it is in his best interests to live with his own people. Though he is strongly connected to Deirdre, Michael, and Bill, Rewa is characterized as having an "easy emotionalism" and "very strong tribal and family instinct natural to the [*sic*] Maori" that means "he adopt[s] his new sister and nephew with ardour" after their initial meeting (260). Deirdre is hurt by Rewa's decision, feeling that he "had seemed to belong to them all, and particularly to herself" (260), which at once casts Rewa as a kind of possession and also implies a kind of familial affection. Rewa shares this sense of belonging and becomes regretful of his decision and reluctant to leave his friends for "strangers": "He did not, could not, love this 'sisiter [*sic*]' as he loved Misdee ["Miss Dee," his name for Deirdre] – he could not take up this new life away from all his friends" (268). For Rewa, the notion of familial belonging and racial identity become inseparable, as he describes Deirdre as his "sister," Michael as his "father," and himself as a "pakeha [non-Māori] boy now": "t'is mornin' I t'ink I te big fool to live like Maori – I t'ink I te pakeha – I go w'ere te white boy go" (271). This suggests that Indigenous identity needs to be erased for the colonial family to embrace Rewa.

The conflict between Rewa's identification with both his Māori family and his *Pākehā* family is solved when Michael invites Aroha to work as a servant on the farm, with her own dwelling provided. The terms of Rewa's residence at Riversdale and his family relationship with his boss/father Michael are manifestly different from those of Deirdre, even though she is not an orphan in its true sense. Nevertheless, Rewa becomes a part of the extended family and is especially involved in the children's adventures. As we explore in chapter 6, the novel exhibits racism typical of the period in its depiction of Māori.[5] Yet it is exceptional in the empathy expressed towards Rewa and his actual inclusion within the broader family group. The presence of Aroha means that Rewa will be raised within a Māori home, and there is no reference to any part that Deirdre might play in educating him or moderating his sister's influence. This distinguishes the novel from more overt – and comically failed – depictions of attempts at "civilizing" Indigenous children, such as Australian author Mrs Aeneas Gunn's accounts of her time on an outback station with Aboriginal girl Bett-Bett in *The Little Black Princess of the Never-Never*

5 When the family travels by train, a group of Māori children on the platform in "modified European dress" with "crude colour effects" are likened to "parakeets" in their "gabbling and babbling and shrill disputes" (Peacocke, *Adopted* 271), while Aroha's son, Alexander, becomes "a pet and plaything with them all" (283).

(1905), in which the girl tears newly sewn clothing into rags to construct a bag and superstitiously refuses to wear a red dress she is given as a gift.

Deirdre is similarly located between two possible families, but more explicitly severs ties with her biological relatives, choosing a transformative family over a dysfunctional nuclear one. When Uncle Michael's visiting nieces taunt Deirdre with the fact that she does not rightfully "belong" to him, Michael comforts Deirdre with the idea that families can be constituted from love alone: "you do belong to me, Kitten, if belonging means *loving*" (288). Both Deirdre and Michael express the wish that he was her "daddy" (288), and the novel concludes with the closest replication of this desire that is possible. On her father's unannounced return to Riversdale after a year's absence with no correspondence, Deirdre is cool towards him. Though Terence works hard to win back Deirdre's affections, she ultimately chooses to remain with Uncle Michael, and her father agrees. While Deirdre still maintains loving feelings towards her father, her connection to Michael and her new home at Riversdale very easily overrides, and almost erases, her familial and national origins. Deirdre has "identified herself with it now"; her new home in New Zealand with Uncle Michael feels to her "as if she had been born and bred there, and [she] loved ever rood of it" (292).

As a story about an Irish girl finding a loving home with an unrelated man in a new country, *The Adopted Family* suggests that New Zealand girls are as easily made as new family connections are. Colonial identities can be assumed without any difficulty for numerous British-born heroines in a range of early twentieth-century girls' fiction. In this novel, Deirdre's Irishness, which is often represented as "wild" in the same way as colonial girls are in British fiction, helps to construct her easy transition to rural life in a distant land.

Like New Zealand author Peacocke, whose novels were regularly published in London, Canadian Dora Olive Thompson published a significant number of novels through the Religious Tract Society. As with much of the fiction we consider, which models a transnational ideal of girlhood that is easily transported and readily consumable around the empire, *Adele in Search of a Home* (1920) flattens any distinguishing national characteristics in its depiction of Canadian children. The protagonist, sixteen-year-old Adele "Dell" Primrose, is originally from England, but only scant reference is made to this period of her life. The novel commences as she moves with her mother into a small cottage in a poor district of what is likely Toronto, after her father deserted the family and left them in a dire financial situation. Dell strikes up a friendship with a neighbouring widow, Mandy O'Neil, and her four children, and not long after their arrival, her mother's grief at being abandoned finally kills her. Mrs O'Neil takes in Dell, who instantaneously fosters a loving rapport with the children, Annette, Bud, David "Davy," and John, which is fortunate given the prompt and perfunctory removal of Mrs O'Neil, who is struck by a car. Her final words to a hospital nurse, which are transcribed onto a piece of paper, are "Dell is with them. Dell will take care of them" (33). The brave and dutiful Dell resolves that all of the children "belong to each other now!" and the novel follows her efforts to maintain a connection between the siblings and find a permanent home for them (39). One of the coloured plates included in the novel (Figure 4.2) positions Dell as a maternal figure at the literal centre of the family group.

In contrast with other novels about orphaned colonial girls, *Adele in Search of a Home* disconnects Dell and the O'Neil children from any relatives, family friends, or associates, and all five children must enter an institution to await adoption. A kindly worker at the institution, Agnes Hudson, recognizes the significance of the connection among the children and is reluctant to separate them, especially as Dell has been such an inspirational figure to many of the orphaned children through her storytelling. Agnes makes arrangements for Dell and Davy O'Neil to be sent to the wealthy Warren family in her own Ontario country town, Lonehill, while the remaining three O'Neil children travel to the elderly Westman couple on a farm near Elliston. Neither home is ideal. Dell and Davy are initially taken for an anticipated period of a year and half, until a permanent home is found for them. The country setting of Lonehill is beautiful and beneficial for Davy, who has always lived in a city. However, Mrs Warren is a distant figure to all of her children and is not enthusiastic about the addition of Dell and Davy to her household; moreover, she shares the class-based concerns of the English aunts in *Harum Scarum* and *A Girl from Canada* and opposes the idea of Dell's telling stories to children from less affluent households within her home. The Westman farm is a dull home for the other three children, as the elderly couple falls asleep in the evenings, and the trio assists with work during the days. Mrs Westman's death conveniently enables the children to be "farmed out" again to families in Lonehill. This creates a scenario in which the discovery of Dell's inheritance from her long-lost father means that she can build her own home that can also accommodate Davy and allow her to help educate the other O'Neil children.

Prior to her death, the O'Neils' mother, Mandy, remarks that Dell's surname, Primrose, that of a quintessentially English flower, was "an

THEY SMILED AT HER CONFIDENTLY, EXPECTANTLY.

4.2 "They smiled at her confidently, expectantly."
Illust. Anne Rochester. Dora Olive Thompson, *Adele in Search of a Home*
(London: The "Girl's Own Paper" Office, 1920).

out of the way name" considering their run-down, urban location (21). Like Dell and her mother, who were originally from England, Mandy could remember "those tiny flowers, starring the English fields" (21). When both English-born and raised mothers die, a space is opened up for Dell, who delights in entertaining and caring for children, to become the lynch-pin of a transnormative family and reject the Warren family's eventual offer to house her and Davy permanently. Though her name marks her as English, Dell is seamlessly transplanted into Canada and is a capable maternal figure for her new siblings. As we will demonstrate in chapter 8, in these colonial stories, it becomes possible for a girl to become a mother without being married herself. At the novel's conclusion, the farm on which Dell is invited to build a home for herself and Davy is named Primrose Farm. Thompson's vision of the Canadian family charges a girl with performing the symbolic functions of both parents in caring and financially providing for the children. While three of the other novels considered in this chapter reassert to varying degrees patriarchal authority through the representation of neglectful aunts and mothers, *Adele in Search of a Home* is preoccupied with how families might survive without a father, whether through death or abandonment. Solid patriarchal authority is present in the figure of the schoolmaster Donald Roberts, whose role is similar to that of the kindly uncles in other novels. His keen interest in Dell ranges from his paying her to tell stories to the children in his school to his offering her land, as well as providing a watchful eye, as appointed guardian, over Dell's new home.[6] The novel suggests that children might find the happiest of families beyond their blood relations and that finding a new family might be as easy as emigrating from England to Canada. The firm barriers around the nuclear family model, and ideas of nationhood, are relaxed in concert with each

---

6 Donald's fatherly role with orphaned or troubled children is highlighted throughout the novel. Not only does he agree to house a troubled boy from the institution, he also takes in the youngest O'Neil, little John. Donald keeps a box full of treasured mementoes of the children he has previously taught in rural schools who have gone on to make valuable contributions to society on an international scale. These include "Henry Desmond, Ontario boy, Rhodes scholar," "Walter Newtown, a Penneville boy, [who] makes [a] scientific discovery honoured by English doctors," "Jack Allan [who was] awarded [a] V.C. for conspicuous bravery on [the] Western front," Jamie Anderson, who was "killed at St. Julien, bringing in his wounded lieutenant" (Thompson 226–7), Dorothy Anderson, "a Red-cross nurse on a hospital ship that was sunk," and "Isabel Martin, the first Penneville girl to study medicine ... out in Ludiana College, India" (228).

other. Moreover, the crucial place of the father in the "natural" British family model is able to be somewhat displaced, as two families headed by single mothers evolve into one symbolically headed by a girl. The embrace of this transnormative structure suggests that a young nation might be built around a family model in which youth and feminine qualities are more significant than masculine authority. The novel's repeated recourse to the phrase "we all belong to each other now" resonates at multiple levels, from the family unit to the adopted nation.

Conclusion

The orphaned colonial girls discussed in this chapter are placed in at least three distinct circumstances after suffering the loss of parents to death or disinterest. Despite the plot variations with respect to the kinds of makeshift or adoptive families into which the girls are initially situated, several commonalities across these novels wholly reinforce the transnormative family as more than an inferior substitute for a traditional one. While the triumphal orphan in historical American children's literature is most commonly understood as a figure that metaphorically asserts America's own youthful individualism, across British and colonial girls' literature, the colonial girl orphan functions quite differently. Family and home are crucial to the narratives of girl orphans across American and British/colonial bounds; however, the novels we have examined all marry a change of nation with a change of family. They evidence the transnational qualities of girlhood that enable colonial girls to operate much like paper dolls, who can be pressed out of the national page from which they originated and then placed against a new back-drop elsewhere in the empire, and interchanged with one another. The shared elements of this idealized model of girlhood are also at the heart of the ways in which these novels readily place colonial girls at the core or helm of transnormative families.

CHAPTER FIVE

Environment and the Natural World

She had grown just as the bush wild flowers grow – hardy, unchecked, almost untended.

–Mary Grant Bruce, *A Little Bush Maid* (1910)

The previous chapters have explored the shared aspects of girlhood that were constructed and facilitated by Australia, Canada, and New Zealand's place within the British Empire and the circulation of print culture throughout the colonies. While particular colonial structures, ideologies, and practices were replicated throughout the empire, contributing to the transnational elements of white colonial girlhood, one aspect of life was thoroughly distinct in each country. Each colony had a natural environment that differed radically from that of Britain and was variously understood as more free and "wild," thereby creating a different setting for the growth and development of young people, as is demonstrated in the chapter epigraph from *A Little Bush Maid.* As a result, as Michael Stone suggests with respect to nineteenth-century Australian children's literature, "settlers' reaction to an environment different from Europe and their contact with the Aboriginal population" are the two dominant themes (322). Betty Gilderdale similarly argues that New Zealand children's literature has two preoccupations, "with the indigenous Maori people and with the Land itself" ("Colonial and Postcolonial" 343). In the Canadian context, and with reference to the nation's literature more broadly, Margaret Atwood suggests that Canadian literature was, from its beginnings, fixated on the idea of "survival," especially with respect to the environment.[1] While New Zealand's landscapes were sometimes favourably compared to those of Scotland in children's fiction, its natural environment was, like Australia and Canada, still understood as "wild." Each unfamiliar location posed various dangers to young people, in particular, through extremes of climate (heat in Australia, cold in Canada), vast distances, and wild weather events, such as flooding and bush-fires.

Colonial environments had a metaphoric relationship with girlhood, most obviously because newly explored and conquered territories tended to be characterized as female, especially in literature. Rebecca Weaver-Hightower notes that "psychological links between *female* bodies and land were used throughout early colonial literature to legitimize acts of colonization by white men" (xvi). The associations between these "new lands" and young women continued to be evident in descriptions of Australia, Canada, and New Zealand as Britain's "daughters" throughout the nineteenth century and into the early twentieth century.[2] Nevertheless, the environments of each colony were also seen as conducive to the formation of distinct types of national character and physicality, and were often related to ideal forms of masculinity. The "bushman" in Australia, for example, became a legendary figure for his mastery of the outback. Across the empire, settler colonies were often utilized as settings for British boys' adventure stories. Similarly, Gail Edwards and Judith Saltman point out that Canada was a favoured location for boys' novels preoccupied with survival and settlement in the wilderness from the mid- to late nineteenth century (25). Canada's wilderness, they argue, "provided the perfect backdrop against which virile young heroes could demonstrate their nobility of character, toughness, and survival skills, and their chaste heteronormative masculinity" (Edwards and Saltman 29). Yet how could girls be situated in these same rugged, colonial natural environments that were used in boys' fiction as testing spaces for masculinity?

---

1 See *Survival: A Thematic Guide to Canadian Literature* (1972).

2 Canada was sometimes described as the "Eldest Daughter of the Empire," as in the introduction to *Songs of the Great Dominion* (1889), an anthology of Canadian poetry edited by William Douw Lighthall. The *Taranaki Herald*, in March 1909, reported on a letter written by the British Empire League in Australia in which "mother and daughter towns" are identified. For instance, the English town of Plymouth is described as having "a daughter in New Zealand" in the form of New Plymouth ("British Empire" 31). Australia was represented as "a fine handsome lass ... who has not yet done growing" in comparison with an older "Mother Country Britannia" in the 1868 *Punch* cartoon "Our Australian Cousin."

In this chapter, we show how early British stories of colonial settlement accommodated girls within environments that were commonly depicted as threatening to young people. Some early children's texts set in Australia, Canada, and New Zealand, including Molly E. Jamieson's *Ruby: A Story of the Australian Bush* (1898), Catharine Parr Traill's *Canadian Crusoes: A Tale of the Rice Lake Plains* (1852), and Mrs J.E. Aylmer's *Distant Homes; or, The Graham Family in New Zealand* (1862), are focused on the processes involved when families settled in dangerous, uncultivated environments. While these largely domestic stories were more clearly directed at a readership of girls in contrast with contemporaneous adventure fiction set in locations such as Africa and aimed at male readers, their girl settler protagonists are constrained in the ways in which they can adjust to the physical demands of colonial life. Their roles are most often confined to domestic work, childcare, and "civilizing" work with Indigenous peoples that keep them safely within the home or schoolroom. Though colonial fiction often developed a relationship between domesticity and successful settlement, these texts by authors who, with the exception of Traill, had likely never visited the colonies nevertheless manifest uncertainty about the place of girls within colonial environments by removing them from potential harm and ensuring that male characters protect their daughters and sisters from the dangers posed by nature. These novels are quite distinct from the girls' adventure fiction we discussed in chapter 3, in which girls are largely depicted as capable and independent in rugged colonial environments.

Fearful attitudes towards the colonial environment can be understood in light of Eric Kaufman's theorization, developed using the examples of the United States and Canada, of the "two ways in which nationalists can apprehend their landscape" (390). Kaufman argues that during what he terms "the nationalization of nature" phase, which is typical in early settler societies, "a nation creates a homeland by settling, naming, and historically associating itself with a particular territory" such that culture determines nature (690). In contrast, through an eventual shift to "the naturalization of nature," the nation "comes to view itself as the offspring of its natural landscape," meaning that nature determines culture in ways that are perceived as positive (Kaufman 690). The idea of the naturalization of nature is a useful means through which to understand the transformation in fictional representations of girls within colonial environments from the late nineteenth century: as colonial populations increase, native-born writers begin to publish fiction that presents natural environments as familiar and integral to the formation of national identity, and emphasizes their beauty rather than their danger. In the early twentieth century, this familiarizing process develops into representations of girls who are more actively in control of the natural environments in which they live, such as Anne of Green Gables (1908), who resides in tranquil Avonlea; Norah, the horse-riding heroine of Mary Grant Bruce's long-running Billabong series (1910–42); and the girls of the Malcolm family in Esther Glen's *Six Little New Zealanders* (1917).

Making Homes in Unfamiliar Lands in British Fiction

Novels for children about colonial settlement published in the second half of the nineteenth century follow the fates of intrepid families who brave the challenges of a new environment. In these stories, girl settlers often experience the natural world fearfully or are shown to be weak and incapable when located within it. Jamieson's *Ruby: A Story of the Australian Bush* is a short novel published by the Society for Promoting Christian Knowledge, addressed to a British readership, which exemplifies this tendency. The protagonists, Ruby, her father, and step-mother, have left the "heather-hilled land" of Scotland for an Australian bush station (Jamieson 11). The environment is harsh, with its "blazing" sun, drought-affected land, and vast "monotonous" stretches of bush (Jamieson 7–8). Bush-fires, in particular, are a threat to the family, and an elderly neighbour is killed and his home destroyed during one blaze. Unlike her father, Ruby is kept safe and never confronts the dangers of the natural environment herself. The novel concludes on a snowy Christmas day in Scotland as Ruby visits family, temporarily displacing any threat posed to the girl protagonist within Australia and refusing the successful integration of a British child within the Australian environment.

Ruby reconciles the conflicts posed by expectations of traditional British femininity within the threatening Australian environment by removing the protagonist to Scotland, rendering it similar to *Queensland Cousins*, discussed in chapter 4, and a small number of similar novels that continued to represent colonial environments as dangerous and undesirable locations for child protagonists.[3] In contrast, much children's fiction published in the second half of the nineteenth century concludes with successful settlement and must resolve the tensions between

3 Haverfield was Scottish but later lived in England. There is no biographical information available for Jamieson, but it is likely that she, too, had never visited Australia.

environment and femininity in other ways. Catharine Parr Traill's *Canadian Crusoes: A Tale of the Rice Lake Plains* (1852) was published in London and explicitly sought to prepare young readers who might settle in the colonies for the new environments they would encounter.[4] The novel's preface, written by Traill's sister Agnes Strickland, a well-known British novelist and historian, encourages English parents to ensure that their children are "prepared with some knowledge of what they are to find in the adopted country; the animals, the flowers, the fruits" (x). It also makes reference to the commonplace occurrence of the loss of children "in the vast forests of the backwoods, similar to that on which the narrative of the Canadian Crusoes is founded" (Traill vii). In the novel, the "Crusoes" of the title, twelve-year-old Catharine Maxwell and her brother, Hector, and cousin, Louis Perron (both fourteen) become lost in the "unbroken wilderness" after spending an afternoon in a meadow gathering strawberries (Traill 2). Hector and Louis despair that Catharine will have to sleep outdoors, but as she is "both hardy and healthy," she does not mind the prospect of sleeping beneath the trees in the summer (Traill 25). Nevertheless, Catharine feels that she must encourage and superintend the construction of a hut so that the boys can play the roles required of male settlers. From the first moments of their isolation, the establishment of a home is crucial to the children. In his explanation of the importance of the domestic to the taming of the wilderness in the Robinsonade, Andrew O'Malley suggests that by "establishing their home-life on the plains, the children are also conquering and subduing the wilds around them" (81). Catharine, in particular, is responsible for fashioning a home and maintaining familiar domestic norms using items from nature. When the group first becomes lost, she crafts beds by cutting ferns and deer-grass (Traill 26), places strawberries in oak leaves pinned together (Traill 41), and creates a "cup" from a mussel shell, while the boys, as early colonial settlers, have acquired the skills to hunt and gather roots. *Shenac's Work at Home: A Story of Canadian Life* (1866), which we discuss in chapter 7, similarly yokes the domestic with the taming of the wilderness (Edwards and Saltman 25), emphasizing the essential place of femininity within the "civilizing" work that underwrites settler colonialism.

---

4 A factual footnote in the novel makes reference to specimens of the Canadian partridge housed in the British Museum, suggesting an implied English reader (Traill 37). Her *The Backwoods of Canada* (1836) was meant for prospective immigrants.

In *Canadian Crusoes*, Catharine works dutifully to reproduce the familiar comforts of domesticity for several chapters. O'Malley points out that the construction of "home" in Robinsonades is performed not only to provide a space of comfort but in order to exclude and "keep out unwanted and dangerous elements" (73). This notion of creating barriers to external dangers has particular relevance within the context of Canadian literature.

In Northrop Frye's influential description of the "garrison mentality," the Canadian imagination was shaped in response to fears about the natural environment and the need to construct psychological barriers or "frontiers" to rationalize the threats it posed (227). The "closely knit and beleaguered [garrison] society," he suggests, arises when "confronted with a huge, unthinking, menacing and formidable physical setting" (Frye 227). In this way, Catharine's repurposing of natural objects into domestic comforts can be seen as a literal enactment of the frontier building that Frye suggests typifies Canadian literature.

The danger of the otherwise idyllic wilderness to girls is nevertheless evident in the novel when Catharine is rendered immobile by an accident. She cries "peaceful tears" at the sight of nature's beauty at night, but is soon shocked by the sight of a "grisly beast," a wolf (Traill 61). Catharine falls down a ravine, injuring her ankle, and must be carried by her brothers until she recovers. The trio encounters a First Nations girl, whom they unimaginatively name Indiana as part of the nationalizing process in which Indigenous people are conflated with nature. In contrast with Catharine, Indiana is more adept at surviving on the land. Indiana is knowledgeable about the location of trees and their useful properties, is able to ice fish and use a tomahawk, and eventually directs the two boys in how to farm wild rice (which was native to North America and grown in lakes). Only Indigenous girlhood is connected with capability in the natural environment, while white femininity is closely associated with the creation of a sheltered domestic space and maternity, as is evident when Catharine cares for Indigenous children when she is taken captive. The Canadian environment helps shape Indigenous femininity, but in Kaufman's terms, nature has not yet been naturalized with respect to white Canadian identity.

To a greater degree than those of Canada and Australia, New Zealand's landscape shared some visual and climatic similarities with that of Britain, and therefore did not give rise to defining mythologies based on human survival and mastery of nature, such as the "garrison mentality" or the iconic Australian bushman. Nevertheless, as Ronda Cooper suggests in *The Oxford Companion to New Zealand Literature*, settler experience commonly found that "nature in New Zealand was wild, primeval and unnervingly evergreen, 'dreary and desolate', 'gloomy forest and repulsive rugged waste'" (n.p.). In his 1969 study of settler reactions to New Zealand, Paul Shepard describes its landscape and biota as a combination of "the familiar and the exotic" (1). Part of this exoticism pertained to the perceived interrelationship between the wilderness and Indigenous people. Shepard explains that establishing orderly pastoral settings therefore had great symbolic, as well as practical, importance: "The necessity of clearing and fencing was inextricably associated with Christianizing the Maoris [*sic*], and indeed, with the creation of a beautiful domesticated environment" (14). This close association between the establishment of ordered farming land and "civilizing" Māori is at the core of Mrs J.E. Aylmer's *Distant Homes; or, The Graham Family in New Zealand* (1862).

Like *Canadian Crusoes, Distant Homes* was one of many pro-emigration children's novels published in the second half of the nineteenth century.[5] In its early pages, the narrator interrupts the story of the Graham family to convey factual details about the New Zealand environment and Māori, including quotations from non-fiction books. These facts initially compete with the fantasies the child protagonists have of life in the British Empire that have been derived from boys' adventure fiction. One of the three sons, George,[6] imagines that he will "hunt Caffirs and elephants, like Gordon Cumming," Scottish soldier and adventurer (Aylmer 4), while Tom asks his father if there will be "wild horses and buffaloes ... [l]ions ... or tigers?" (6). The narrator's description reinforces the benefits of New Zealand's favourable weather and lack of reptiles and "larger wild animals, such as lions or tigers" (Aylmer 16). This mirrors the view that Shepard describes among settlers like William Yates, who interpreted the absence of lions and tigers in the country as indicative that it "was preserved by Providence for man" (Aylmer 6). When the family's ship arrives in port, the beautiful scenery of New Zealand, which resembles "home," is disappointing to boys in search of adventure, but more obviously signals its suitability for British Christian settlers.

5 See Moruzi, "The freedom suits me." Aylmer had never visited New Zealand, but Betty Gilderdale notes that she was related to the Graham family and likely based the story on her correspondence with them ("Children's Literature" 526).

6 George remains behind as he has two years remaining at Cambridge, but has exacted a promise from the bishop "that he would give him work to do in the colony" (Aylmer 11).

The Graham family labour throughout the novel to establish a cottage and farm on land thirty miles from Christchurch. This work is divided on gendered lines with Captain Graham and his son Tom setting out on an overland journey ahead of Mrs Graham and daughters Lucy and Beatrice in order to establish the home in a "pretty valley, watered by a broad silvery river, and bounded by a magnificent forest" (Aylmer 79). Farming in New Zealand is described as relatively easy and devoid of hardship; within two years, the Grahams bring the "pretty little farm homestead with its garden and fields ... out of the wilderness" and have a plentiful supply of produce and a growing contingent of livestock (Aylmer 177). As in the similar novel *The Redfords* (1886) by Mrs George (Ann Jane) Cupples, which we discuss in chapter 7, the daughters Lucy and Beatrice perform domestic chores and assist with feminized farming tasks such as milking cows, feeding chickens, and producing butter. There is a broader uncertainty about what their true purpose is within the colonial environment in comparison with masculinized tasks such as fencing. The answer supplied by Aylmer is that girls could be most usefully employed by "learning how to teach the native children," and Lucy proposes to learn Māori language in order to do so (53). When the family grants permission for friendly local Māori – who wish "to be like" the English (Aylmer 137) – to situate their *pa* (village or settlement), without the customary fortifications, only a mile from the family's home, Lucy is pleased that it will give her an opportunity to teach the children. The Grahams construct both a school and a church on their land so that Māori can be domesticated and civilized in the same way as the land they have already altered. As Patricia Grimshaw notes, prior to the Treaty of Waitangi in 1840, through which the British Crown assumed political control of New Zealand, Anglican, Methodist, and Catholic missionaries had already ensured that Christian Māori communities were widespread ("Women and the Legacy" 172). Nevertheless, tensions over land escalated to armed conflict in 1845 and escalated in 1860, and the 1862 story of the Graham family retains its pro-emigration message by depicting education and religion as the answer to peaceful coexistence with Māori.

While the righteousness of white settlement in a country "preserved by Providence" is reinforced by the ease with which the Grahams transform their property and establish a positive relationship with Māori, nature still occasionally threatens the family, as is typical of children's settler narratives of this period. For instance, there are warnings of the unfamiliar natural dangers posed by a country located on the Pacific

Ring of Fire when a volcano erupts and an earthquake is felt while the family is still on board their emigrant ship. On two occasions, children almost drown. These incidents prefigure the major threat posed to settlements by flooding. Yet, while readers are warned that "floods are more sudden and destructive than people living in England can possibly imagine" (Aylmer 132), the threat is displaced onto neighbours' homes, signalling potential risk but ultimately leaving the pro-emigration message and environmental transformation – as culture triumphs over nature – uncompromised within the narrative. Like *Ruby* and *Canadian Crusoes, Distant Homes* does not question the rightfulness of white settlement of the British colonies, but the natural world remains a hurdle to be overcome, rather than an element that is integral to the production of Australian, Canadian, or New Zealand identity. While these struggles provided the foundation for male heroism in adventure fiction, in domestic novels of settlement, the place of girls within unsettling and unfamiliar natural environments is more difficult to conceptualize.

Diminishing Threat: The Environment in Colonial Girls' Fiction

All of the novels discussed in the first section of this chapter were published in England, in part because they appeared prior to the establishment of significant colonial presses, and two were written by authors with no lived experience of the colonies. In contrast, the authors of the fiction we will now consider, L.M. Montgomery, Mary Grant Bruce, and Esther Glen, were born in Canada, Australia, and New Zealand, respectively, while the fourth author whose work we examine, Ethel Pedley, emigrated to Australia from England with her family as a girl. Their fiction is exemplary of a greater familiarity with colonial environments in the early twentieth century and an increased confidence about the interaction of children with the natural world. Much of the hard work of settlement and the transformation of the colonial landscape into cities, towns, and farming land had been achieved by this period. Moreover, the white settler population of these colonies had reached a critical mass, diminishing the perception of these nations as composed of a small number of hardy settlers pitted against the untamed wilderness. At the beginning of the twentieth century, Canada had attained a population of 5 million, Australia 4 million, and New Zealand, with its much smaller land mass, 1 million (Censuses of Canada; Dunlap 48). There were multiple reasons for Canadians, Australians, and New Zealanders to feel increasingly confident about their nations and content with their "rightful" place within their country's environment.

The most popular and enduring Canadian girls' novel, *Anne of Green Gables* (1908), is marked in its contrast with fiction such as *Canadian Crusoes* in its representation of nature.[7] As Owen Dudley Edwards and Jennifer H. Litster briefly note in their work on Montgomery's depiction of war throughout the series, on Prince Edward Island, "even nature (consistently portrayed as the 'enemy' in Canadian fiction) was devoid of much of its hostility" (43). Moreover, *Anne of Green Gables* resonates with domestic fiction for girls published in Australia and New Zealand in the period. These works represent a contented life on farms and diminish the threats posed by the land, animals, and climate. Montgomery begins the novel with a description of the idyllic situation of the homes of Avonlea within the landscape:

> Mrs Rachel Lynde lived just where the Avonlea main road dipped down into a little hollow, fringed with alders and ladies' eardrops and traversed by a brook that had its source away back in the woods of the old Cuthbert place; it was reputed to be an intricate, headlong brook in its earlier course through those woods, with dark secrets of pool and cascade; but by the time it reached Lynde's Hollow it was a quiet, well-conducted little stream, for not even a brook could run past Mrs. Rachel Lynde's door without due regard for decency and decorum; it probably was conscious that Mrs Rachel was sitting at her window, keeping a sharp eye on everything that passed, from brooks and children up. (*Anne* 1)

The natural features surrounding the Avonlea homes not only are harmless to humans but almost capitulate to their desires for order and civility, with the brook's rushing pace and potential danger of "dark secrets of pool" curtailed once it passes beyond the woods. Both native trees and exotic, introduced flowering shrubs like the fuchsia ("ladies' eardrops") coexist to produce beauty in a natural environment reshaped by white settlement. The aesthetic pleasures of nature extend to the transformations wrought on the land by agriculture, such as the Lynde's orchard ("a bridal flush of pinky-white bloom" [2])[8] and the sweet "breath" of apple orchards permeating the air along the "pretty road" to Bright River (Montgomery,

7 *Canadian Crusoes* itself was subject to substantial transformation as environmental perceptions changed towards the naturalization of nature with respect to nation. The 1882 Nelson edition, retitled, *Lost in the Backwoods*, was reworked to emphasize "the romance of conventional wilderness both in its preface and in its illustrations" (New, *A History* 56).

8 Anne likens a wild plum tree to "a bride all in white with a lovely misty veil," repeating the associations between natural beauty and the innocent young woman (Montgomery, *Anne* 17).

Anne 11). Indeed, nature is repeatedly personified, especially by Anne, who names houseplants in order to make them "seem more like people" (Montgomery, *Anne* 43). Similarly, natural features are likened to the most sophisticated or symbolic human structures in ways that situate nature and culture in mutually beneficial harmony. For instance, when Anne is afraid that Matthew might not collect her after she travels by train from the orphanage, she decides that she will sleep in a wild cherry-tree that is in bloom and imagines that it would be as though "you were dwelling in marble halls" (Montgomery, *Anne* 14). The view of the sky from the avenue of apple trees near Newbridge is "like a great rose window at the end of a cathedral aisle" and gives Anne an indescribable sensation of pleasure, "a queer funny ache" (Montgomery, *Anne* 21, 22).

While *Canadian Crusoe*'s Catharine cries "peaceful tears" at the beauty of the Canadian wilderness, its uncultivated state does not allow the girl heroine to take simple pleasure in nature in the same ways as Anne. Whereas Catharine must work to shape a domestic space that keeps out the dangers of the natural world and maintains the standards of civility that underwrite the process of settler colonialism, the domestication of Avonlea frees Anne to merely play with the idea making a home out of nature. Together with her best friend, Diana, Anne creates a playhouse that she names "Idlewild" – a name that draws together the notions of both an idyllic and a wild setting – on a neighbouring piece of land with a ring of white birch-trees. Seen through their eyes, natural objects in the house are transformed into furnishings: "We have great big stones, all covered with moss, for seats, and boards from tree to tree for shelves. And we have all our dishes on them ... There's a piece of a plate with a spray of red and yellow ivy on it that is especially beautiful. We keep it in the parlour and we have the fairy glass there, too" (Montgomery, *Anne* 114).

While romantic conceptions of childhood associated young people with nature, nineteenth-century British children's literature set in the colonies was instead preoccupied with the threats that nature posed to children. Montgomery's novel refashions these connections, with Anne resident in a Canada in which she can create the fantasy space of Idlewild, and bestow natural features like ponds with romanticized ancient English names such as "Willowmere" and "Violet Vale."[9] With

9 Through Idlewild, the Canadian environment evokes Old World European settings and elements such as the ancient moss-covered stones and ring of trees. Moreover, the names that Anne gives to the places that surround her derive from ancient English terms ("mere" is Old English for "pond," and "vale" is Middle English for valley).

the lack of any danger, or even evidence of the intensity of changing seasons in a cold climate, Anne and Diana are compelled to invent a kind of threat in order to experience a sense of adventure. With Avonlea being what Anne describes as "so – so – *commonplace*," the girls determine that the spruce grove contains ghosts and that a murdered child haunts a place near Idlewild. The only aspect of the natural environment that causes fear for Anne is a figment of her imagination, which highlights the domestication of the Canadian environment and displaces preoccupations with survival. The comforting representation of Avonlea fits the transition that Edwards and Saltman identify in Canadian children's books, in which its "peoples, land, and wildlife and their relationship to each other" come to be represented as "domesticated and familiar, rather than alien and exotic" (30).

Two of the most famous girl protagonists in Australian children's literature are intimately connected with the natural environment in similarly positive ways. The eponymous heroine in *Dot and the Kangaroo* (1899), a young girl who becomes lost in the bush and is rescued by a kangaroo, and Norah of the Billabong series, who resides on an outback station, are indicative of a transition in depictions of the environment as more children's literature by Australian authors was published. *Dot* was one of a number of children's fantasy fictions that was more sympathetic in its representation of the Australian landscape and fauna.[10] By this period, time had also made evident what Thomas R. Dunlap describes as "the limits of conquest" with respect to colonial environments (126). He argues that by the late nineteenth century in Australia, Canada, and New Zealand, there was a "turn toward native nature ... in the settlers' search for a place in the land" (Dunlap 126). Settlers and subsequent generations came to realize that there was a limit to how far land could be remade "by killing the wildlife, destroying the forest, plowing up the ground, and bringing in familiar plants and animals" (Dunlap 126). Fictions like *Dot and the Kangaroo* began to critique adversarial attitudes towards Australian fauna, in particular, and to shift anxieties about the threat of nature towards children to concerns about the human impact on nature.

10 See also J.M. Whitfeld's *The Spirit of the Bush Fire and Other Australian Fairy Tales* (Sydney: Angus & Robertson, 1898); and Olga D.A. Ernst's *Fairy Tales from the Land of the Wattle* (Melbourne: McCarron, Bird and Co, 1904). There were also earlier nature writings that attempted to educate children about Australian fauna, such as Louisa Ann Meredith's *Tasmanian Friends and Foes: Feathered, Furred and Finned* (1880).

Pedley plays on the familiar trope of the "lost child" in colonial Australian print culture. In addition to depictions of lost children in fiction, several high-profile cases of children who became lost in the bush were closely followed by the public.[11] Peter Pierce proposes that the lost child symbolized "essential if never fully resolved anxieties" among white settlers (xi). In contrast with the colonial Australian fixation on children lost and harmed in the natural environment, *Dot and the Kangaroo* explicitly rejects fears about the dangers of the bush to children.[12] The narrative enables dialogue between humans and animals and lingers on the beauty of nature that, unlike Anne's Prince Edward Island, cannot remotely mimic that of England. The kangaroo who befriends Dot is a harmless representative of nature in her protection and care of Dot when she is lost. And Dot herself enjoys enhanced insight into the animal world, as she is given berries that allow her to understand the sounds of nature. As the kangaroo transports Dot in the safety of her pouch, they visit a series of animals that are petrified of humans. The pigeons, for instance, are afraid to drink at the waterhole because of humans and their "bang-bangs," meaning that they face the choice of either being "murdered" or "dying of thirst" (Pedley 11). The animals' use of the term "murdering" suggests that there is no justification for these animal deaths. The "kookooburra" [*sic*] points out to Dot that it is "easy" to live in the bush "without hurting anyone," "and yet Humans live by murdering creatures and devouring them. If they are lost in the scrub they die because they know no other way to live than that cruel one of destroying us all. Humans have become so cruel, that they kill, and kill, not even for food, but for the love of murdering" (Pedley 20). The kookaburra pointedly differentiates the "black" humans from the white, because, though they kill and eat animals, Indigenous people do not "delight in taking our lives, and torturing us just as an amusement" (Pedley 20). Here Pedley likely distinguishes between the necessary killing of animals for human survival and the kinds of hunting and culling that devastated species for the sake of profit and agricultural expansion.

11 For detailed accounts of this subject, see Peter Pierce, *The Country of Lost Children: An Australian Anxiety* and Kim Torney, *Babes in the Bush: The Making of an Australian Image*.

12 See Michelle J. Smith, "Transforming Narratives of Colonial Danger: Imagining the Environments of New Zealand and Australian Children's Literature, 1862–1899," *Children, Childhood and Youth in the British World: Historical Perspectives*, ed. Simon Sleight and Shirleene Robinson (Houndmills, UK: Palgrave Macmillan, 2015), 183–200.

In contrast, realist Australian girls' fiction exhibited little concern about environmental harm and degradation, while sharing similarities with Pedley's story regarding the Australian girl's place within the environment. The "bush girl," who was comfortable in both the feminized space of home and the masculinized bush, as Gillian Sykes explains, "was frequently celebrated as a feminine version of this idealized Australian [the bushman]" (3). Grant Bruce's *A Little Bush Maid* (1910), the first novel in the Billabong series, depicts a girl heroine, Norah Linton, as a "born bushmaid" who is capable and confident on the land surrounding her family's sheep station in northern Victoria (76). Figure 5.1 dramatically illustrates Norah's skill on horseback and her capacity to hold her own among boys and men when riding on the property. As in *Anne of Green Gables*, the homestead setting harmoniously marries the aesthetically pleasing natural environment ("a wide plain, dotted with huge gum trees and great grey box groves" [Bruce, *Little* 7]) and the cultivated homestead, which follows a European model, with its "well-kept vegetable garden and orchard" maintained in an orderly state by two gardeners (Bruce, *Little* 7). Orphan Anne has had no parents to raise her until her adoption, while Norah has been influenced by her father and brother, Jim, but has had no mother to instruct her in domestic chores and accomplishments. Norah is comfortable within the home, but she is most content in the homestead's stables, when riding her pony, and while exploring the scrub. Indeed, not only is Norah confident and adept in the bush but her maturation is explicitly compared to wild, yet delicate, aspects of nature: "She had grown just as the bush wild flowers grow – hardy, unchecked, almost untended" (Bruce, *Little* 12). In this series, the idealized Australian girl takes on the characteristics of the bush.

Norah's confidence with her horse – which she rides on a hunting saddle while wearing a divided skirt, as shown in the book's illustrations – affords her freedoms and capabilities within the bush that were usually reserved for mythologized masculine figures like the drover. Her riding ability is at the core of the most iconic episode in the novel, when she braves a bush-fire to save sheep on the station. When a grass fire erupts, Norah is quicker than the male station hands to saddle her horse and ready herself to assist the men. However, as she is a girl, she is ordered by her father to stay back from the area closest to the fire and to refrain from attempting to put it out, while the men set off with fire beaters and a water cart. The men heroically battle the flames, and are capably in control with their methodical approach, despite the challenges of

5.1 Frontispiece. Illust. J. Macfarlane. Mary Grant Bruce, *A Little Bush Maid* (London: Ward, Lock & Co., 1910).

the wind and falling branches. One tree, however, cannot be felled, and the branches send sparks and blazing limbs towards the home paddock, where valuable imported English and Tasmanian sheep are housed. Unlike in *Ruby*, where homes are endangered by fire that men struggle to bring under control, the Billabong homestead is safe from danger because the paddock has been cleared. Nevertheless, this domesticated portion of land surrounding the home provides a space for Norah to demonstrate her confidence in the Australian outdoors. Norah is the only one in a position to save the expensive sheep, and she drives them to safety while on horseback. Jim proudly narrates the event: "She banged them with sticks, and the last old ram she fairly kicked up the hill. They were just out of the gully when the fire roared up it, and a minute or so after that we got to her" (Bruce, *Little* 69). Norah's face is blackened, her eyes swollen with smoke, and a small hole is burnt in her riding skirt, but she is more concerned with whether her father might be upset because she had promised not to touch the fire. Expectations of feminine behaviour constrain Norah's heroism to a limited space near her home, yet her skill and bravery in riding and mustering the sheep signify a major development in how girls are represented interacting with the bush in fiction. The helpless fears of a protagonist such as Ruby, who is only safe within the home, grow into depictions of girls such as Norah, who exhibit some mastery over nature and its potential threats. Nevertheless, the Billabong station, as we have noted, is an overwhelmingly bucolic setting that Norah describes as "the loveliest part of the world!" (Bruce, *Little* 7), and such disruptions are understood as rare and manageable when tackled with the pluck of hardy Australians.

This is not to suggest that Australian girls are represented as controlling the natural environment in the same ways as boys or men are. In Ethel Turner's *Seven Little Australians* (1894), the iconic and rebellious Judy attempts to mow the unkempt lawn at her family's suburban Sydney home with a large scythe, slicing off part of her dress and the top of a rosebush in the process. Judy struggles against the limits placed upon her by her age and her gender, and her aspirations rest in the masculine sphere of the bush (she talks of being an *aide-de-campe* to her brother, Pip, should he become a stockman), rather than in the home. There are two instances in the novel in which nature checks Judy's behaviour: the first when she runs away from boarding-school and the long walk home sees her struck down with consumption, and the second when a rotting gum-tree crashes on her back and kills her. While the natural environment is used to punish unconventional femininity in *Seven Little Australians,* the later New Zealand novel it inspired, Esther Glen's *Six Little New Zealanders* (1917), presents a different relationship between girls and the natural environment. The novel was published in London by Cassell & Co., and its presumed audience lies beyond New Zealand, as the narrator, 12-year-old Ngaire Malcolm, encourages readers to consult a map of the world in order to find "three funny little crinkly islands" where the story will take place (Glen, *Six* 1). The six Malcolm children have been raised in the city of Auckland and travel to the South Island to stay with their three uncles for a year at Kamahi sheep station while their mother receives treatment from a doctor in England. The novel is comedic in its depiction of the siblings getting into various "scrapes" on the farm, and minimizes fears about children and the natural environment. Unlike Mrs Malcolm, who needs to be taken "home to England" to recover from her increasing frailty (which is unexplained but seemingly owes something to the environment), this generation of native-born white New Zealanders is comparatively resilient (Glen, *Six* 5).

Fire is one of the most frightening natural threats in children's literature set in the Antipodes, yet it is dealt with differently here from the way it is in earlier British novels. In *Six Little New Zealanders,* the woolshed catches alight because of a cigarette discarded by Ngaire, who is encouraged to smoke by her brother Jock and sister Pipi. Not only is a girl responsible for the fire, rather than it being a non-specific natural threat, the children also join the adults in helping to stamp out the blaze, an activity that Ngaire describes as "awfully exciting," rather than frightening (Glen, *Six* 115). While the fire does destroy "the swaggers' whare" (Glen, *Six* 116), haystacks, and fences, the wind dies down, and the rest of the property is spared. Rural New Zealand is no longer represented as a place of danger for children, but rather as the scene of pleasure and adventure.

Similarly, the "lost child" trope, as represented in *Dot and the Kangaroo,* is overturned when Jan and Ngaire run away from a lunch at a distant property at which they disgrace themselves. The girls resolve to walk home, but become lost and spend a rainy night in a shed near an abandoned house, which is rumoured to harbour ghosts. Though the night is unpleasant in some respects, the girls feast on pears in the orchard – indicative of the cultivation of non-native plants thanks to settler colonialism – before returning unharmed to Kamahi in the morning. Significantly, the house belonged to "an Englishman named Morrison," who had established and readied the house for the arrival of his wife and three children. All four fell ill and died immediately after their arrival in New Zealand, and Mr Morrison promptly sold the property and returned to England. This amplifies the contrast, which begins with the Malcolm children's absent and sick mother, between English-born emigrants who are rendered sick, or endangered, by the New Zealand environment and hardy children born in the colonies. The illustration depicting Jan and Ngaire during their journey back to Kamahi, with its picket fence and pretty flowers and the relaxed demeanour of the girls visually representing their harmony with the landscape (Figure 5.2), collapses any real distinction between the pleasant English countryside and the New Zealand environment.

This is further illustrated by the novel's treatment of the familiar danger of rivers and creeks, which tends to show these environmental risks as manageable for colonial children. The children become stuck in the river when bathing, but are soon rescued (Glen, *Six* 63–4). Uncle Rob initially warns that a ford on the property has risen suddenly and drowned several men and "one poor girl" (Glen, *Six* 30). Later in the novel, it is briefly explained that the girl who drowned was Uncle Stephen's fiancée, who was caught in the rising river while riding on horseback. Eldest daughter Kathie is moved by the story of the lost girl, which drives her resolution to renew her engagement to Uncle Dan. She is emblematic of a new generation of young New Zealanders who can easily adapt to country life, just like the Malcolm siblings, who rapidly transform their naiveté into survival and farming skills: "We knew the signs of the river, and could trace a ford by the colour and flow of the waters; we had been flooded twice, and snowed up once. We could round up sheep, tell a Merino from a Cross-bred, and ride any of the horses barebacked" (Glen, *Six* 239). The Malcolm children are both skilled in traversing the natural environment and knowledgeable about and adept at farming, mirroring the broader process of environmental colonization.

At the core of colonialism is the acquisition and settlement of land, and settlers' establishment of homes in that natural environment is integral to the formation of national identities and narratives of belonging. The three colonies we consider in this monograph each encompassed radically different geographical features, flora and fauna, and climate from those of Britain. In girls' fiction, however, early attitudes towards these unfamiliar lands are relatively consistent across Canada, Australia, and New Zealand, with adversarial representations of nature rendering the place of girls within them uncertain. As each nation emerges with

5.2 "We laughed and laughed till it hurt to go on any longer." Illust. Noel Harrold. Esther Glen, *Six Little New Zealanders* (London: Cassell & Co., 1917).

a distinct sense of self, the natural world becomes a valued and unique part of being a Canadian, an Australian, or a New Zealander (although, quite often, the natural environments of these new nations are mapped onto European models). Indeed, these natural features can even help define a sense of superiority or good fortune. As Anne Shirley remarks during the Canadian spring, "I'm so sorry for people who live in lands where there are no Mayflowers" (Montgomery, *Anne* 197).

CHAPTER SIX

Race and Texts for Girls

[Nakinna] will soon be a little English girl in all but complexion.
–Anne Bowman, *The Kangaroo Hunters* (1859)

In Anne Bowman's novel of adventure, *The Kangaroo Hunters* (1859), Nakinna, a young Australian Aboriginal girl befriended by the Mayburns, an English family, learns English and religion at the hands of sixteen-year-old Margaret Mayburn. The relationship between these two figures, Nakinna and Margaret, encapsulates how relations between white and non-white girls are represented in colonial texts. It is assumed, first, that Nakinna possesses no knowledge or traditions of her own, and that she will be consigned to barbarism if she does not receive an education in English and Christianity, and second, that Margaret's role is that of teacher and potential mother of the nation. But young readers are not to imagine that once she has learned English and the rudiments of Christianity, Nakinna will be "a little English girl"; her complexion will always mark her inferiority.

The example of Nakinna is a stark reminder that the models of girlhood promoted in colonial books for girls were grounded in theories of race common in Europe at the time. The imperial girl protagonists who feature in the texts we discuss come from British stock; while these girl figures may be treated as having distinctive Canadian, Australian, or New Zealand qualities, they are defined by their gender, their connections to empire, and their race. In contrast, non-white girls appear as peripheral and secondary figures who mark the boundaries between superior and inferior races, colonizing and colonized populations. As gendered subjects, they perform versions of femininity that alert readers to the superior claims of white imperial girls who are destined for maternal roles in emerging nations. In some of the texts we discuss, non-white girls may appear to take on the manners and practices of their white sisters, but routinely, these narratives' conclusions revert to depicting a world in which whiteness is valorized and non-white girls fade into obscurity or death. Nevertheless, representations of non-white girls disclose many of the cultural tensions that surround formulations of girlhood, Indigeneity, and the imperial project. This is especially the case when texts address interracial relationships. At one extreme, romantic relations between non-white girls and white boys or young men play out the fear of miscegenation common in colonial societies through narrative outcomes in which non-white girls die tragically. At the other extreme, epitomized by the figure of Indiana in *Canadian Crusoes*, the "native" girl is assimilated into white society through her marriage, in Indiana's case, to the young settler Hector Pemberton.

As Marilyn Lake and Henry Reynolds observe, whiteness gained ascendancy as a global force during the nineteenth century, effecting a "mode of subjective identity that crossed national borders and shaped global politics" (2). The "imagined communities" of New World nations based their aspirations and identities on "scientific" arguments predicated on the supposition that white races were further evolved than non-white, and that white rule was the normal and proper mode of government (Anderson 1991).[1] A corollary of these arguments was the widespread belief in the "doomed race" theory, which invested non-white cultures and peoples with pathos and a sense of hopelessness.[2] When Australian, Canadian, and New Zealand texts feature non-white girl characters, they rehearse these norms, as well as the reflexively masculinist underpinnings of the imperial project, which privilege white men over white women and over non-white men. The figure of the non-white girl is thus doubly marginalized, lacking both the pre-eminence of masculinity and the standing of white girls and women, whose adherence to imperial

---

1 The strength of this transnational alliance was evident at the Paris Peace Conference of 1919, when leaders from Britain, the United States, Australia, South Africa, New Zealand, and Canada defeated Japan's proposal that a clause on racial equality be incorporated into the Covenant of the League of Nations.

2 The "doomed race" theory was almost universally embraced in Australia; in New Zealand, the doctrine was hotly debated (McGregor 2006), as was also the case in Canada (Rowse 2014). Proponents of the theory were influenced by shifts in racial science and attitudes to religion, which varied across nations and time periods.

values is demonstrated by their willingness to embrace the maternal roles necessary for the development of "white men's countries" (Lake and Reynolds 7). The non-white girl is, however, not a universal or essentialist figure, since she is attributed with the characteristics associated with particular places and cultures. In this chapter, we compare depictions of Indigenous girls and young women in Canadian, New Zealand, and Australian texts, attending both to the purposes to which they are put in relation to agendas of nation building and also to the significances they carry in particular national contexts.

In line with their emphasis on girls' roles as future mothers, texts for girls and young women often draw on the binary logic of race to construct relationships that depend upon the attribution of maternal or teacherly qualities to white girls who are charged with the training or education of "native" girls. Folded into these depictions of white benevolence are assumptions about the childishness of subjugated people, whose inferior state requires that they be subjected to the civilizing mission implemented by white girls and women. Discourses of benevolence and charity are frequently marshalled to add weight to the notion that the imperial project, at its core, intends only the good of subjugated peoples, and especially of non-white girls, who need to be liberated from their barbarism or primitiveness by the indefatigable efforts of conscientious and godly white girls. Books, magazines, and annuals for girl readers in the nineteenth and early twentieth centuries, like all children's texts, were shaped by the values of the societies in which they are produced. Produced by adults for children and young people, they are necessarily implicated in socializing agendas, promoting behaviours and ideologies deemed desirable for readers who will be the future wives and mothers of new nations. But it would be a mistake to assume that texts for the young adhere seamlessly to a univocal set of principles, values, concepts, and emotions. Rather, they are prone to the doubts and inconsistencies that attended the imperial project, especially when they address the future of young nations whose Indigenous populations must be "managed" in both fictive and real-world settings.

A crucial aspect of such "management" relates to relationships between the young white characters who feature as protagonists and focalizers and the non-white characters they encounter. As Mieke Bal notes, readers typically respond to characters by locating them in relation to "relevant semantic axes" (127). The white/non-white axis is of fundamental importance in settler-colony texts because it mobilizes the cultural givens of imperialism: the negative logic underpinning hierarchies of race and the deployment of this logic as a means of cementing the status of whiteness. Depictions of non-white girls present knotty problems of representation in texts for the young, which are directed to relatively inexperienced readers. While discourses of miscegenation form a prominent aspect of settler culture debates and concerns, episodes involving sexual relations are absent from texts for girls. This, however, implies not that sexuality is entirely out of bounds in these texts but rather that romantic and sexual relations between white and non-white characters are treated obliquely and sometimes metaphorically. Texts for the young are, as we have noted, always imbued with the preoccupations of the adults who produce them, and there is no more fraught aspect of imperial discourse than its ambivalence about interracial sexuality, particularly in narratives directed to white girls.

In selecting the focus texts for this chapter, we have sought out works that go beyond the merely formulaic depictions of non-white girls that appear as caricatures in much fiction. Canadian, New Zealand, and Australian texts concern themselves principally with the adventures and experiences of white girls, since they are directed to white readers. Thus, although the corpus of texts we canvass throughout this book is extensive, fewer suit our focus in this chapter. As we noted in the introduction, the production of children's texts in New Zealand was limited by the country's small population and the constraints encountered by local publishers; for this reason, there are quite simply more Australian and Canadian texts to consider. This chapter covers a range of genres, from books for young children, such as Grey Owl's *The Adventures of Sajo and Her Beaver People* (1935), to novels of settlement, romance, and adventure, including G. Mercer Adam and A. Ethelwyn Wetherald's novel, *An Algonquin Maiden: A Romance of the Early Days of Upper Canada* (1887). The texts cover a range from the nineteenth to the early twentieth century, from *A Mother's Offering to Her Children* (1841) to Frank Dalby Davison's *Children of the Dark People* (1936).

Embodying Inferiority: Specularity and Non-White Girls

While concepts of race predate colonialism, they proved to be of high utility to the imperial project. Bill Ashcroft, Gareth Griffiths, and Helen Tiffin remark that "despite its allegedly scientific grounding and application, the term 'race' has always provided an effective means of establishing the simplest model of human variation – colour difference" (200). Typologies of race, whether based on the Great Chain of Being,

Enlightenment stage theory, or Social Darwinism,[3] consigned the "black races" to the lower echelons of human development. Australian Aborigines were commonly located at the bottom of these hierarchies, whereas Native Americans were accorded a higher status and Polynesians (including Māori) a still higher one, and Europeans were located at the pinnacle of humanity (Freeman 44). Texts for girls take up these hierarchies in their constructions of character and of social relations in settler societies, building their narratives on the central binary that underpins concepts of race: white/non-white.

Skin colour is prominently on display in these texts, enforcing distinctions between "races" and marshalling associations that emphasize the superiority of whiteness. When non-white girls take up elements of European dress or behaviour, readers are often positioned as observers of scenes in which inferiority is coded through bodily behaviours and actions.

In *An Algonquin Maiden: A Romance of the Early Days of Upper Canada*, the action revolves around romances between two pairs of characters: Allan Dunlop and Rose Macleod and Rose's brother Edward Macleod and Hélène de Berczy, young people whose families belong to the gentry (English and French, respectively) of Ontario society. Despite the novel's title, the Algonquin maiden, Wanda, is merely a foil to the principal players: Edward Macleod falls prey to Wanda's charms despite himself, Hélène rejects Edward because of this relationship, and Wanda kills herself when she realizes that he is romantically attached to Hélène. Writing as "Garth Grafton," Sara Jeannette Duncan's review of *An Algonquin Maiden* in *The Globe* signals Wanda's relative insignificance. The review commences with a coy reference to the longed-for arrival of the book: "The 'Algonquin Maiden' has ceased to dally with the printers and the proofreaders; her fleet, brown foot has covered all the distance between Montréal and Toronto; and her moccasin lightly prints every one of the snowy pages that come to us" (6). Having delicately alluded to the Algonquin maiden's brown foot and moccasin, the remainder of the review focuses squarely on those elements deemed more notable: the novel's romantic tone and its evocation of Canadian nature.

Wanda is introduced to the narrative when Edward travels to his family home to bid farewell to his dying mother. As he nears the house, he perceives an "apparition," a "dark, lissome creature, beautiful as a young

3 See Russell McGregor, *Imagined Destinies: Aboriginal Australians and the Doomed Race Theory, 1880–1939*.

princess, but a princess in the disguise of a savage" (Adam and Wetherald 18), a "dusky Diana" whose face and body impress themselves on him despite his preoccupation: "his mind retained only a general impression of a face, perfect-featured and olive-tinted, and a form robed in a brilliant and barbarous admixture of scarlet, yellow, and very dark blue" (Adam and Wetherald 19). The language of this description is overloaded with colour: Wanda is dark, her face olive-tinted and her clothing multicoloured. Presented through Edward's focalizing perspective she embodies mutually exclusive qualities, since he views her both as a princess and also as a savage; her clothing is both brilliant and barbarous; and he compares her to the Roman goddess Diana, but notes that her skin is "dusky." This insistence on the coloration of Wanda's body and clothing, pervasive throughout the novel, enables multiple comparisons between Wanda and Hélène, whom Wanda refers to as "the Moon-in-a-black-cloud" because of the paleness of her skin and the dark luxuriousness of her hair (Adam and Wetherald 47). Hélène's "cool graceful black and white propriety" (Adam and Wetherald 81), set against the heated and highly coloured person of Wanda, constructs an opposition that both reinforces the white/non-white binary of race hierarchies and also signals the dangerous seductiveness of the native girl.

When Edward invites Wanda to a picnic on the shores of Lake Simcoe, his sister Rose fixes on a strategy to ensure that Wanda's inferiority will become evident to her brother: she presents Wanda with a pink cambric dress, gloves, and a straw hat. Wanda embellishes this ensemble, tearing off the hat's trim and substituting it with "wampum, gorgeous feathers, the stained quills of the porcupine, with tufts of moose hair, dyed blue and red" (Adam and Wetherald 191). Her lack of taste and decorum is exposed through comparison with Hélène, who wears a filmy black garment that exudes "invisible radiations – the luxurious sense of refined womanliness" (Adam and Wetherald 193). If Hélène's picnic garb exposes the vulgarity of the other young (white) women at the picnic, it is doubly eloquent in its commentary on Wanda's failed and pathetic attempt to pass herself off as a lady. The narrative lingers on Wanda's propensity for making "an object" of herself: she muddies her gown, loses her hat, discards her gloves, and entertains the children at the picnic by demonstrating her prowess in climbing trees (Adam and Wetherald 193). The narrative alerts readers to Edward's embarrassment at this demonstration of Wanda's irremediable inferiority as he remonstrates with her about her lack of propriety. This episode draws attention to Wanda's alignment with the natural world, which supplies her with adornments including wampum, feathers, porcupine quills, and moose hair. In comparison, Hélène is oriented towards a world of culture and refinement, her pale face and elegant attire attesting to her superior status.

Episodes of this kind, in which Indigenous girls take on European clothing and manners, are pervasive across settler-society texts for the young. They reassure readers of the gap between primitive and civilized, nature and culture, non-white and white. Homi Bhabha's formulation of "colonial mimicry" is apposite to this narrative trope in that the mimicry performed by non-white girls "emerges as the representation of a difference that is itself a process of disavowal" (126). One of the best-known Australian representations of a non-white girl occurs in Jeannie Gunn's *The Little Black Princess of the Never-Never* (1905), her account of "living among blacks" as the wife of the manager of a cattle station in the Northern Territory of Australia (62).[4] Gunn traces her project of educating one particular "little black princess," the eight-year-old girl she names Bett-Bett, whose relationship with the narrator, the "little Missus," shapes the trajectory of the narrative. Gunn's untroubled usage of the term "nigger" to describe Bett-Bett is in itself indicative of the absolute distinction between white and black that informs the narrative, and of the text's implied readers: white children and adults who might be assumed to find the term unproblematic. Wanda, the Algonquin maiden, is compared to a princess because of her beauty, even if her princess-like appearance is vitiated by her inferiority. In contrast, Gunn's use of the term "princess" is heavily ironic: "Bett-Bett must have been a princess, for she was a king's niece; and, if that does not make a princess of any one, it ought to do so" (9). The king in question is a man known as "Goggle Eye," and his kingly status is described as follows: "He didn't have a golden sceptre. Australian kings never do; but he had what was quite as deadly – a 'magic death-bone,'" which causes death when pointed at an enemy (Gunn 22). The playfulness of the narrative and its tone of amused superiority construct the narrator as pioneer, amateur ethnographer, and chronicler of the quaint customs of Bett-Bett and her people. Wanda, who occupies a rung several steps higher up the hierarchy of races than Bett-Bett, might almost seem like a princess if her race was not at issue, whereas Bett-Bett is not and could never be considered a princess except through the narrative's jocular and patronizing allusion to her "royal" heritage.

4 *The Little Black Princess* was widely used in Australian schools up to the 1960s, often in an abridged form, and was anthologized in school readers such as the *Victorian Reader*.

Bett-Bett is readily suborned as a (conveniently prepubescent) representative Aboriginal girl whose education at the hands of the "little Missus" might function as a test case. The question of clothing is central to this process, since if she is to be housed in the homestead, decorum requires that she wear clothes. Provided with a blue-and-white singlet, she "dressed herself in it at once, and looked just like a gaily-colored beetle, with thin black arms and legs" (Gunn 13). Her delight in the singlet is itself a sign of Bett-Bett's primitive state, encoded in the comparison to a beetle. In contrast, the narrative lingers on the maternal qualities of the "little Missus" as she diligently sews clothes for Bett-Bett: a blue dress, some white petticoats, and a red dress, which the girl refuses to wear on the grounds that the colour red will encourage the "debbil-debbil" associated with thunder-storms to kill her. The narrative contrives at once to mock Bett-Bett's superstitious belief and to promote the benevolence and patience of the "little Missus": "When I heard this, of course I made a pink dress, as I didn't want the Thunder debbil-debbil to run off with her" (Gunn 15). At the end of *The Little Black Princess*, Bett-Bett succumbs to a state identified by the "little Missus" as homesickness for the bush, "for anything that would make her a little bush nigger once more" (Gunn 122). Her restitution to primitivism is symbolized by her abandonment of the clothes she has worn in the homestead. Nevertheless, she gives the "little Missus" the token of a mussel shell, which promises that "in a little while, Bett-Bett would need her 'Missus,' and come back bright and happy again" (Gunn 124). This closure, wrapping up the narrative by anticipating Bett-Bett's return to the station, positions readers – especially the child readers who were introduced to the narrative in educational settings – to regard such an outcome as the only possible happy ending to the story of Bett-Bett.

Educating the "Lesser Races"

While *The Little Black Princess* foregrounds the magnanimity of the "little Missus," other narratives focus on relationships between pioneering white girls and the non-white girls whom they encounter in colonial settings. Fiona Paisley notes that during the first decades of the twentieth century, social reformers emphasized the importance of education and training: "as mothers and civilizers of children generally, middle-class white women were enjoined to bring civilization also to the child-like lesser races" (242). Narratives featuring girl settlers who take on this civilizing role promote the value of education in Christianity, literacy, and domestic crafts and its capacity to lift non-white girls to new levels of achievement. Nevertheless, there exists a considerable gap between young teachers and their native charges, since hierarchies of race always trump stories about the educability of non-white children. Such hierarchies are clearly visible in W.H.G. Kingston's *Milicent Courtenay's Diary* (1873), in which the protagonist, visiting the cattle station of the wealthy Radland family, encounters some of the local Aboriginal people and concludes, "We should try to win their regard, for the purpose, if possible, of benefiting them" (356). Milicent is, however, pessimistic as to her prospects of engaging the children in systematic education: "though they take in with considerable intelligence what they are taught, they seldom remain long enough to benefit much" (Kingston 456). Just as Bett-Bett cannot resist the call of the bush, these children are prone to "come and go as the whim seizes them" (Kingston 456), thus demonstrating their incapacity for the discipline required of students, a weakness integral to their membership to an inferior race.

Like Kingston, Anne Bowman was an armchair traveller whose adventure narratives ranged across imperial settings. In *The Kangaroo Hunters*, the widowed Mr Mayburn and his family are shipwrecked on the west coast of Australia and embark on a wholly implausible overland journey to the east coast. During their progress, they rescue a young Aboriginal woman, Baldabella, whose husband has been killed by an escaped convict. Sixteen-year-old Margaret takes responsibility for Baldabella's education and that of her little daughter, Nakinna, both of whom prove to be adept at learning English. Margaret imparts "lessons of civilization and religion to the lively little Nakinna, and, through the child, poured the words of truth into the heart of the mother" (Bowman 271). When the Mayburns reach the east coast of Australia, they join their wealthy friends the Deverells, who have established a feudal society where Aboriginal servants "not only wear clothes and live in huts, but speak English, behave quietly and honestly, and attend prayers regularly with the other work-people" (Bowman 443). Margaret assumes the role of teaching the young daughters of these workers and intends to integrate Nakinna into this group so that she will "learn with them, and soon be a little English girl in all but complexion" (Bowman 458–9). That is, Nakinna may be exposed to the lessons that Margaret provides these little English girls, but her "complexion" will always consign her to the lower echelons of the hierarchy of races. Bowman treats Nakinna as an exemplary figure rather than an individualized character, sliding over any description of an intersubjective relationship between Margaret and Nakinna. Authors such as Kingston and Bowman, whose settings and plots locate British protagonists across a wide range of imperial contexts, produce texts that are ineluctably Anglocentric, privileging the virtue and benevolence of white girls, who are treated as conspicuous examples of British femininity and whose virtue is rewarded by marriage in Australia. In comparison, the non-white girls to whom they minister are to various degrees locked into a state or stage defined in terms of its racialized inferiority.

The emphasis of *Milicent Courtenay* and *The Kangaroo Hunters* is squarely on the advantages of migrancy to well-brought-up English girls; the Aboriginal girls and young women who feature in these narratives are accorded little individuality or agency. In comparison, the non-white girl characters of Kingston's *Waihoura, the Maori Girl* (1872) and Catharine Parr Traill's *Canadian Crusoes* (1852) are "naturally" more attuned to European culture than are Baldabella and Nakinna, since they belong to more "advanced" races. The eponymous Waihoura and the young Indigenous Canadian woman Indiana in *Canadian Crusoes* are attributed with cognitive and affective capacities that enable them to form friendships with the white girls who act as their teachers, even if these friendships play out the unequal power relations of colonialism. Waihoura, brought to the camp of the pioneering Pemberton family because she is ill, is nursed back to health by fifteen-year-old Lucy Pemberton. In *Canadian Crusoes,* Indiana is rescued by Hector, who, with his sister Catharine and cousin Louis, becomes lost in the forests of Upper Canada (Figure 6.1).[5]

The illustration "Hector Bringing the Indian Girl" depicts Hector Maxwell accompanying Indiana to a clearing in the forest; in the background, Catharine and Louis look on, and in the foreground, the Maxwells' old dog, Wolfe, approaches Hector and Indiana. The effect of light falling on Hector's face both emphasizes his watchful expression and serves to contrast him with Indiana, dark-haired, downcast, and dressed in clothing coded as Indian. The dog's posture as he barks at Indiana is wary rather than welcoming, although Hector's calm gaze seems to persuade the dog to withhold his judgment. The young settlers occupy the forest as though native to these environs; indeed, they seem more "at home" than Indiana, who has been captured and left to die by a group of Indians. The composition of the group, with Louis and Catharine looking on, constructs Hector as Indiana's saviour as he supports her protectively. When, a page or so later, he gives Catharine and Louis a

5 Hector discovers Indiana wounded and bound, in retaliation for her attempt to kill the "Ojebwa [*sic*]" chief responsible for the massacre of her Mohawk tribe.

6.1 "Hector bringing the Indian girl." Illust. "Harvey." Catherine Parr Trail, *Canadian Crusoes: A Tale of the Rice Lake Plains* (London: Arthur Hall, Virtue & Co., 1852).

graphic account of the cruelty meted out to Indiana, the implications of the illustration are amplified: the young settlers are Indiana's true family.

Unlike Indiana, Waihoura is attributed with an aristocratic genealogy that marks her out from other Māori girls. She is conspicuously not dark-skinned; the daughter of the chief Ihaka, she is "much fairer than ... any of her companions, scarcely darker, indeed, than a Spanish or Italian brunette" (Kingston 19). Having learned English from a missionary, she is capable of conversing with Lucy, who adopts a quasi-maternal attitude towards her, although the two girls are around the same age. Waihoura's aristocratic standing locates her within a trope common in New Zealand literature and culture: that of the Māori princess, a fixture in romance novels for adults.[6] Modified for young audiences in *Waihoura,* the "Māori princess" trope provides a ready explanation of Waihoura's evident superiority over other Māori figures, and constructs her as an appropriate companion for Lucy. The Pembertons' servant, Mrs Greening, remarks that she is "a sweet young creature, and I little expected to find such among the savages out here" (Kingston 31). In line with her superior status (for a Māori), Waihoura is an attentive student who quickly gains fluency in English following Lucy's tutelage. Lucy herself learns Māori from Waihoura, so that "at length the two girls were in a limited degree able to exchange ideas" (Kingston 39).

Nevertheless, the narrative takes pains to emphasize the limitations of Waihoura's understanding. Lucy employs "a homely way of speaking such as her Maori friend was likely to understand" and reassures Waihoura, who laments her lowly standing as a heathen: "God no love Maori people" (46, 47). The sturdy binaries of colonialism reassert themselves in a narrative strand based on Ihaka's decision that Waihoura should marry the young chief Hemipo, who is staunchly opposed to Christianity and who carries out numerous acts of violence against the English. In contrast, Rahana, "chief of a numerous tribe," is both Christian and also "on friendly terms with the English" (Kingston 88). The two young chiefs thus represent opposing attitudes to Christianity and the English, a conflict resolved in the outcome of the novel, when Ihaka disavows his loyalty to Hemipo and gives Waihoura in marriage to the virtuous Rahana, who in turn advises Hemipo to align himself with the English, abandon the "cruel customs" of the Māori, and convert to Christianity (Kingston 124). Thoroughly incorporated into the ambit of the Pembertons' model settlement, Waihoura and Rahana live in a house "built after the English model" and live as "true and earnest Christians" (Kingston 126, 127).

6 See Bradford, "'My blarsted greenstone throne!': Māori Princesses and Nationhood in New Zealand Fiction for Girls," 95–6.

Waihoura possesses skills and knowledge that locate her securely in the natural world: she is adept at finding her way through the forest, knows the names of numerous birds and plants, and negotiates her way by canoe through gorges and swift-flowing rivers. Similarly, in *Canadian Crusoes*, Indiana is an expert at making clothes from animal skins, harvesting and cooking wild rice, and hunting game, as well as possessing many other skills. In both cases, non-white girls progress from creatures of nature to mature women through tutelage provided by girls their own age. Yet both Waihoura and Indiana are depicted as childlike, so that the narratives flatter girl readers by imputing superior maturity to white girl protagonists. Andrew O'Malley notes that *Canadian Crusoes* frequently refers to Indiana as a child, so that "colony becomes 'home,' colonizers become 'parents,' and Aboriginals become 'children'" (79). Accordingly, Catharine's labour in teaching Indiana is treated as a virtuous and womanly duty, rewarded when Indiana says, "My white sister, I kiss you in my heart; I will love the God of my white brothers, and be his child" (Traill 117).

Fiction for the young is commonly structured by narratives of personal development in which protagonists progress towards a higher degree of self-actualization or agency. Indiana's progress is defined by her gradual assimilation into European culture. The novel introduces Indiana by drawing attention to her intellectual limitations: the "dreamy apathy" of her expression (Traill 172); her inferiority as a conversationalist compared to Catharine, "the offspring of a more intellectual race" (Traill 172); and her occasional "lapses" into what Louis refers to as "the young squaw's '*dark hour,*'" when "the savage nature seemed predominant" (Traill 173). Indiana's progress as a subject is instantiated by the scene, towards the end of the novel, when Hector, Catharine, and Louis are restored to their families and Catharine introduces Indiana to her parents: "It is my Indian sister … She also must be your child" (Traill 343). Catharine's profession of sisterhood is borne out when, at the end of the novel, Indiana is first baptized and then married to Hector. This turn of events is notable for the baldness of its narration, which leaps forward to some years after the return of the protagonists to their home. In deference to the youth of its implied readers, the narrative does not incorporate any episodes of romance between Hector and Indiana, and their marriage is presented as a wholly unremarkable event. As O'Malley notes, Indiana's marriage to Hector is the logical outcome of her domestication at the hands of Catharine, who tames and trains her in Christianity and, as a consequence, in European models of domesticity (84).

Troubling Relations

If Indiana's marriage to Hector in *Canadian Crusoes* is depicted as unexceptional, romantic and sexual relations between non-white girls and white men comprise a lively site of tension in many texts for girls. Angela Woollacott notes that across colonial regimes, "interracial sexuality was a messy and blurred liminal area in which gender relations were shaped in the most intimate and telling ways – across racial boundaries as well as within and across class divisions" (*Gender* 81). Transnational debates about interracial relations during the nineteenth and early twentieth centuries were inflected by what Lake and Reynolds (following W.E.B. DuBois) refer to as "apprehension of imminent loss" (2), the unease experienced by white inhabitants of countries where "the black and yellow races" increased in number and influence (3).[7] While our focus here is on depictions of relations between Indigenous and European individuals and cultures in Australia, Canada, and New Zealand, we acknowledge that debates about interracial relations in these nations were complicated by broader questions relating to border control, national identities, and immigration.

Settler society texts for the young between 1840 and 1940 carry the ideological freight of their socializing imperatives, but are also constrained by the necessity of catering to audiences whose sensibilities must be considered. Clear instances of self-censorship occur in the first Australian-published book for children, Charlotte Barton's *A Mother's Offering to Her Children* (1841), in which a colonial mother, Mrs Saville, conducts a series of conversations with her four children, covering topics ranging from flora and fauna to mines and maritime disasters and concluding with a chapter entitled "Anecdotes of the Aborigines of New South Wales," which opens with a reference to the death of an Aboriginal girl: "Little Sally the black child has been accidentally killed" (197).

This bland announcement about Sally's death leads Mrs Saville to describe Sally's mother, Nanny, who "also met with an untimely death. These poor uncivilized people, most frequently meet with some deplorable end through giving way to unrestrained passions" (Barton 197). The passions in question are specifically sexual, since Sally is "a half-cast, or brown child, as you call them" (Barton 199), the issue of a relationship

7 This phrase, quoted by Lake and Reynolds, is drawn from *National Life and Character: A Forecast* (1893) written by Charles Pearson, a Liberal politician in the colonial parliament of Victoria, Australia.

between Nanny and a white man. Nanny has died at the hands of her brother, who killed her because of his "great objection" to her insistence on "living among white people" (Barton 209). This euphemism both discloses and conceals the fact of interracial sexuality, and the story functions as a cautionary tale about the dangers of relationships with Aboriginal girls. The girl Sally, six years old at the time of her death, had been informally adopted by Jane, "a young married woman, who had lost her only child sometime before" and who "took a fancy to little Sally" (Barton 199). In this vignette, the first "Stolen Generations" episode in Australian children's literature, Nanny's readiness to give her daughter away is attributed to her belief that the child will be better cared for by Jane than "wandering about the forests, in search of precarious food" (Barton 202). As Anna Haebich notes, this rationale relies on a racist assumption common in Australia from the nineteenth to the twentieth centuries: that "the Aboriginal family was deemed to be a site of danger and neglect for children" (1036), so that assimilation into white society was a benevolent act of rescue, especially for mixed-race children like Sally. The sad story of Sally's accidental death is folded into a warning about miscegenation, framed by Mrs Saville's conviction that Aboriginal women are hostages to "unrestrained passions."

Indeed, the death of non-white girls is a common feature of narratives involving interracial romance. In *An Algonquin Maiden,* Wanda is figured as a threat to Edward's romance with Hélène. Following the death of Edward's mother, Hélène gives him a bouquet of hothouse flowers to place on the grave. The "pure tender curves of the white camellias" remind him of Hélène, who is herself "the flower of an old and complex civilization" (Adam and Wetherald 41). When he reaches his mother's grave, he discovers Wanda there and observes her while she places on the grave an armful of flowers gathered from the forest. The contrast between Hélène and Wanda, symbolized by the distinction between hothouse and forest flowers, places Edward in the position of one who must choose between the two. In a somewhat heavy-handed cue to readers, the narrative describes how, following Edward's fruitless pursuit of Wanda, "one of the pure buds that Hélène had given him had fallen from his breast, on which he had pinned it, and had been rudely crushed beneath his heel" (Adam and Wetherald 45). From this point on, the narrative lingers on Edward's developing obsession with Wanda and his disregard for the feelings of Hélène, who is far too restrained to reveal her suffering when Edward neglects her.

At several points in the novel the action is filtered through a narrative perspective that describes Edward as he observes Wanda, notably in a scene in which he watches while she disrobes and dives into the lake, "graceful as a young maple in autumn, standing in beautiful undress" (Adam and Wetherald 61). Having been depicted as a voyeur, Edward next takes advantage of Wanda's proximity to bestow "a lingering kiss upon the lovely curve of her cheek" (Adam and Wetherald 65), whereupon she slaps him, bruising his brow. Questioned about this bruise during family breakfast on the following morning, Edward is indignant when his father assumes that he may have sustained the injury in a tavern fight: "The idea was loathsome to him. He had not a single low taste or trait of character" (Adam and Wetherald 70). This disjunction between Edward's view of himself and his harassment of Wanda positions readers to view him as something of a bad boy, even if a likeable and attractive one. His progress from a feckless young man to a solid Canadian citizen is tracked in relation to his fluctuating affections for Wanda and for Hélène, resolved at the end of the novel by Wanda's suicide and Edward's marriage to Hélène.

Wanda is an ambiguous and troubling figure, exemplifying what Bhabha refers to as "the ambivalence of colonial authority," which "repeatedly turns from *mimicry* – a difference that is almost nothing but not quite – to *menace* – a difference that is almost total but not quite" (132). She is, as we have seen, almost but not quite like a white girl in the pink dress that Rose gives her to wear at the picnic; but she is utterly unlike one when she climbs trees and drags the dress through the mud. Wanda's behaviour towards Edward lurches from coquettish to aloof, as though the narrative cannot make up its mind whether she is a temptress or a wronged innocent. Indeed, the language with which she is described yokes together terms that convey this doubleness: she is a "sweet womanly savage" (Adam and Wetherald 149), a "sweet little squaw" (Adam and Wetherald 153), consumed by desire for Edward but vulnerable because of the ingenuousness with which she articulates her love for him.

It is when Edward tells Rose that he intends to marry Wanda that the narrative discloses the colonial hierarchies on which it is based. Rose warns him that Wanda's beauty is fleeting: "After that you will have for your wife a coarse ignorant woman, forever chafing at the restrictions of civilized life; angering, annoying and humiliating you in a thousand ways, a woman whom you cannot admire, whom it will be impossible for you to respect" (Adam and Wetherald 189). The narrative then proceeds to demonstrate the accuracy of Rose's prediction: Wanda shames Edward before his friends at the picnic. On a second occasion, she offers herself to Edward as his bride (again publicly humiliating him), and when he rebuffs her, she takes to her canoe, rowing into the lake to die in a fierce storm. At the end of the novel, Edward and Hélène stand together before Wanda's body, which is now, perversely, a sign of their mutuality: "And so, with clasped hands, they bent together and kissed the beautiful still lips that could never utter an accusing word against them. Their love founded upon death had suddenly become as mysterious and sacred as the life of a child whose mother perishes when she gave it birth" (Adam and Wetherald 235). Readers are positioned to acquiesce to the logic of a narrative closure in which the sacrifice of the non-white girl is the precondition for the happiness of white characters who have wronged her. Bhabha argues that colonial discourse is definitively split so that "two attitudes towards external reality persist; one takes reality into consideration while the other disavows it and replaces it by a product of desire that repeats, rearticulates 'reality' as mimicry" (132). The narrative enunciates the harsh facts of Wanda's marginalization in a colonial regime. At the same time, it treats her body as a "product of desire" whose mimicry of the white body constitutes a menace to propriety and order. Wanda is at once a "poor child of the wilderness" and a signifier of Indigenous presence, now ushered from the scene to be displaced by Edward and Hélène, true natives of a young nation (Adam and Wetherald 234).

Native girls are, similarly, attributed with a problematic range of significances in Mona Tracy's short story collection *Piriki's Princess and Other Stories of New Zealand* (1925). The collection is framed by the perspective of a first-person narrator, most of whose stories are gleaned from an old Māori woman, Hina Kaihau. This claim to authority ascribes a quasi-documentary flavour to the stories, which hinge upon relations between Māori and *Pākehā*, several of them focusing on romantic liaisons between Māori girls and white men. From the standpoint of the 1920s setting in which the narrator listens to Hina's stories, these narratives of doomed Māori girls are set in pre-colonial or colonial times. Hina is, however, thoroughly assimilated into European life: she "despises what she calls 'Maori living,' and her passion for cleanliness is such that Tomaki, her husband, must go slippered within the house" (19). The effect of this play of temporality is to enforce a sharp contrast between Māori village life and modernity, between the lack of agency experienced by Māori girls in the past and Hina's own independent life in her impeccably clean house.

Two of the stories, "A Deserted Settlement" and "Four Tons of Flax," present stridently negative depictions of Māori attitudes towards young women. In "A Deserted Settlement," the action revolves around a feast at which the villagers set up a swing on which people fly out on ropes over a sheer drop to a wild river, in an early version of extreme adventure sports. The beautiful Takiri decides to attempt this feat, but when she is in mid-flight, the shawl that is her only covering comes loose and falls far down to the river. The onlookers jeer and laugh at Takiri, who is so shamed by her nakedness that she kills herself by relinquishing her hold on the rope and is hurled into the river. At this, her betrothed, the young chief Te Whetu, shoots himself. "Four Tons of Flax" features Hina's great-great-grandfather, Ruatuna, who promises his daughter to the captain of a cargo ship in exchange for muskets. Both Ruatuna and the young warrior who is betrothed to his daughter kill themselves in despair. These stories of cruelty to young women position young female readers as indignant observers of a barbaric, patriarchal system. The British men who feature as shadowy figures are predatory and unreliable, but traditional Māori society is treated as irremediably rigid in its treatment of girls and women. In contrast, the figure of Hina Kaihau reassures audiences as to the benefits of colonization and modernity. The empty villages that remain adhere to a common trope in the Māoriland tradition of the late colonial period in New Zealand, where, as Jane Stafford and Mark Williams note, "the landscape is both peopled by the ghosts of Maori and emptied of their actual presence as they are figured in terms of the 'dying race' topos" (39).[8]

Two stories, "The Coming of the Grey Bird" and "The Ghost Canoe," feature Māori girls who abscond from their villages to follow white men. In the former, Mara and Pipitea run away to offer themselves to sailors on the boat *The Grey Bird*, who, in Mara's words, may wish for "kumaras and pork. It may be, also, wives!" (Tracy 12). When the girls fail to return, the women of the tribe wail "the terrifying *tangi* for the dead" (Tracy 16). "The Ghost Canoe" tells the story of Reni the Beautiful, who falls in love with a British soldier on the strength of his good looks and scarlet jacket. The soldier has killed a member of the ship's company and is imprisoned in the ship prior to being handed over to the law. Reni repeatedly takes her canoe out to the ship to see him, until it sails, whereupon she kills herself. Robert Young notes that theories of race in the nineteenth century "focussed explicitly on the issue of sexuality and the issue of sexual unions between whites and blacks. Theories of

8 "Māoriland" is the term given to New Zealand literature of the late colonial period, that is, from 1880 to a decade or so before the publication of *Piriki's Princess*.

race were thus also covert theories of desire" (9). "The Coming of the Grey Bird" and "The Ghost Canoe" reiterate these nineteenth-century theories, attributing sexual desire to Māori girls who reject their families and tribes because they are powerless to overcome their inordinate desire for white men.

Only one of the stories in *Piriki's Princess,* "The Weka," features a mixed-race girl, Moira, whose first-person perspective distinguishes this from the other stories in the collection. Brought up in the bush, Moira attends a local school where she effortlessly learns Māori and is befriended by the Māori pupils who attend. In particular, she forms a close friendship with a Māori boy, Tai Raupaki, who sings a love song to her:

> A love-song, I thought idly, and said as much to him. "So!" he answered simply, and we sat in silence for some moments. The thin call of a weka [native wood-hen] drifted up from the scrub. "There is no answer ..." said Tai, after a little while. "No answer," I echoed; and as I met his straight brown gaze I rose hurriedly and fled along the track towards the house. (Tracy 89)

This moment is heavy with symbolism relating to the call of the weka and Moira's "no answer," which seems to terminate her romance with Tai. The illustration accompanying this episode (Figure 6.2) locates the two children firmly in the bush, with an emphasis on the ferns, rocks, and pond where they enact their games of fantasy. The boy Tai is bare-skinned to the waist, while Moira is demurely dressed; his face is coded as Māori, while hers is "European" or at least indeterminate. Their expressions are pensive; they are engrossed in their fantasy world. This picture seems to depict the two as prepubescent children playing happily together. It leads into the episode above, when Tai's love song pushes their relationships into new terrain, which is unwelcome to Moira.

Years later, living abroad with her mother and young sister Nonie, Moira discovers that she is not the daughter of the white couple who have brought her up. She was a foundling, "a little half-caste baby" (Tracy 89), laid on her parents' door-step. Vying with Nonie for the affections of a young white man, Moira realizes that she does not belong in the European setting or with a white partner, and she resolves to return to the bush, where "it may be that Tai Raupaki, grown to strong brown manhood, will come to the edge of the clearing and call." The story ends on this note: "So ... another little weka will go back to the bush" (Tracy 92). While this story does not evidence the horror of interracial romance

6.2 "We played through the immortal legend." Mona Tracy, *Piriki's Princess and Other Stories of New Zealand* (Auckland: Whitcombe & Tombs, [1925]), 87.

conveyed in "The Coming of the Grey Bird" and "The Ghost Canoe," it hints at a concern for racial purity that is wholly consistent with the enthusiastic promotion of eugenics by New Zealand women's organizations during the first decades of the twentieth century. As a "half-caste," Moira's destiny is to marry a brown man, thereby protecting the "future of the white 'race'" (Wanhalla 166).

Moira represents one extreme in a continuum of mixed-race figures in the texts we consider in this chapter: the narrative proposes that she embrace her "natural" identity as a Māori girl, relinquishing her white ancestry and her associations with her white foster family. At the other end of the continuum, the sad death of the "half-caste" child Sally in *A Mother's Offering* is linked to her parentage, an Aboriginal mother and a white man. In literature for adult readers, the figure of the mixed-race woman is commonly associated with a state of being neither/nor, which commonly results in her tragic death. A version of this trope surfaces in texts for the young, although, as we have seen, depictions of mixed-race girls generally address interracial sexuality obliquely and through allusion.

L.M. Montgomery's short story "Tannis of the Flats," from *Further Chronicles of Avonlea* (1920), demonstrates all too clearly that the trope of the tragic mixed-race woman is limned with racism. This story was first published in outlets directed to adults, including *The Canadian Magazine* (1914), but was incorporated in *Further Chronicles* after a protracted legal battle between Montgomery and her publisher, L.C. Page. Carole Gerson notes that *Further Chronicles* was an "unauthorized collection issued by Page" and that it was "presented as an Anne book" ("Dragged" 158n.29). Whereas the story as it appears in *The Canadian Magazine* does not mention Avonlea or any of its inhabitants, the version in *Further Chronicles* begins squarely with an Avonlea reference: "Few people in Avonlea could understand why Elinor Blair had never married. She had been one of the most beautiful girls in our part of the Island and, as a woman of fifty, she was still very attractive" (Montgomery, *Further* 280). The narrator is Elinor Blair's former neighbour, and the story is framed as an explanation for Elinor's unmarried state, which is a consequence of an unhappy episode when she was in her twenties and visited her brother Tom in the town of Prince Albert. Lacking a protagonist with whom young readers might identify, and written in a style that sets it apart from Montgomery's writing for girls, the story is clearly not "for girls" but is included in a collection marketed to girls.

•

The catalyst for Elinor's lifelong sadness is Tannis, the daughter of a "French half-breed and whose father was a pure-bred Highland Scotchman" (Montgomery, *Further* 284). This "atrocious mixture" has produced a young woman of spectacular grace and beauty (Montgomery, *Further* 284), whose father provides her with an education that leaves her with "a very thin, but very deceptive, veneer of culture and civilization overlying the primitive passions and ideas of her nature" (Montgomery, *Further* 285). Tannis is, then, irremediably degraded by virtue of her mixed race. She falls in love with an Englishman, Jerome Carey, who is employed as manager of the telegraph office at the Flats, a trading station inhabited by "skulking breeds and Indians" fifteen miles from Prince Albert (Montgomery, *Further* 283). Carey is at first attracted to Tannis but quickly abandons her for Elinor Blair. Fatally shot at the Flats, Carey beseeches Tannis to fetch Elinor from Prince Albert in order that he might see her before he dies.

Despite her resentment and anger, Tannis embarks on a dangerous ride through stormy conditions from the Flats to Prince Albert, returning with Elinor and Tom in time for a tender farewell scene. In the final tableau, Tannis sits, wrapped in a shawl, on the floor outside the room where Carey lies dying, attended by Elinor. The narrative, lingering on Tannis's appearance, represents her as "exactly like a squaw" (Montgomery, *Further* 300), an expression that clearly delineates the distance between Tannis and Elinor. At the end of the story, Tannis claims Carey's body for burial at the Flats, where, she says, he will be "mine – all mine" (Montgomery, *Further* 300). Both Elinor and Tannis are tragic figures; but Tannis's tragedy proceeds from her mixed race, which consigns her to the sordid setting of the Flats. Elinor, wistful as she is, enjoys the privilege of living in Avonlea, a privilege that derives from her whiteness. This curious story exposes a deep unease about miscegenation through its representation of Tannis, the "handsome, sullen girl" whose despair stems from the knowledge that she will never be the equal of a white girl (Montgomery, *Further* 299). If the figure of the mixed-race girl is presented in muted forms in texts for girls, "Tannis of the Flats" offers a reminder of the negative associations that surround depictions of interracial sexual relations well into the twentieth century.

In Their Place: Non-White Girls and Indigenous Cultures

Few children's texts from the period between 1840 and 1940 locate non-white girl characters within Indigenous cultures, since most such characters are peripheral figures in narratives set in white society.[9] In the 1930s, two texts that departed from this pattern were published: Grey Owl's *The Adventures of Sajo and Her Beaver People* (1935) and, in Australia, Frank Dalby Davison's *Children of the Dark People* (1936). In both cases, the action involves a young girl and a boy who feature in quest narratives that emphasize environmentalist themes. Grey Owl (Archibald Belaney) was a prominent Canadian example of white people who "go native," taking on Indigenous identities and often profiting from them. Dressed in leather clothing and moccasins and claiming to be part Apache, Belaney conducted lecture tours across Canada, the United States, and Britain, speaking on environmental issues and the value of wilderness. After his death, it was established that Belaney was British, that he had no Indian ancestry, and that he had invented a life story that enabled his self-production as an Indian conservationist who, as Daniel Francis says, "spoke with the accumulated wisdom of the people who had inhabited the eastern woodlands for thousands of years" (139). From 1906, when he migrated to Canada, Belaney developed relationships with Ojibwe Indians, learning their language, narratives, and rituals, which enabled him to pass as Indian. Nevertheless, his depiction of girls and women in *The Adventures of Sajo* is based on European and British conceptions of gender norms. Similarly, Davison's treatment of Aboriginal femininity in *Children of the Dark People* is inflected by beliefs about the subservient role of girls and the domestic and maternal roles attributed to them.

The preface to *The Adventures of Sajo* clearly identifies the book's implied readers: non-Indigenous children who will gain from "this simple story of two Indian children and their well-loved animal friends" an appreciation of "the joys and sorrows, the work, the pastimes and the daily lives of the humble little People of the forest, who can experience feelings so very like their own" (Grey xiv). These "humble little People" live in the northern wilderness, a space redolent with mythic significances in colonial and post-colonial Canada. The novel's emphasis on the majesty of northern landscapes and the everyday lives of animals is reminiscent of two narrative forms popular in early Canadian writing for the young: adventure stories set in the northern wilderness and the realist animal stories of Ernest Thompson Seton and Charles G.D. Roberts.

9 In Australia, Canada, and New Zealand, it was not until the second half of the twentieth century that Indigenous authors produced texts for young people that treated the values and practices of Indigenous cultures as normal and usual (see Bradford, *Unsettling Narratives*, 47–59).

Whereas adventure narratives typically trace the progress of young settlers as they leave the safety of home or school to embark on dangerous journeys in remote parts of Canada, *The Adventures of Sajo* follows its protagonists' voyage from the northern wilderness to an urban location referred to as "the city." Eleven-year-old Sajo lives with her brother, Shapian, and her father, Big Feather, near the Indian village O-pee-pee-soway. During a hunting trip, Big Feather rescues two beaver kittens from an otter that destroyed their dam and gives them to Sajo as pets. Big Feather is forced to sell one of the beavers to a zoo so that he can pay his debts to the store owned by "the Company," and Sajo and Shapian travel to the city to rescue the young beaver.

The novel defines Sajo's identity in relation to a masculine order in which she is relegated to the domestic sphere, cooking for Shapian and Big Feather and cleaning the family's cabin. The beaver kittens, Chilawee and Chikanee, are surrogate children to Sajo, who tells them stories, provides them with food, and comforts them when they are sad. In contrast, Shapian sometimes regrets that he is both masculine and also older than Sajo: "he wished – very privately of course – that he was not quite such a man" (Grey 76). Such formulations of feminine and masculine identities are suggestive of traditional social orders and perhaps speak to a nostalgic vision of gender relations prior to the emergence of the New Woman. In this novel, regimes of power are dominated by male figures: the trader who forces Big Feather to trade Chikanee for provisions; the missionary, "tall and strong-looking, with bright yellow hair and blue eyes" (Grey 147), who collects money for the children so that they can continue their quest; the policeman who directs them to the amusement park where Chikanee is an exhibit; and the owner of the park, who restores the beaver to Sajo.

During their hazardous journey to the city, during which the children negotiate a forest fire and wild rapids, Shapian acts as "captain of their little ship" (Grey 117), issuing orders to Sajo and soothing her when she is fearful; Sajo's role is to care for Chilawee, whom the children take with them. When Shapian's eyebrows are burned off by the fire, Sajo laughs at his appearance, prompting Shapian to reflect that "it was just like a girl ... to worry about a little thing like eyebrows when they had all so nearly lost their lives" (Grey 134). By focusing on these contrasts between Sajo and Shapian, the narrative enforces gender hierarchies in which boys are active and agential while girls are dependent and emotional. It is certainly the case that girl readers of *The Adventures of Sajo* are positioned to admire Sajo's skills at negotiating the forest and bravely facing the dangers

6.3 "Sajo ran home with Chilawee in her arms." "Grey Owl," *The Adventures of Sajo and Her Beaver People* (London: Lovat Dickson & Thompson, 1935).

she encounters. Nevertheless, these skills are in the main coded as feminine, revolving as they do around the mother-like care that Sajo invests in Chilawee and Chikanee. When the beavers whimper and cry as kittens, Sajo, "who had never forgotten her own mother and knew why they were lonesome, would take them in her arms and croon softly to them, and try to comfort them" (14).

The illustration entitled "Sajo ran home with Chilawee in her arms" (Figure 6.3) depicts Sajo running through the forest carrying Chilawee. The focus of the picture is Sajo's face, which stands out from the sketchy background as the most developed element of the illustration. Sajo's expression suggests resolve and concentration as she clutches the young beaver in her arms. The context of this image is that Sajo, enjoying her favourite place near the waterfall, believes that she hears her mother's voice speaking to her and urging her to go to the city to rescue

Chikanee. Impelled by her mother's words, Sajo snatches Chilawee up and runs home to relay her mother's message to Shapian. A sense of urgency is suggested by Sajo's energetic movement, visible in her swinging braids and billowing clothes. She is defined in relation to her maternal and nurturing instincts, heightened by her preternatural access to her mother's voice.

Distinctions between female and male experiences and identities pervade Davison's treatment of the girl and boy, Nimmitybel and Jackadgery, in *Children of the Dark People*, whose prologue announces the imminent demise of Aboriginal people: "This story [is about] two children of the dark people who once roamed the Australian bush, who were so few and who have now almost passed away" (n.p.). The names of the children and the spirit figures who feature in the narrative are based on white versions of Aboriginal place names, just as the novel's depictions of Aboriginal practices are based on hearsay and imagination.

Children of the Dark People constructs a version of Aboriginal culture characterized by superstition and cruelty: the premise of the narrative is that an evil "witch-doctor" in the children's tribe plans to abduct them and take them to a distant tribe from which they will not be able to return. He tricks the children into embarking on a journey, during which they become lost and rely on spirit figures for assistance. Like Sajo, Nimmitybel makes up her mind that she is "the little girl and the housekeeper" and that she is responsible for the children's domestic needs, while Jackadgery's duty is to protect her (Davison 25). He hunts for food, makes weapons, creates cave drawings, and carries Nimmitybel on his back to disguise the children's tracks from the witch-doctor, who pursues them. Thoroughly socialized into these gendered behaviours, Nimmitybel feels sympathy for Jackadgery, "because no matter how frightened he might be he was the one who had to do something" (Davison 110). She is as attuned to animals as Sajo is, making a pet of a possum, which she carries with her on her journey. In effect, both Sajo and Nimmitybel are represented in line with gender norms that attribute power and authority to boys and men. Unlike the young white girls we discuss in chapter 9, whose robust independence anticipates their futures as modern women, Sajo and Nimmitybel are consigned to a time and space that predates modernity and where gender relations are fixed and immutable; in both novels, power and authority reside with men and boys. In his study of time in the discipline of anthropology, Johannes Fabian argues that colonial discourses locate societies on "a temporal slope" (17), on which modern, white societies occupy the apex and Indigenous peoples are placed on the lower realms, associated with mythology rather than history. In line with Fabian's argument, Sajo and Nimmitybel are precluded from the drive towards modernity exemplified by their white sisters, and they must play out the subservient roles attributed to Indigenous girls and women in *The Adventures of Sajo* and *Children of the Dark People.*

The texts we have discussed in this chapter promote the virtues of British culture and the superiority of white over non-white peoples. Their transnational commonalities are most evident in their treatment of white girls who act in quasi-maternal roles towards Indigenous girls, who are universally depicted as childlike, exemplifying the inferiority of non-white cultures. However, the Indigenous girls who appear in these texts adhere to a variety of representational modes and imperial ideologies. One factor that shapes depictions of non-white girls is the extent to which authors have first-hand experience of the settings and cultures in which the narratives are located; for instance, Bowman treats the young Aboriginal woman Baldabella as a kind of all-purpose Native figure who might substitute for an equivalent character in various imperial settings. In contrast, Gunn's depiction of Bett-Bett is inflected by her experience as the mistress of a homestead on a large cattle station in the Northern Territory of Australia. This is not to say that Gunn's treatment of Bett-Bett can be seen as "accurate," but rather that it is shaped by lived experience as well as by colonial discourses. These discourses do not manifest a uniform set of values beyond their shared commitment to imperialism and their espousal of hierarchies of race; they are contingent and often contradictory. Imperial fiction for girls gives voice to widespread distinctions between the "black races" and those deemed "less black," or brown, so that Māori girls are accorded a higher status than Australian Aboriginal girls. Discourses of miscegenation are particularly unstable: in *Canadian Crusoes,* Indiana marries Hector, whereas mixed-race romances in *Piriki's Princess* and *An Algonquin Maiden* end, with a sense of inevitability, in the death of non-white girls. All the texts we discuss position girl readers – colonial and British – to acquiesce to the belief that to be white is to enjoy a status denied to non-white girls, who may aspire to be white but who rarely rise above their racialized inferiority. As Lake and Reynolds observe, the decades from the late nineteenth century to the twentieth were marked by "the spread of 'whiteness' as a transnational form of racial identification" (3). In this chapter, we have demonstrated how national and cultural inflections shape depictions of Indigenous girls and young women while locating them firmly within this transnational ideology. In the texts we discuss in the next section of this book, narratives produced over the first decades of the twentieth century, Indigenous girls are largely conspicuous for their absence. In fiction addressing education and work, war-time girlhoods, and modernity, non-white girls are, it seems, relegated to the past, where they play out their role as remnants of doomed races.

SECTION THREE

Modernity and Transnational Femininities

CHAPTER SEVEN

Work and Education

A girl [should be] fitted to earn her own living whether she ever has to or not.
–L.M. Montgomery, *Anne of Green Gables* (1908)

In *Anne of Green Gables*, Marilla's comment that a girl must be educated to earn her own living, even if she is never required to do so, reflects the central questions of colonial girlhood: what will the colonial girl be required to do in the future and what skills and attributes will she need to be successful? Girls' fiction and periodicals in white settler colonies have many similarities, especially as they answer these questions. Colonial girls' fiction is often preoccupied with the need to raise colonial girls to become capable wives and mothers and with identifying the knowledge and skills a girl needs to be successful in these roles. Ideas about education and work are similar in girls' print culture throughout the colonies, yet they vary significantly over the century under consideration here. The earlier fiction focuses on settler colonialism and tends to be more progressive than later fiction in how it approaches girls' education and work. Although the mid-nineteenth-century novels typically conclude with girls' demonstrating domestic expertise and eventually marrying – attributes valuable to the building of these nations – they nonetheless demonstrate the need for skilled, educated women. By the 1910s, however, anxiety about women's roles is much more evident in girls' fiction, particularly in Australia and New Zealand. Only with the increased popularity of the girls' school story, which flourished in the 1920s and 1930s, does this anxiety diminish. The school story reflects modern attitudes towards girls' education, but the girls in these stories generally occupy a space separate from the real world and rarely consider where their education might take them in terms of future employment.

Although girls' texts did not often position themselves as feminist, they nonetheless engaged with questions of women's work and education, which remained an important topic throughout the nineteenth century and into the early twentieth century. Patricia Grimshaw explains that "the two basic elements of nineteenth-century feminism were the education of girls and women at all levels and the undertaking of paid employment by an increasing number of women, who thus shared with the male population the task of breadwinning" (*Women's Suffrage* 31). Attitudes towards girls' work and education shifted between the 1860s and the 1920s. These changes were transnational in the sense that we can see similar concerns in Canadian, Australian, and New Zealand texts. Yet they also reflected local concerns about women's roles and responsibilities in these emerging nations.

Education, Work, and Suffrage

Attitudes towards girls' work and education in Canada, Australia, and New Zealand varied based on the nations' respective colonial settler histories. In Canada, education and women's rights and suffrage were formalized through provincial legislation throughout the late nineteenth and early twentieth centuries. Public education was crucial to the establishment of civil order and public stability, especially in a period of profound social change. Schools established during this period were expected to "cultivate the students' sense of citizenship, loyalty, respect for property, and deference to authority" (Axelrod 25). Free, compulsory public schooling helped to restore and reinforce public order. Although provinces established secular and religious (Protestant and Catholic) schools, for many children (especially those living in rural areas), schools could be difficult to access, and attendance was irregular (Davey 109).

Curricula differed somewhat by province, but in Ontario in the 1880s, girls were taught English, history, modern languages, science, the classics, and mathematics; they comprised almost half of secondary-school enrolments (Axelrod 61). Women's access to higher education began in 1872, when Mount Allison University in New Brunswick first granted entry to women. Over the next decade, most other Canadian universities opened their doors to women, and the barriers to women's entry gradually began to fall. The American example of women's higher education provided a co-educational model that could be emulated in Canada and elsewhere. In addition, educated women were perceived to bring "cultural refinement" to their communities (Axelrod 96). Thus, by the 1920s, Canadian girls and young women "had gained the rights to equal access to education" (Pierson 21). Most Canadian women worked in domestic service, in sewing-related occupations, as teachers, or in sales, with relatively few jobs available to them, especially after they married (Connelly n.p.). Women were expected to "bear primary, if not exclusive, responsibility for child rearing" (Pierson 17). This remained a constant idea throughout the nineteenth and early twentieth centuries in Canada, New Zealand, and Australia.

In New Zealand, the first women graduated from the University of New Zealand in 1877, and by 1893, women comprised over half the university students in the country (Grimshaw, *Women's Suffrage* 33). Although women and girls nominally had equal access to education from the 1870s, formal equality was compromised by the University of New Zealand Senate's regulation in 1916 that required female candidates for matriculation to show they had completed domestic-science training (Nolan 13–14). According to Melanie Nolan, this regulation, and another in 1917 mandating domestic science as part of the curriculum, ensured that, "at least for the first quarter of a century, [the university] 'confirmed the stay-at-home role' of these future wives and mothers" (14).

Australian girls' secondary schools were established in the final decades of the nineteenth century with the aim of preparing girls for university and public life (Lake 37). While women were first admitted to the University of Melbourne in 1880 and the universities of Sydney and Adelaide in 1881, women's higher education was not a dominant concern in Australian culture. The relatively high marriage rate in Australia meant that there was less pressure for single women to support themselves through professional careers, despite the fact that between 1891 and 1901, the number of women aged twenty-five to twenty-nine who remained unmarried doubled to more than ten per cent in all colonies excluding Tasmania (Magarey 111). In response to this decline in marriage rates, various attempts were made to limit women's economic freedoms and reassert the idea that their primary responsibility was as wives and mothers. Changes to recruitment during the 1890s made it illegal to hire married women in a range of roles in which women had traditionally been employed.[1]

Alongside better access to education was the emergence of progressive suffrage campaigns. In 1893, New Zealand was the first country in the world to grant women the vote, with a feminist movement "comparable to movements elsewhere in the world" and, like in Canada, connected to the work of the Women's Christian Temperance Union (Grimshaw, *Women's Suffrage* 4). Australia's suffrage campaign followed New Zealand's, with South Australia granting women's suffrage in 1894; other states followed, with Victoria finally granting suffrage in 1908. In 1902, the Australian federal franchise was granted to all white women. Angela Woollacott suggests that Australian women consequently viewed themselves as "politically more modern than even British and American women" ("White Colonialism" 50). The comparatively early granting of white women's suffrage meant that the Australian Woman Movement directed its energies towards addressing other issues of gender inequality in the first decades of the twentieth century, particularly seeking to reduce their economic dependence on men.[2] Women's suffrage in Canada proceeded much more slowly, with several provinces granting women the vote during the First World War. In 1919, federal enfranchisement followed for women who were British subjects and at least twenty-one years of age.[3]

Unsurprisingly, the progress in women's education during the sixty years of Queen Victoria's reign was a prominent focus of the 1897 Victorian Era Exhibition, held in London, which was designed to coincide with Victoria's Diamond Jubilee. In addition to arranging displays on the topic of women's education, Frances Evelyn Greville, the Countess of Warwick, also organized an educational congress and a series of

1 These roles included teaching in New South Wales and Victoria. Elite areas of the clothing, boot-making, and printing trades were also closed off to women; apprenticeships were denied to women in most areas; and clothing outwork was eliminated. Low rates of pay in the early twentieth century also prompted a decrease in the number of women employed in factories (Magarey 132–5).

2 The Australian Woman Movement was not a formal organization; the name is used to describe feminist activity in Australia and New Zealand in the period. See Magarey for more detail.

3 This act did not allow women to stand for election, although this right was granted in July 1919. Women were denied the right to be appointed to the Senate until the successful resolution of the 1929 Persons Case.

conferences, the proceedings of which were printed in an edited collection, *Progress in Women's Education in the British Empire.* In her preface, the countess remarks that

> the quality of any woman's education is not to be tested by the amount of knowledge which she possesses, but rather by her capability to use that little knowledge which it is in the power of the very least of us to acquire. One sees with rejoicing the ever-widening field which is opening up for women everywhere, giving to all those who possess a trained capacity for work, their opportunity; and it should be remembered that *trained capacity*, wherever it exists, is always in demand. (Warwick xii–xiii)

Warwick unites the idea of education with work when she explains that women have a useful role in society based on their training. Moreover, this educational ideal is imperial in its focus.[4] The celebration of the British Empire provided the opportunity to bring together a number of speakers to explore the progress in women's education.

The tone of the conference is quite positive, with the countess remarking that "one of the most pleasing features ... was the great interest taken in the proceedings by visitors from the colonies" (Warwick xxii). Representatives from Canada, Australia, and New Zealand provided updates about the status of girls' education in their respective colonies. Lord Loch, former governor of Victoria, observed that "all the great self-governing colonies have educational Acts" with one of the "underlying principles" being that the system should be compulsory (286). Yet he acknowledged that in some colonies it is "more difficult to carry out that compulsory system than in others, owing to the great distances which separate people from each other" (Loch 286).

Loch's comments highlight two important points regarding girls' education in the colonies. First, although all colonies had education legislation, none had a national framework for it. Instead, colonial education was regional in its orientation. Canadian provinces, Australian colonies, and New Zealand regions each separately contributed to the emerging education systems in their respective colonies. The Honourable W.P. Reeves, formerly minister of education in New Zealand, explains

4 Late in the century, discussions of women's work and education had shifted to focus on the importance of training, an upper- and middle-class requirement wherein girls and women needed proper skills to enter the workplace.

that New Zealand's "decentralized State system" has emerged from the "geographical conditions of the colony" (308), with the result that "for many years the different settlements of New Zealand were cut off from one another, and the education grew up in accordance with the ideas and capacities of the settlers in different places" (309).

The second important point about education, and girls' education in particular, is that geography had an effect on whether one received an education, and of what quality it was. The Marquis of Lorne, governor general of Canada from 1878 to 1883, remarks that "the colonies have had much advantage over the Mother-land, inasmuch as they have been able to proceed very much upon a blank sheet. [Education systems] have been built up from the ground" (289). This freedom meant that each colony could decide what kind of education system it wished to implement, and they all emphasized the importance of educating both boys and girls.

By the time of the exhibition in 1897, higher education in the colonies was relatively accessible for white upper- and middle-class women. The development of girls' (or co-educational) secondary schools and a system of university entrance exams helped to encourage girls to pursue their education. Although education "was a key site through which notions of empire were to be disseminated ... there was no coherent formal policy for British colonial education" (Stephenson 24). This meant that Canadian, New Zealand, and Australian governments, typically at a state, provincial, or regional level, were free to develop independent education policies.[5]

In this chapter, we draw on this history of education, suffrage, and employment to examine a number of Canadian, Australian, and New Zealand texts. These stories address the importance of girls' education and work and the extent to which the focus of education and the opportunities for work shift over time. Transnational similarities are reflected in the colonial preoccupation with ensuring girls were able to handle the harsh demands of settlement while also being appropriately educated to fulfil their civilizing mission. This chapter is divided into three sections

5 Patrick Walsh argues a contrary view based on his examination of the role of schoolbooks in Ireland and Ontario, claiming that colonial education systems were strongly influenced by the British system. He asserts that "among the most long-lasting of the influences of British imperialism and its administrators on colonised countries were the educational systems they founded and passed on at independence to the new native governments" (645).

that reflect the shifting perspectives on these themes over time. In the first section, on colonial settlement, we discuss two early Canadian texts, *Shenac's Work at Home: A Story of Canadian Life* (1866) by Margaret Murray Robertson and Henrietta Skelton's *Grace Morton* (1873), alongside Ann Jane Cupples's 1886 novel, *The Redfords: An Emigration Story*, which is set in New Zealand. All three texts focus on the importance of female domestic skills. In the next section, we examine the discomfort with and uncertainty about girls' education in Australian fiction appearing in the 1910s. In Henry Handel Richardson's *The Getting of Wisdom* (1910), the protagonist struggles with the ways her boarding-school fails to prepare her for the future, and Vera G. Dwyer's *With Beating Wings* (1913) examines the ways in which patriarchal oppression limits girls' opportunities. These stories, published prior to the rise of the Australian girls' school story of the 1920s and 1930s, place little importance on girls' education, although domestic work remains a significant focus.

In the third and final section, we discuss school stories published in the 1920s and 1930s. In the Canadian school stories *Judy of York Hill* (1922) by Ethel Hume Bennett and *The Girls of Miss Clevelands'* (1920) by Beatrice Embree, the educational focus is much less domestic than it is in nineteenth-century Canadian fiction. At the same time, however, these texts contain little discussion of girls' post-school employment. This attitude is echoed in other 1920s school stories, such as Constance Mackness's *Di-Double-Di* (1929), set in Australia, and Phillis Garrard's *Hilda at School: A New Zealand Story* (1929), the earliest New Zealand school story. Another New Zealand novel, Isabel Maud Peacocke's *Brenda and the Babes* (1927), displays a concern that women might forget their responsibilities to their homes and their families if they take on work outside the home.

Through our comparison of these novels, we demonstrate how the feminine ideals embodied by their female protagonists are inevitably intertwined with the needs of the nation. The similarities in attitudes towards work and education in girls' fiction from different colonies relate to the ways in which such attitudes were influenced by transnational ideas about education, suffrage, and employment while also reflecting differences based on unique national concerns.

The Nineteenth Century and Colonial Settlement

In one of the earliest of the novels we discuss in this chapter, Robertson's *Shenac's Work at Home: A Story of Canadian Life*, work and education ultimately become entwined, although work is initially at the forefront.[6] Published first by the American Sunday School Union of Philadelphia and then by the Religious Tract Society in London (Waterston, *Rapt* 241), the novel highlights the importance of religious faith, which Shenac originally lacks.[7] The domestic nature of Shenac's work is evident in the novel's title. Yet the story differs from other domestic fiction because of the importance it places on the land as a vehicle for family prosperity and as a symbol of familial ties.

The novel follows the MacIvor family as they emigrate from Scotland to settle in Canada. Through an unlikely set of circumstances, Shenac is forced to take responsibility for the family fortunes: "the youth portrayed on the Canadian backwoods farm is not frolicsome or flirtatious; it is sombre, dominated by harsh necessities of productiveness" (Waterston, *Rapt* 240). Land use is crucial to the family's survival, and Shenac not only works in the fields but also does heavy chores around the home after her mother's strength fails following the death of her oldest son and her husband. When her cousin tells her to move to the nearest town and "take a [domestic] situation," Shenac insists that the family "must keep together ... and the land must be kept" for her oldest brother to inherit when he returns from the gold-fields (Robertson 54).

Although her role as the head of the household is temporary, Shenac is understood to be "doing a woman's work" (Robertson 54), rather than a girl's. Indeed, she has to be reminded that "she [is] not an old woman, burdened with care, but a young girl not sixteen, to whom fun and frolic might be natural" (Robertson 49). As a young girl full of youthful energy, she is enabled in her success by her good health. The farm could not succeed without Shenac's labour, and she prefers to be working in the fields instead of spinning wool. The narrator reminds the reader that the need for girls and women to help with fieldwork is a common feature of the Canadian farming landscape:

> It must not be supposed that because Shenac was a girl she had no part in the field-work. Even now, in that part of the country, the wives and daughters

---

6 The 1889 reprint of this book is retitled as *Shenac: The Story of a Highland Family in Canada*, thus removing the focus on work at home.

7 Waterston concludes that the novel's "wider appeal ... is evidenced in the fact that the major publishing house of Nelson in London and Edinburgh reissued the novel in 1889, with reprints in 1892, 1901, and 1904. In Canadian terms, it was a best-seller" (*Rapt* 241).

> of farmers help their fathers and brothers during the busy seasons of spring and harvest; and for many years after the opening up of the country the females helped to clear the land, putting their hands to all kinds of outdoor work as cheerfully as need be. (Robertson 42)

Although working the land is understood as primarily a male occupation, girls and women are required to help when necessary, a task they perform willingly.

Yet Shenac's determination to keep the farm means that she sacrifices some markers of her femininity. She eschews traditional feminine skills and cuts her hair when it proves to be "such a trouble" (Robertson 58). This lack of femininity symbolizes the tension between work and responsibility. She is prepared to sacrifice almost everything, including feminine attributes, such as her long hair, to farm the land. This exacerbates her neglect of her responsibilities to her mother and to God: "In the eagerness with which she devoted herself to her work, she forgot higher duties ... the duty owed to God" (Robertson 84). The work she performs causes her to become "hard and bitter" (Robertson 45), which the narrator attributes to the unnatural responsibility that has fallen on her shoulders:

> It is never well to take girls quickly out of their childhood, and it was especially bad for her to have so much the guidance of these affairs, for she naturally liked to lead, – to have her own way; and, without being at all conscious of it, there were times when she grew sharp and arbitrary, expecting to be obeyed unquestioningly by them all. (Robertson 84)

In taking on this leadership role, Shenac expects her decisions to be obeyed, a quality that makes her less agreeable and less feminine.

This lack of femininity becomes more explicit over the course of the novel. By the time Shenac is almost nineteen, her appearance has changed significantly: "You are thinner than you used to be, and sometimes you look pale and very weary; and you are a great deal older-looking" (Robertson 166). Her work has caused her to age and lose the beauty that came with health and physical labour. Only when Shenac comes back to God do "peace and comfort" return to her (Robertson 167). This epiphany accompanies a change in the family fortunes, with the return of her older brother, Allister, for whom the land is intended. The narrator explains that "the welfare of all the family had depended on her strength and wisdom while they kept together, and the responsibility had been too heavy for her. How much too heavy it had been she only knew by the blessed sense of relief which followed its removal" (Robertson 185). Although Shenac has performed bravely and capably in his absence, Allister's return means that she is able to return to domestic duties, in which she now takes "pride and pleasure" (Robertson 188). The narrative makes clear that Shenac's decision to take up farming was the right one at the time, just as later relinquishing farm work and taking up more feminine duties was the appropriate action.

Upon Allister's marriage, his new wife handles these domestic duties, and Shenac begins to look towards employment outside the home: "I think there must be work somewhere that I could do better, more successfully, than I can do on the farm" (Robertson 214). Her brother Hamish's illness and eventual death provides her with an opportunity to work as a caregiver, for which she is an obvious and appropriate choice, as the role represents the final dimension of her "work at home" (Robertson 246). Upon his death, this work is deemed complete, yet it leaves Shenac with no obvious future employment. When Hamish's friend Stuart, a minister, comes to visit, he asks her to marry him, a seemingly satisfying solution to the problem of her work. Yet Shenac knows that she is "not fit" to be a minister's wife, because, she explains, "I am not educated … I have never been anywhere but at home. I can only do common work" (Robertson 253, 254). She sympathizes with his ministerial work and would "like it to be [hers] in a humble way" but knows that she needs more education (Robertson 258). As the narrator concludes, attending school at her age is not an impossibility, because the farm has become a success: "In Shenac's country, happily, it is not considered a strange thing that a young girl should wish to pursue her education even after she is twenty: so she had no discomfort to encounter on the score of being out of her teens … She spent all the money … but she was moderately successful in her studies, and considered it well spent" (Robertson 261). Her education, in this case, and somewhat unusually, comes after her work, but together they provide her with the skills and knowledge she needs to perform her role as a minister's wife with grace and strength. For Shenac – and other Canadian girls who might follow in her footsteps – formal education enables work as a wife and, eventually, as a mother.

In contrast, the work performed in *Grace Morton* (1873) is much more domestic from the outset, although these domestic skills are learned at school rather than in the home. Grace, nearly sixteen, is delicate and often feels ill when studying. Her lack of usefulness within the home results in her being sent to a school "where better habits might be formed, and those nobler qualities which she really possessed be called forth into action, and become all that is lovely in women, and be a blessing to [her father] in his old age" (Skelton 17). The school to which she is sent "finishes the education of young ladies, and so prepares them for the duties of life, that they will be blessings to the homes they occupy, and a credit to the country" (Skelton 18). Through her education, Grace will be prepared for her future work, looking after her father and, eventually, her husband. The domestic space, the home, has failed to prepare a girl for her future roles as wife and mother. Instead, the school environment becomes the proper place to obtain domestic skills that can be put to work in service of both the home and the nation.

Published just six years after Confederation, the book's connection between domestic knowledge and nationhood is perhaps unsurprising, but it also relates to issues of class. The headmistress echoes this sentiment, explaining that "in a new country like this, where efficient servants are so difficult to obtain, ... if the mistress is not acquainted with all the details of a house, it must necessarily bring on the family a great amount of discomfort, and even sometimes misery" (Skelton 20). The realities of housekeeping in Canada, where obtaining domestic servants can be difficult, mean that Grace must be educated to manage the household with efficiency and economy. Initially, however, she wonders why she should "learn things which are not fit for a lady to do" (Skelton 22). Her father represents Canadian attitudes, while also foreshadowing his reversal of fortune, when he answers that "no work however humble degrades a true lady or gentleman" (Skelton 22). Grace ultimately proves to be transformative within the household when she and her friends take to the kitchen to prepare food. The servants, and especially the cook, appreciate this help. Yet the ease with which Grace interacts with the servants is part of the reason why her aunt, on a visit from England, decides to return home. We explored this phenomenon, in which colonial girls are typically more willing to interact with and assist servants, in chapter 4. Only British immigrants who adapt to changing circumstances will thrive in Canada.[8]

The girl's parents have a duty to ensure she is ready for the responsibilities adulthood, and possibly marriage, entails. The narrator observes

8 Published in Toronto, this novel was likely distributed primarily within Canada. Thus it seems unlikely that it was read in England, suggesting that this message of Canadian adaptability was a form of self-congratulation for successful Canadian emigrants.

that Grace's mother "did not think it fashionable for a young lady to learn to be useful. Oh how many foolish mothers are answerable for their daughter's wretchedness" (Skelton 84–5). Her father, "a true and sensible man, although weak in some points" (Skelton 17), can see that his wife has failed in the raising of their daughter. The changing fortunes of Grace's family mean that she will have an opportunity to put her budgeting skills to the test, emphasizing that girls have an obligation to work hard while at school to become useful and productive members of society. The narrator wonders at the frequency with which girls at school, "instead of employing their time in gaining useful knowledge … [spend] it in idleness and frivolous nonsense" (Skelton 33). Skelton dedicated the novel to the pupils of the Bishop Strachan School in Toronto, Canada's oldest boarding- and day school for girls, founded in 1867. Her message about productivity and usefulness is clearly aimed at the real schoolgirls to whom the book is dedicated, as well as to the implied readers. They should recognize the sacrifices being made, both financially and emotionally, to enable them to obtain a superior education. Not only will this education allow them to be useful within the parental home, it will also improve their prospects for marriage.

The connection between domestic skills and marriage is a common theme in the novel. The capability of these school graduates means that they would make eminently suitable wives: "What a prospect for the sons of Canada, should they in the future ever be fortunate enough to obtain the hand of any of my fair young friends; in them they will certainly find a real help-meet" (Skelton 61). Yet marriage is not the only prospect available to girls. When the family of Violet, Grace's friend, loses its fortune through a bank failure, Violet immediately decides that she will not return to school, for she is "quite competent to earn a livelihood" as a clerk or a teacher (Skelton 162). She quickly finds a position as a governess and companion to a little girl, and they sail to Europe. Notably, Violet regrets that her employment means she will have to leave her family. The decision to work can only be to help others, not because of a selfish desire to be independent. The tension between a girl's duty to her family and her ability to obtain gainful employment can be ameliorated only if the employment is intended to contribute to the family finances.

The connection between domesticity and marriage also appears in *The Redfords: An Emigrant Story* (1886). Although seventeen-year-old Maud has been away at school in London, she is recalled home when her father's fortune is ruined after a bank failure. The family discusses emigration and concludes that New Zealand is "a much better field for enterprise [than North America or Australia] ... in the case of those who have little money" (Cupples 23). Maud, who is already known as "old mother" for her maternal role as the oldest sister (Cupples 16), is determined to prove herself useful in the colonial setting. She is resolved "to be the head of the home department, and look after the cow we shall have, and all the work indoors" once they settle in New Zealand (Cupples 24), although she does not yet have the necessary domestic skills. In the brief months before they depart, she and her sister quickly receive "instruction from the housekeeper in the art of cooking and other housewifely occupations" (Cupples 29). Domestic skills required for emigration are quickly and easily learned and vital to the family's success in the colony. When Maud laments being unable to help with some of the more physically demanding tasks in New Zealand, her father reminds her that the boys and men would not "work so well if [they] had to cook [their] own food, and look after the house" (Cupples 69). Maud readily adapts to the new environment, making the house look nice and demonstrating her feminine accomplishments by playing the piano, while also performing necessary settler tasks like rising early to start the kitchen fire, making the daily bread, and arranging the dairy to raise additional income through the sale of butter. Eventually, she marries a nearby settler, thus reinforcing her marital and (eventual) reproductive role.

Tension around Education and Work

In contrast to these nineteenth-century texts, which appear relatively early in the history of colonial girls' print culture, Australian texts featuring girls and their education appear only in the early twentieth century and are less explicitly supportive of education and work. In *The Getting of Wisdom* (1910), one of the most enduring Australian novels, a country girl from a poor family is sent to a boarding-school in Melbourne.[9] Not a traditional novel for girls, this *Künstlerroman* nonetheless features many

9 Although this novel is one "by which most younger readers know her" (Probyn and Steele xxi), *The Getting of Wisdom* is not typically considered a girls' novel. Instead, as Clive Probyn and Bruce Steele note, its ironic and iconoclastic tone and its incorporation of a lesbian relationship mean that "this was never a novel for schoolgirls: it was always a novel for adults set in a school" (xxxvi). Like *An Algonquin Maiden*, which we discussed in chapter 6, this novel is nonetheless about girlhood and speaks to the porous boundaries between texts for girls and those for women.

school-story tropes as well as a school-aged female protagonist struggling to come to terms with the limitations imposed on her at school. It differs substantially from typical British school stories in its depiction of the repeated persecution of heroine Laura Tweedle Rambotham as she unsuccessfully attempts to adapt to the modern, urban space of the boarding-school. *The Getting of Wisdom* is emblematic of the way in which a number of later Australian school stories, such as Lilian Turner's *The Girl from the Back-Blocks* (1914), were built on the premise that girls from the bush required education in Sydney or Melbourne to appropriately feminize them.

Written by Henry Handel Richardson, the pseudonym of Ethel Florence Lindesay Richardson, *The Getting of Wisdom* is semi-autobiographical, reflecting the challenge of being an educated Australian woman at the time, when education was defined in typically masculine terms.[10] It begins with Laura telling a romantic tale where "Wondrous Fair" passively waits for her prince, but Laura is awkwardly positioned in this role. She struggles to adapt to the world of the boarding-school, finding that her previous schooling and her upbringing have made her ill-suited to boarding-school life. Although she has a vivid imagination, she soon discovers that "true knowledge" comes from "facts that were the real test of learning" (Richardson 77). These facts are defined as "masculine" (Pratt 7), as when a teacher criticizes a schoolmate for having "a real woman's brain: vague, slippery, inexact, interested only in the personal aspect of a thing. You can't concentrate your thoughts, and, worst of all, you've no curiosity – about anything that really matters ... It makes me ashamed to belong to the same sex" (Richardson 75). Thus Laura comes to understand that "it mattered tremendously that [Mount Kosciuszko] was 7308 and not 7309 feet high: that piece of information was valuable, was of genuine use to you; for it was worth your place in the class" (Richardson 77). Although Laura's conclusions are correct within the confines of her school, the narrator's ironic tone implies that such information is useless in the wider world. While this education helps Laura fit in, it fails to prepare her for the future, an irony of the narration that also critiques the wider world to which Laura struggles to adapt.

10 Miles Franklin's *My Brilliant Career* (1901), although not a book for younger readers, similarly addresses the difficulties facing a young woman whose opportunities are constrained by a life of poverty.

Unlike those of Grace and Shenac, for whom education is vital to their success, Laura's narrative is "deliberately indeterminate" (Pratt 8), and closure is intentionally withheld. Laura is happy to be "done with learning," although she is "unclear" about her future (Richardson 227). She is not attracted to the idea of life at home, where she fears she will be expected to instruct her younger brothers, but she "[does] not know in the least where she really belong[s]" (Richardson 227). According to Mandy Treagus, Richardson "makes use of an open ending to create opportunities" for Laura "while outlining the many forces aligned against her" (174). Laura has, the narrator explains, "the uncomfortable sense of being a square peg, which fitted into none of the round holes of her world" (Richardson 230). The novel concludes with her running down the road, growing smaller and smaller, until she turns at a bend in the path and disappears. Unlike the earlier Canadian stories, where the narratives conclude by laying out the future marriage prospects of the protagonists, Laura's future is "lost to sight" (Richardson 233). Although the narrator reassures the reader that "even for the squarest peg, the right hole may be ultimately be found" (Richardson 230), Laura's future is unclear.

The uncertainty surrounding girls' work and education is paramount in other Australian texts of this period as well. Lilian Turner's *Paradise and the Perrys* (1908) reinforces domesticity as a method of earning money without traversing the boundaries of the home. In this novel, four sisters unsuccessfully attempt a variety of different jobs. The eldest, Addie, works as a governess but finds it "dull" and unenjoyable (L. Turner 16). Theo is employed as a typist, but her employer skips town without paying her wages. After unsuccessfully searching for further work in the same area, Theo decides to try nursing. A series of mistakes in a real first-aid situation, however, lead her to conclude that she is ill-suited for that occupation. Theo desires a professional career, an unusual aspiration in Australian girls' fiction from this period, but the return to the domestic sphere as a source of income was in keeping with concerns about the declining marriage rate among women of childbearing age in the last decade of the nineteenth century.

If the domestic space can be transformed to enable paid employment, girls can both earn money and uphold the feminine ideal of duty to one's family. The girls are able to mobilize their domestic skills when they establish a profitable business selling refreshments to travellers and cyclists. This enables them to raise themselves out of poverty and eventually hire additional workers to help with some of the chores, such as waitressing and washing up. Formal education is never seen as an option or a desirable goal for these girls, who instead capitalize on already existing domestic capabilities.

Education is treated much more favourably in Vera G. Dwyer's *With Beating Wings: An Australian Story* (1913), although the protagonist must push the boundaries of behaviour deemed acceptable by her traditional father. The novel follows the fortunes of the Pemelby family as the impractical, stubborn, and old-fashioned father loses his job, has to pay legal fees, and is unable to find further work. Despite this setback, he refuses to let his daughter Gwen get a job and prevents his family from socializing because he imagines everyone is socially inferior to him. In one of the book's illustrations (Figure 7.1), the power relations of family life are reflected in the depiction of Gwen and her father. He sits alone at the breakfast-table enjoying the food and drink prepared through the unpaid domestic labour in his household. This man, who has caused the family's precarious financial situation, benefits from their labour even as he refuses to allow the girls to seek paid employment to improve the family's finances. Gwen stands with her head turned down and to the side in face of his wrath at her daring to ask his permission to seek work. Her standing position places Gwen above her father and foreshadows her refusal to accept his dictates. Gwen's writing talent is enhanced by her subject matter, stories about her home life. Like Brenda's mother in *Brenda and the Babes* and Anne in *Anne of Green Gables*, women writers are successful when they write about what they know. Because of Gwen's connection, through her writing, with the editor of a journal, she is easily able to find work when it becomes crucial that she help support her family.

Freedoms, both social and economic, are fundamental issues for Gwen and her sister Pat. As Pat explains,

> Work is all very well – I would hate to be a mere empty-headed butterfly, – but I do want something else besides, while I am young. I want a big, wide horizon! I want to know people – crowds of people. I can feel myself growing stupid in this groove, where we never meet anybody in our own sphere of intellect from one year's end to the other. I want to know something of the lovely jumble of characters that go to make up the world, instead of being hidden away in my corner – a particularly dark corner, too – wasting. (Dwyer 140)

Pat and Gwen know that they can contribute to the household through their talents and education. While their father believes in

7.1 Frontispiece. Illust. Victor Prout. Vera G. Dwyer, *With Beating Wings* (London: Ward, Lock & Co., 1913).

the importance of their formal education, he is unable to see that his attitude prevents them from accomplishing all that they could. He believes he has the "right of ownership" and "will uphold [his] authority over [them] at any cost" (Dwyer 181). This prevents Gwen from being a "real help" to her mother and contributing to the household finances (Dwyer 177). When she finally rebels against her father and begins working for the journal, she enjoys herself: "It was lovely work. Every moment of her day was now full of keen interest and enjoyment" (Dwyer 193). Girls' employment is rewarding not only for the financial rewards but also for the interest and challenge it provides. Moreover, because her father eventually reads Gwen's manuscript, he realizes the effects of his tyranny and understands that he has been wrong to restrict his children's activities. Girls' and women's work outside the home is desirable and necessary if girls are to develop fully into mature adults with the freedom to make their own choices. This contrasts with nineteenth-century novels, in which work is only undertaken because of family necessity – as in *Shenac's Work at Home* – and not for the girls' sense of fulfilment.

In comparison to *The Getting of Wisdom*, which seems to have received little attention in the Australian press, *With Beating Wings* received more promotional support.[11] Publisher Ward, Lock & Co. announced in March of 1913 that it had accepted the first story of the new "Australian authoress" Vera G. Dwyer ("With Beating Wings" 4), a news item that was repeated at least twenty-four times in colonial newspapers between 6 March and 28 March.[12] The British firm evidently felt Australian readers would be interested in new fiction from an Australian woman writer. By promoting the book in advance of its publication, they hoped to encourage readers to purchase it when it appeared in local shops. When the book appeared later that year, Ward, Lock & Co. advertised it alongside three other Australian girls' books – Lilian Turner's *Stairway to the Stars*, Mary Grant Bruce's *Norah of Billabong*, and Evelyn Goode's *The Childhood of Helen* – resulting in a number of favourable reviews in the Australian press. *The Register* writes that this first novel "contains much good work, and is full of promise ... Miss Dwyer writes sympathetically and evenly"

11 *The Getting of Wisdom* was published in London by Heinemann, which may account for the lack of attention in Australia.

12 Some of the colonial newspapers that reprinted the story include *Zeehan and Dundas Herald*, *The Traralgon Record*, *The Naracoote Herald*, *The Horsham Times*, *West Gippsland Gazette*, and *The Mildura Cultivator*.

("A New Writer" 4). The *Examiner* calls it a "bright, readable story that will find many admirers" ("Literature" 8). Although none of the reviews are exceptionally enthusiastic, one reviewer notes that the characters are "types of nicely educated Australian girls, whose characters are strengthened by their battles with the world, and their charming account of their experiences – lone and otherwise – will provide very wholesome reading for the growing girls of the period" ("New Novels" 13). Although the novel features Gwen's rebellion against her father, reviewers were not concerned about this behaviour. Instead, in the 1910s, this fiction is seen to be entirely appropriate for "girls of the period" in Australia, and elsewhere.

In interview with a Sydney journalist, Dwyer explains that "the gates of wisdom are open" to a girl who has aspirations in art, literature, or science ("What a Girl May Do" 7). Dwyer connects this freedom specifically to her nationality, asserting that she is a "true Australian" and that she lives "in an atmosphere of freedom and independence" ("What a Girl May Do" 7). As the reviewer in *The Advertiser* writes, "very few [readers] will wish to put the book down without ascertaining for themselves the outcome of Gwen's determined effort to win economic independence" ("New Novels" 13). Contemporary reviewers understood Gwen's desire for economic independence as an admirable endeavour central to the plot of the novel.

The need for girls to be able to earn money to support themselves is a concern in all three countries. Gwen's desire for paid employment to support her family is echoed in Montgomery's Anne of Green Gables series, where Anne's success at school enables her to win a scholarship and obtain her Bachelor of Arts. Unlike Gwen, whose father is financially able to give her the education she needs but prevents her from using it, Anne's family is uneducated but understands its importance. Anne must attend school to obtain the learning necessary to become a teacher. Moreover, to attend university, Anne must work harder and take extra classes, all of which are enabled by a lessening of her domestic duties. As we discussed at the beginning of this chapter, Anne's adoptive mother, Marilla, fully supports Anne's desire to obtain a degree. Marilla's attitude reflects the Canadian feminist concern that women should be able to support themselves. Education and the resulting employment are desirable outcomes for Canadian girls because they enable girls to be well prepared for the future. To Anne – and the broader Avonlea community – education is important both for its intrinsic value and for its contribution to their future employment prospects.

Girls at School

In the years following World War I, the girls' fiction appearing in all three countries reveals remarkable consistency in attitudes towards girls' education and work. Although the war years offered numerous opportunities for girls, as we discuss further in chapter 8, the post-war years depict the importance of girls' education, but demonstrate little concern with what they can and should do after school. Girls' education in the 1920s and 1930s seems to have been universally approved of, but girls and women in the workforce were expected to give way to returning soldiers in the post-war years. This may account for the shift from pre-war texts (like *Anne of Green Gables* and *With Beating Wings*) to post-war fiction. In the former, education is pivotal to girls' ability to obtain paid employment; in the latter, either girls are ensconced within the protective space of the school or the importance of the domestic space is reasserted.

As a consequence, girls' literature during this period is characterized by the increasing popularity of school stories. Particularly in Australia, girls' fiction privileges the "world of girls" found at girls' boarding-schools, where domestic duties give way to a space where homosocial bonds are predominant.[13] Louise Mack's *Teens: A Story of Australian Schoolgirls* (1897) was the first school story to be published in Australia, and the first juvenile title issued by Angus & Robertson in Sydney. Few Australian authors wrote more than one story in the genre until the 1920s, when writers such as Constance Mackness and Lillian Pyke became well known. The importance of friendship and the exciting possibilities offered by the school setting are particularly evident in this novel. The story, set in a Sydney day school, focuses on the development, and testing, of a strong friendship between high school girls Lennie and Mabel. The girls take the tram and exchange visits to each other's homes, but the school itself is the most important location for their new experiences. It was

> a great, strange world. A new world, unbounded, … indented with a hundred thousand episodes, of great importance to every dweller in the new world; broken up by rivers – of tears; or by mountains – of detentions, bad marks, punishments; covered with exquisite fruit and flowers, friendships

---

13 See Kristine Moruzi and Michelle J. Smith, "'A Great Strange World': Reading the Girls' School Story," *Girls' School Stories, 1749–1929*, vol. 1, ed. Kristine Moruzi and Michelle J. Smith (London: Routledge, 2014), xiii–xxxii.

> and fancies, competitions, winning, and losing, and laughter; and one larger, lovelier blossom than all the rest, the flower of Fun. (Mack 33)

Mack uses evocative landscape imagery to describe the exciting world of girls' education. In the context of colonial girls' school stories, it is reminiscent of the similarly exciting space described by noted British school-story novelist L.T. Meade in *A World of Girls: The Story of a School* (1886). Like Meade, Mack depicts an intellectual space where girls are free to enjoy girlhood communities that celebrate learning, accomplishment, and friendship. Even girls who are not especially scholarly should be allowed to explore these new educational horizons. The relatively early publication of this school story accounts for its atypical generic conventions.

Teens is an unconventional school story in that the girls do not board, and its Sydney setting is emphasized. Later Australian school stories focus more extensively on the school experience. By the 1920s, the conventions of the girls' school story were firmly established. In a 1927 discussion of the school story in the *West Australian*, the author explains that the link between Australian girls and the British boarding-school tradition was enabled by their shared ideals of girlhood:

> Only a small percentage of girls in Western Australia experience boarding-school discipline. But, although life at a girls' boarding-school in England is totally different to the school days of the average Australian girl, the chronicled doings of English girls in and out of school and their holiday adventures, are very popular in Australia. This is an indication of the link that binds the Commonwealth to the Homeland: the ideals that govern English girls' schools, reflected in tales which ever advocate honour and truth as against deceit and selfishness, are the ideals of Empire. Such stories are welcomed by succeeding generations of girls in Australia as in England. ("Woman's Interests" 8)

The values imparted in the school story are seen to be universal, as we discussed in chapter 3, bringing together colonial girls and their British heritage. These girlhood ideals are maintained by the separation of the world of school from the lived spaces of the colonies. The boarding-school space becomes a signifier of girlhood that is independent from specific geographic or cultural realities. It can be difficult to remember where a specific story is set unless the girls have a Christmas or term holiday on which they travel from school to home. Otherwise, the generic school spaces of the classroom, bedroom, library, and dining hall function as the setting in which girls perform rituals and relations of girlhood.

In Ethel Hume Bennett's *Judy of York Hill* (1922), for example, most of the action takes place at a school, and the school is rarely concerned with the realities of everyday life. Instead, it is the setting for understanding the rules and regulations of Canadian girlhood. An ethic of work exists in the novel, insofar as girls are expected to succeed in their studies, but the domestic framework of the earlier nineteenth-century Canadian novels has disappeared. Instead, these girls are expected to participate in a variety of different activities, including sports and drama clubs, while also attending to their studies. Bennett dedicated the novel to those in "the old school" (n.p.), presumably the girls she taught as a head teacher at Havergal College in Toronto from 1908 until her marriage in 1916 (*Canada's Early Women Writers*). She includes a portion of a poem by Henry Newbolt entitled "Clifton Chapel" extolling the virtues of student collegiality. Supporting the school is more important than individual recognition: "the School and you are one" (Bennett n.p.).

The headmistress and teachers of the fictional York Hill school believe in the importance of service and encourage the students to think of what they can do for others: "Social service of some sort or other, after one left school, was an established fact like unlimited tea-parties and dancing partners" (Bennett 68). The upper-middle-class ethic operating in this text reinforces the girls' future roles as charity workers and caregivers. One such example is former student, Nursing Sister Ruth, who worked as a nurse during the First World War. She observes that "wherever [she] found a York girl ... whether she was a V.A.D. ambulance driver, a nurse in hospital, a Y.W.C.A. secretary, or a Child's Welfare worker, always the record was the same, that when a York Hill girl undertook something, she *put it through* – especially if it were a hard job!" (Bennett 71). Judy is convinced that she must "put through ... hard study" (Bennett 72), but she discovers pursuing one activity exclusively is inappropriate. She is initially reluctant to participate in a drama performance because she wants to study for an exam instead, but she comes to understand that she must forgo her individual achievement to support the school and her friends. The community to which she belongs is more important than individual excellence.

Attending school makes girls more capable in both academic and domestic settings. Judy soon learns that she is "required to think for herself in order to take part" in class discussions (Bennett 22), and her "delight" in lessons steadily increases throughout the novel (Bennett 148). Unlike Laura in *The Getting of Wisdom*, Judy is encouraged to pursue genuine knowledge rather than memorizing useless facts. On a visit to see her aunt and uncle, moreover, Judy willingly and cheerfully takes on domestic duties when their maid unexpectedly departs. Her uncle observes that Judy "couldn't have tackled the pots and pans last year the way she does now" (Bennett 179), but her aunt, also a York Hill girl, knows that "Judy has had to tackle all sorts of things this year, more things than she ever dreamed of, and she's caught the York Hill spirit of putting through any sort of job that her hands find to do" (Bennett 179–80). Like Grace Morton, Judy's education facilitates her maturity and her ability to contribute to the domestic sphere. The difference for Judy is that this contribution is not framed by marriage. Instead, her usefulness is a sign of her increasing alignment with the ideal of girlhood modelled within and by her school.

The future possibilities for York Hill girls include useful employment that helps make the world a better place, ideas that the girls have incorporated into their thinking when they discuss careers in nursing, art, and teaching. The conclusion of the novel, featuring a wedding and a reunion of the "Old Girls," emphasizes the range of possibilities available to educated Canadian girls. Former graduates include a New York singer, a Juvenile Court judge, a matron of a large hospital, and a commander of a woman's hospital unit in Serbia. These working women are placed alongside those in more traditional female roles as wives and mothers, but each option is equally viable for the current students. As Judy explains, "we're going to be women that York Hill will be proud of when we come back" (Bennett 257). More important for these girls is that they be the best women possible as they leave the school setting and move into the future.

In another Canadian school story, Beatrice Embree's *The Girls of Miss Clevelands'* (1920), girls' ambition has become normalized. Dedicated to "Canadian School Girls – Past and Present," the novel features a series of loosely connected episodes of Canadian (and some American) girls, coming from locations across the country – from Vancouver to the Maritimes – who have travelled to Toronto for their education. The protagonist, Mabel, is "a picture of healthy, happy girlhood" who wants to attend Miss Clevelands' school because of its egalitarianism (Embree 2). As one mother explains, "money seemed to make no difference – you couldn't tell which girls had money and which hadn't" (Embree 4). The school offers a range of activities, including domestic science, physical culture, music, art, dancing, elocution, and a variety of sports. Although the girls work hard academically, the novel is primarily concerned with the schoolgirl community that is formed through the shared experiences of boarding-school life. This community is enabled by spaces like the "Girls' Own Sitting-room" (Embree 24), with echoes of the popular nineteenth- and early twentieth-century British girls' periodical the *Girl's Own Paper.* As the narrator explains, "here the girls might lounge and talk and read in any free time. There was a large fire-place, flanked by book-stands containing magazines … and books, new and old, dear to the hearts of girls in their teens" (Embree 24). The school community is created through spaces in which girls might talk, laugh, and read.

Like the girls in *Judy of York Hill,* the girls at Miss Clevelands' also casually discuss their desires to become teachers, doctors, and nurses. Letty envisages her future in charity work, in which she distributes flowers from her garden "to the hospitals and to the poor folks" (Embree 153). Another girl, Babs, sees her future in social work, since, she explains, "I just love studying people and seeing what you can do for them" (Embree 155). Only one girl suggests that her social activities may prevent her from attending university or obtaining a career: "Mother says I'm to be home for a year at least … I may go to the University after that, but between my piano, housekeeping, and running, and 'coming out', I won't have much time for a career" (Embree 154). Yet, like other typical school stories, the book does not follow these girls beyond the world of school. Importantly, however, these narratives do not conclude with marriage. As Laura finds, in *The Getting of Wisdom,* the future is open.

The school-story genre is central to the formulation of this unconstrained future, since it presents a world in which girls occupy the main roles in the story. Constance Mackness's *Di-Double-Di* (1929) follows the adventures of two boarding-school girls named Diana. One Diana, also known as "Buzz," is "an active young person, who climb[s] tall trees and [rides] anything on four substantial legs … with a smile that [is] mingled kindness and fun" (Mackness 1). She arrives at her first boarding-school "all eager interest for the new life" to be experienced at Sydney's Brentwood College (Mackness 1). Although she has "an unusual amount of general knowledge," she also has "an unusual ignorance of many things a thirteen-year-old is expected to know," because of an undisciplined upbringing under her father's "indulgent" eye (Mackness 2). The school once again offers an opportunity for education, friendship, and community, especially after Buzz meets the other Diana, "Monkey."

Two of the girls' teachers fall in love with men and marry. For these Australian women, both of whom are active, engaging teachers, marriage means the cessation of work. Rachel, who has recently finished school, unexpectedly finds a job as sports mistress at the girls' school. As she explains, "Here was I, good at nothing but games, and thinking my market price wouldn't be fifty pounds a year, unless I took to scrubbing floors and washing pots. And I'm actually to get a hundred and fifty, with board and residence thrown in, just to teach … games and gym" (Mackness 151). Although her education is seemingly inadequate for future employment, she is able to find a job that is perfectly suited to her skills and temperament. When she gets engaged to a medical student who must move to Edinburgh to complete his training, she wonders how she will keep herself occupied: "My job will be to keep my man's nose to the grindstone and make him study hard … I'm thinking out things to take up, to keep me occupied – millinery and china-painting, to begin on. I wish I didn't cook quite passably, or I'd take a cookery course. We'll have a tiny flat … but keeping that spick and span won't take long" (Mackness 281). Undoubtedly responding to the expectation that married women did not work in paid employment, Rachel does not entertain the possibility of keeping her job, or of finding similar employment while overseas. Instead, she begins thinking of suitably feminine occupations to keep busy.

Although the two Dianas are part of this feminine world of marriage, they will remain within the school for the foreseeable future. They enjoy school and the challenges placed before them. As Buzz explains after her class gets a new English teacher, "I'm going to suck up knowledge here like a sponge drinking in water. Honestly, I'm keen on learning, and she makes learning a delight" (Mackness 45). The other Diana, Monkey, wants to be a writer and is also eager to learn more. Yet, like characters in other school stories, the girls wonder whether the next school year can possibly be as good as the current one. They worry that the next year will be "dull and lonesome" (Mackness 249), but inevitably, the positive environment of the school wins them over: "some of the newbies are bound to be interesting, and it's rather thrilling to have two new teachers to try out" (Mackness 294). They can see the positive results of change and are happy to remain at school, where they will continue their learning. Moreover, although love and marriage are important themes in the novel, they are depicted as appropriate only for adults, not for schoolgirls like themselves. They have not yet progressed beyond the "world of girls" into a world of adult romance and responsibility.

The idea of the school as a space for girls to grow and develop was a common feature in the girls' school stories that dominated the shelves in Australia and New Zealand and that were typically based on models from British girls' school stories. In Phillis Garrard's *Hilda at School* – the first New Zealand school story, appearing in 1929 – Hilda actually spends relatively little time at school. As Betty Gilderdale writes, "Characteristically, books about day schools lack the cloistered atmosphere of those set in boarding schools: out-of-school activities are equally as important as in-school activities" ("Children's Literature" 535). Hilda's adventures primarily occur in the real world because these experiences help her understand the world as it is. Early in the novel, Hilda has an important realization that "she was really and truly living in the world and going to live and grow up … She saw the long years stretching before her – adventurous, terrifying, marvellous years just because they were going to be hers" (Garrard, *Hilda* 29). The remainder of the novel explores the ways in which Hilda encounters her world. The narrative includes aspects of Hilda's school life, and especially her gradual understanding that school is a place in which to be challenged to work harder and achieve more. Hilda also learns to empathize with others, including a new student who struggles to adapt to New Zealand country life. Although Hilda does not understand why he is unhappy, her father encourages her to "just try and *imagine*" (Garrard, *Hilda* 175). Her increasing empathy, and remaining true to her own moral code, is part of her gradual maturity throughout the novel.

Hilda comes to understand that "it's a big world" and she is but a "tiny centre of no account in such hugeness" (Garrard, *Hilda* 192). In the accompanying illustration (see Figure 7.2), the immensity of the landscape is highlighted by a large tree against a vast sky. Hilda and her father, on horseback, are identifiable but somewhat small and indistinct characters in the foreground. This moment is almost sublime for Hilda, who is initially frightened at the vastness of the world but realizes that "it's rather thrilling to be so insignificant and up against such a big, ruthless, uncaring world … To prove [her] own small courage in the face of such tremendousness" (Garrard, *Hilda* 196). The world, and a girl's world, in particular, is to be explored with courage.

Yet the future for these girls could be at risk if they end up neglecting their domestic duties, as Brenda's mother does in Isabel Maud Peacocke's New Zealand novel *Brenda and the Babes* (1927). Non-domestic work is unacceptable if a woman ignores her caregiving responsibilities. Fourteen-year-old Brenda is horrified to return home from school to

7.2 "It's a big world." Illust. Radcliffe Wilson. Phillis Garrard, *Hilda at School: A New Zealand Story* (London: Blackie & Son, [1929]).

discover that her young siblings have been neglected for the day while their mother works on her book. In the accompanying illustration (see Figure 7.3), Brenda is clearly depicted as a schoolgirl, complete with school uniform, tie, hat, and satchel full of schoolbooks. Yet her care and concern for her younger siblings is evident as she leans towards the two young children, who have been left to their own devices while she was away at school. She returns home after the school day to find her siblings filthy and unfed, to say nothing of the daily chores left undone. Although Brenda loves her mother, she can see that Mrs Guyon's writing interferes with her other duties. As Brenda and her older brother Wilfred observe, when they were children "she was quite different. She looked after us well enough … but ever since she got that story accepted by that piffling magazine in Sydney, she thinks she's a George Eliot, or something" (Peacocke, *Brenda* 17). Brenda spouts traditional feminine ideals when she says, "If she's a mother, she is a mother, and should act as such, not to mention a wife. Here's the house not swept, the beds not made and she sits scribbling in there, and poor old Dad will be home for his dinner soon, and the joint's hanging in the safe, and no time to cook it" (Peacocke, *Brenda* 17). Yet part of the problem is that her writing is of poor quality. Her stories are, as Wilfred explains, "tripe" and have been regularly rejected for publication (Peacocke, *Brenda* 19). These circumstances could be easily overcome if the family finances would permit the hiring of a servant to look after the house and the younger children, but the Guyons are "hatefully hard up" and cannot afford to hire additional help (Peacocke, *Brenda* 19).

Mrs Guyon is infantilized in the narrative. She is described as "slim and girlish" with "limpid and innocent eyes" and "youthful looks … so like an ingenuous child" (Peacocke, *Brenda* 20, 21). From the beginning of the novel, Brenda is already positioned as the more appropriate feminine ideal, a girl who understands the care required of the family and home. This role reversal is made explicit when Brenda forces her mother to eat before she will let her go back to writing. Yet Brenda feels guilty for forcing her mother into the maternal role, even though she knows her mother is "in the wrong" (Peacocke, *Brenda* 22). No one "ever seems to hold [Mrs Guyon] responsible for anything," even though they can all see that she is neglecting her duties, even her husband: "his wife's irresponsible neglect of her children and her household duties … was a real trouble to him" (Peacocke, *Brenda* 22, 27). He also understands the implications of her abdication of her responsibilities: the situation "was not fair to Brenda … who was only fourteen and working hard at school,

7.3 "*Babes!* What in the world are you doing?" Illust. Harold Copping. Isabel Maud Peacocke, *Brenda and the Babes* (London: Ward, Lock & Co., 1927).

and it was only fair she should have her relaxations like other girls, and not have to come home, as she so often did, to an untidy house and neglected little brother and sister" (Peacocke, *Brenda* 27). In contrast to earlier narratives, in which the extended nature of girlhood was neither possible nor desirable, Brenda's role in the household is based on her education and her need for leisure and relaxation. Although she is capable of performing the role of mother and housekeeper, both Brenda and Mr Guyon see this as unnatural and inappropriate because Mrs Guyon should be performing these duties.

Brenda proposes that her mother go away for three months to dedicate herself to her writing and determine if she can be a successful writer. Brenda stops attending school in order to facilitate this plan and looks after the children and the house without any concern for her schooling. Domestic duties are clearly privileged in relation to girls' education. Although Brenda's mother's book is published successfully and to some acclaim, she never writes again, because, during her sojourn away, she ignores her young son, who gets lost in the bush. His loss is punishment for her neglect, and she finally realizes, upon his return, that her desire to write has been replaced by "a higher, dearer, sweeter interest ... in [her] children and their happiness, in [her] home and its well-being" (Peacocke, *Brenda* 236). This text reinforces the "state backlash," beginning in the 1910s, against women's education in New Zealand (Nolan 13).

Like *With Beating Wings*, *Brenda and the Babes* was published by Ward, Lock & Co. Unlike Dwyer's novel, it received relatively little publicity, being reviewed only briefly in New Zealand newspapers and receiving scant mention in the Australian press. The New Zealand *Evening Post* explains that "the character of the mother is a little strained – she is very sweet and she cannot write at all. The combination of charm and neglect of little children would be hard to find in any mother in New Zealand" ("New Zealand Writers" 21). *The Australasian* incorrectly identifies Peacocke as Australian in its brief mention of this "domestic story" that is "far from being tame" ("Christmas Gift" 8). The *West Australian* describes it as a "charming home-life story" ("Woman's" 8). As late as 1944, Annie Rooney of Mia Mia writes that she received *Brenda and the Babes* as a book prize at a school picnic ("Children's Corner" 5), suggesting that the book still had a place on girls' shelves, presumably because of its portrayal of traditional female roles.

Although by the 1940s novels like *Shenac's Work at Home* and *Grace Morton* were no longer being read, girls' school stories such as Louise Mack's *Teens* remained popular. In Mack's 1936 obituary, the *Western Mail* asserts that *Teens* and its sequel, *Girls Together* (1898), "are still read by modern schoolgirls who enjoy the author's pictures of school life 30 years ago" ("Louise Mack" 35). Phillis Garrard continued to publish more Hilda stories, including *The Doings of Hilda* (1932), *Hilda's Adventures* (1938), and *Hilda, Fifteen* (1944). The school story undoubtedly reflected a more modern sensibility that spoke to girl readers of the twentieth century. In contrast, colonial texts of the mid- to late nineteenth century addressing issues of colonial settlement demonstrate the extent to which ideas about girls' work and education shifted between the 1860s and the 1920s. These changes were both transnational, in that they were felt throughout the British colonies, and distinctly local, reflecting national concerns about suffrage, childbearing, and female roles and responsibilities in these emerging nations. Moreover, they share few similarities with British fiction of the period that represented girls of the empire as a relatively homogenous, adventure-loving type, as we saw, for example, in Bessie Marchant's adventure fiction, discussed in chapter 3. Canadian, Australian, and New Zealand writers for girls in the early twentieth century began to shape unique conceptions of national femininities. From an initial sense of the importance of girls' education to the performance of their roles as wives and mothers in settler colonies, attitudes shifted to reflect the widening world of education and work, although girls' fiction generally shied away from depicting paid work outside the home. If girls and women did work outside the home, it tended to be only until they married, at which time these fictional girls happily gave up the challenges of paid employment to become wives and mothers.

In the next chapter, on girls' experiences in the First World War, we turn to fictional depictions of girlhood to show how girls took on new responsibilities as a generation of young men went off to fight. Their education and work, which had been so hotly contested prior to the war, became subsumed by patriotic rhetoric that encouraged girls to do their part in supporting the war effort.

CHAPTER EIGHT

Girlhood and Coming of Age during the First World War

Mother, I want to do something. I'm only a girl – I can't do anything to win the war – but I must do something to help at home.

–L.M. Montgomery, *Rilla of Ingleside* (1921)

In the introduction, we noted that within the space of the colonies, girls were subordinated by factors that related to both their gender and their age. War time only magnified these gendered issues of power. Within the American context, Andrea McKenzie describes girls in war time as suffering "a double reduction and silencing": as "girl children who are unable to become soldiers, they become exponentially marginalized" (n.p.). This marginalization is evident in the gendering of war fiction. Across the empire, war fiction for boys was plentiful, and girls rarely feature in these male-authored novels. Yet some British novels for girls, such as Bessie Marchant's *A Girl Munition Worker* (1916) and Brenda Girvin's *Munition Mary* (1918), and a range of American novels[1] drew on the growing involvement of women in roles that directly supported the war effort by placing them close to the heart of the action as Voluntary Aid Detachment and Red Cross nurses, and as workers in the manufacture of munitions. Although relatively few Australian, Canadian, and New Zealand novels feature girls in war time, those that do nonetheless exhibit a consistent sense of what female support for the war effort should entail. While most historical and fictional girls were almost entirely removed from combat zones, their work at home and

1 See Celia Malone Kingsbury's chapter "VADS and Khaki Girls: The Ultimate Reward for War Service" in *For Home and Country: World War I Propaganda on the Home Front.*

within their communities was understood as vital to maintaining the future of these young nations. L.M. Montgomery made particular reference to the "bravery, patience and self-sacrifice" of Canadian girls during the Great War, dedicating *Rilla of Ingleside* to them, and flagged their "duty and privilege to shape and share" the country's "destiny" ("How I Became a Writer" 3).

The propaganda associated with the First World War was instrumental in fostering strong nationalist sentiment in Australia and in Canada, a sentiment reflected in these countries' girls' fiction. The two most popular and prolific authors for girls in Australia in the early twentieth century, Ethel Turner and Mary Grant Bruce, published war-time novel trilogies that placed their girl protagonists in the international theatre of war. In Canada, L.M. Montgomery published *Rilla of Ingleside* in 1921, after the conclusion of the war; it is one of the most significant contemporary depictions of Canadian women during the war and focuses on the contribution that girls could make to the war effort at the local level. The female protagonists in these novels symbolized their respective countries' growth into nationhood while also becoming emblematic of the nations themselves. Yet even as these girls embodied distinct national identities, they also exemplified a transnational subjectivity based on shared ideas of war, duty, and courage.

As Kristine Alexander suggests, young people's roles in war had both discursive and practical functions, "as symbols of national virtue and as sources of patriotic labour" (174). While the fiction we will discuss in this chapter largely connects its girl protagonists with this notion of "national virtue," the periodicals of the era contain actual attempts to mobilize children in "patriotic labour." New Zealand's fledgling publishing industry produced no war fiction for either girls or boys, yet in all three countries, children's periodicals aimed at readers of both sexes responded quickly to international developments on the battle-field and regularly encouraged young readers to support the war effort. In Canada, the weekly *Grain Growers' Guide* emphasized the contribution of rural, farming communities to feeding British and colonial soldiers, and the Presbyterian Sunday-school weekly, *The King's Own*, included adventure stories set in Canada that featured girls in war time. Throughout the conflict, both the New Zealand *School Journal* and the Victorian *School Paper* regularly included war-related content. Some of the Australian magazine's war content was reproduced in the New Zealand publication, indicating a shared outlook on the subject in some respects, particularly given the camaraderie fostered between the two nations through the Australian and New Zealand Army Corps (Anzac). However, unique New Zealand-authored content about the war also provided a local perspective on New Zealand's participation.

In this chapter, we contrast fictional depictions of the First World War from Australia and Canada with its representation in periodicals published between 1914 and 1918 to show how young people were encouraged to answer the empire's call for soldiers and caregivers and to understand their nation's war-time role and the sacrifices made by its people. These publications encouraged support for the war in the form of domestic and caregiving responsibilities as well as monetary contributions to patriotic and charitable causes. Australian, Canadian, and New Zealand children's war-time experiences were imagined in print culture as pivotal to their coming of age and intimately related to their identification with nation, empire, and transnationalism.

Fictional Girls on the Home Front

Colonial responses to the First World War in children's literature were patriotic and imperialistic, yet also reflective of the ways in which Australia and New Zealand were defining themselves as newly federated nations. The commonalities across these nations' works of fiction, in particular, demonstrate the extent to which colonial girlhood can be seen transnationally. The war-time texts read by girls were written, often in highly nationalistic terms, in Canada, Australia, the United States, and England and then shared across borders through the circulation of print culture. Reviews of girls' war fiction reflect the transnational appeal of these texts. *The Spectator*, a British weekly periodical interested in providing a wide range of material, often included reviews of literature for young people. On 9 December 1916, for example, it discussed gift books for girls and included brief reviews of Marchant's *A Girl Munition Worker* and Bruce's *Jim and Wally*, both of which featured war-time themes. The review begins by noting that "there is an abundant supply of new stories for girls this season, and many of them are very readable. The war of course enters more or less directly into a number of these stories, but we are inclined to think that most young girls will prefer the unwarlike domestic variety" ("Gift-Books" 737). Whether or not girls preferred domestic fiction to war fiction, the presence of two books featuring models of war-time girlhood – one by a British author, the other by an Australian author – together in a British review suggests that readers could, and should, read both books.[2]

In all of the war-time books we examine, girls were encouraged to respond in very similar ways to the challenges of war time. In Ethel Turner's war-time trilogy (*The Cub, Captain Cub,* and *Brigid and the Cub,* published in 1915, 1917, and 1919 respectively), Mary Grant Bruce's three war-time Billabong books (*From Billabong to London, Jim and Wally,* and *Captain Jim,* in 1915, 1916, and 1919 respectively), and L.M. Montgomery's *Rilla of Ingleside* (1921), the British Empire is one of the key motivating factors in the protagonists' participation in the war and, indeed, reflects the reality that each of these colonial nations was automatically drawn into the war after Britain made its declaration. As historian Jonathan Vance explains, "The children of Mother Britain have been scattered around the globe yet remain tied to England by bonds stronger than steel. When the call goes out in August 1914, they all answer 'Ready, aye, ready' and come running to the aid of Mother Britain" (150). Notably, in British boys' war fiction, "the sons of empire" are "part of the supporting cast rather than leading players" (Paris 105). In Australian girls' novels, however, Australian soldiers are elevated in importance and are portrayed as essential to the Allies' success. Moreover, the maturation inspired by war is entwined with the characters' development and identification as Australians. Such narratives of the heroism of Australian soldiers are integral to the mythology that evolved around the figure of the Anzac soldier, which galvanized national pride. Girls and women were excluded from the Anzac myth, yet in these two girls' war series and in *Rilla of Ingleside,* war provides the back-drop for girls, who are symbolic of the nation and its future through their maternal potential.

Colonial girls' war fiction tends to assign females a supporting role. Peter Hunt points out gendered differences in which "girls were exhorted to support the male cause, whereas the rollicking formulas of pre-war boys' stories were adapted to this new battlefield" ("Retreatism" 197–8).[3] Indeed, Mary Cadogan and Patricia Craig, in *Women and Children First: The Fiction of Two*

2 Their presence in a British periodical was undoubtedly facilitated by Bruce's British publisher, since, as we mentioned in chapter 2, advertising was often based around a series of books issued by a particular publisher.

3 More recently, Kimberley Reynolds makes the important point about the multiplicity of attitudes in boys' books pertaining to the war, observing that "in writing for boys the attitude to war was far less stable than has been suggested, and the messages about war, patriotism and empire in the books, comics and periodicals available to boys were susceptible to many possible interpretations, including resistant and subversive readings" ("Prostitution" 123).

World Wars (1978), conclude that "girls' war-time fiction was not particularly impressive ... [because] girls were simply encouraged to worship the male heroes at the front, and to knit comforts for them" (59). Their critique, however, fails to acknowledge the significance of these texts in constructing models of war-time girlhood. More recent scholars, such as Jane Potter, emphasize the importance of popular fiction for children, and especially girls, which "reinforced the existing war effort" as "fictional representations ... drew on increasingly familiar and instantly recognizable images: wounds, khaki, women in uniform, public mourning, family grief" (7).

As we will discuss in chapter 9, the Billabong series tended to privilege the Australian bush over what it depicts as the potentially harmful effects of civilized living, and in many ways, the Billabong station setting was both bucolic and timeless. However, the advent of the war disrupted the established pattern of life at the station to mirror real-world expectations that all citizens should contribute to the nation's war effort to the best of their capabilities. Bruce, recently married to a British army major at the time of writing, demonstrates a clear belief in the validity of the war effort, the need for all able-bodied young men to enlist, and the requirement that women fulfil their roles in the war effort by supporting the soldiers through homemaking, nursing, and childcare.

The heroine, Norah Linton, travels with her father; her brother, Jim; and their friend Wally to London, where the boys enlist in the British army. Crucially, Jim and Wally must fight – against parental restriction and age limits respectively – simply to participate in the war. As armed combat was constructed as a route to manhood, *From Billabong to London* sets up a degree of tension with the movement of its central boy characters into the theatre of war. The preceding narratives set at the Billabong station contain few reminders of the progress of time and the aging of the protagonists. Yet the war-time trilogy irrevocably sets in motion the movement of Jim and Wally from boyhood to manhood as well as Norah's development into womanhood (see Figure 8.1). Their coming of age is also related to national and imperial identities, which coexist in Bruce's novels. "The Empire" calls Jim and Wally to serve (Bruce, *Billabong* 244), but Norah connects the individual with the national when she realizes that one's honour is subsumed into "the nation's honour" during war (Bruce, *Billabong* 250). These competing identifications are also evident in descriptions of England as "ours" and as "home" (Bruce, *Billabong* 43), while the ship *Perseus*, on which the Lintons travel, carries aboard an Australian magpie and a sulphur-crested cockatoo as comforting reminders of Australia (Bruce, *Billabong* 194).

8.1 "They strolled across the grass to the railings, and looked up and down the tan ribbon of Rotten Row." Illust. J. Macfarlane. Mary Grant Bruce, *Captain Jim* (London: Ward, Lock & Co., 1916), 16.

Despite a variety of adventures, in which Norah discovers a nearby warship and later helps to capture a German submarine, she is left temporarily helpless in face of the boys' sacrifice. She wants to know how she, too, can contribute to the war effort beyond making care packages for the boys and providing a refuge from the horrors of the front when they return on leave. Jim sympathizes with her perception of her role as "a tiny little share" by reminding her that not everyone can "do a big thing," yet "everyone has got some sort of little row to hoe, and everyone's row counts" (Bruce, *Billabong* 254). For a girl like Norah, who has always participated fully in the running of Billabong (although never in an official capacity as Jim, as the son of the owner and heir to the station, has), the sharply gendered nature of war, which renders her contribution uncertain, is vexing. She remarks, "It's awful to be a girl!" when she cannot take an active role in the confrontation of a German spy on board the ship that takes the family to England (Bruce, *Billabong* 130). Only when she receives the gift of a house and land in England in the final book of the war-time novels can she see that her role is to establish a "Home for Tired People," where she can provide soft beds, good food, and wholesome outdoor activities for soldiers, primarily Australian, who are too far from home to return there to recuperate during the war. Norah's war-time role is to develop her housekeeping and nursing skills and, when Jim is thought killed in action, to respect his sacrifice while continuing to help other "tired" Australian soldiers. Donna Coates argues that Norah and other Australian female protagonists, including Turner's Brigid Lindsay, achieve little through their war-time adventures, effecting "only flights of escape, not acts of rebellion. Rather than moving towards emancipation or autonomy, they merely tread water, and hence cause scarcely a ripple in the surface of the patriarchal structures which keep them submerged as subordinates in the war effort" (Coates 121). While this reading accurately points to Norah's position within the patriarchal structures of Billabong, it neglects to account for the ways in which her war-time action enables her maturation and development as a young woman.

Turner's series concentrates on a young Australian man, John Calthrop (nicknamed "the Cub"), and his burgeoning romance with an English girl, Brigid. Like Norah, Brigid despairs about her inability to support the war effort. When the Cub enlists and sails away on a transport ship, Brigid "must go home and wait. There is nothing else for women to do" (E. Turner, *The Cub* 255). Similarly, the adult women in Turner's series, such as the Cub's mother, can only passively participate in war by allowing their sons to enlist. Nevertheless, Brigid's heroism is evident in the opening chapters of the first novel, in which she sees a mother, father, and newborn baby murdered and narrowly escapes death herself. She flees from occupied Belgium with the murdered family's orphaned child, Josette, and her experiences transform her into a young woman ready to take up a mother's responsibilities and duties, much like Rilla is transformed in *Rilla of Ingleside.* In Canada and Australia, both "young" emerging nations, the connection between maternity and independence for girls signals an important shift from an imperial identity to a national one. Brigid is frustrated by the inactive role ascribed to women in the war effort, and in the final novel, she obtains a humble role at a French orphanage, having abandoned all pretensions to fashionable clothing in order to be accepted in the austere facility (see Figure 8.2). Brigid willingly sacrifices her own comfort to aid the children affected by war, which contrasts with the actions of wealthy Mrs Calthrop, who donates token amounts of money to the war fund but has not learned "that in true giving one gives one's self" (E. Turner, *Brigid and the Cub* 70).

While both series discussed above contain similar depictions of maturity through war-time sacrifice, Turner does not provide the same kind of narrative reassurance about war as Bruce. The Cub does not initially display fantasized heroism and bravery; he does not wish to go to war, because it "doesn't appeal" to him (E. Turner, *The Cub* 105). In this ambivalence about the war, Turner's first book is similar to *Rilla of Ingleside,* in which Rilla's brother Walter, too, is uncertain about the validity of the war and the sacrifice it will require. Yet both boys ultimately appreciate the importance of being willing to sacrifice oneself to the war effort, an ideal that the girls in the novels come to understand as well. The death of the Cub's brother, Alec, in combat and his mother's resultant anguish leads Paris to argue that *The Cub* is rare in its status as "a book for young readers that actually dared to ask if the human cost of the war could really be justified" (24). Indeed, out of a male population of three million, almost four-hundred thousand Australians served, and of these, more than sixty thousand were killed, over eight thousand at Gallipoli, an ill-fated battle that Grant Bruce's protagonists avoid through their enlistment in England rather than Australia and that the Cub and his friend Galileo survive.

While the depiction of Brigid implicitly establishes her future suitability to be a wife and mother, the Cub, like Jim and Wally, is granted the status of a man through combat. A *Sydney Morning Herald* reviewer writes that while the Cub was always a mature character, "when he dons

8.2 "I am one of those who want to help fight – if you will let me." Illust. Harold Copping. Ethel Turner, *Brigid and the Cub* (London: Ward, Lock & Co., 1919).

khaki, fights at Gallipoli and in France, and earns promotions for his efficient work, he attains the full stature of manhood though still a boy in years" ("New Fiction" 8). War therefore proved to be the ideal backdrop against which to set stories of the maturation of Australian boys and girls. Involvement in the First World War not only enables the individual growth of Jim, Wally, Norah, the Cub, and Brigid but, through the novels' international settings, symbolically affirms Australia's own coming of age as a nation on the world stage.

Canada's own maturity into nationhood is embodied by Rilla's transformation from girl into woman in Montgomery's *Rilla of Ingleside*. Readers around the empire were imagined as sharing a common interest in war fiction from other dominions. *Rilla of Ingleside* was published in an edition for distribution in Australia and New Zealand by the Australasian Press in 1921. The Adelaide *Mail*, in a review of the novel, suggests that "there is much of kin to any Briton beyond the seas in this tale of Canadian war work" ("Anne's Daughter" 10). Similarly, *The Queenslander* comments on Montgomery's representation of the part of "Canada, her country," in the war, but notes that the novel "will awake a responsive chord wherever the Empire holds its sway" ("Other Novels" 3). However, the explicit identification of Rilla as having resonance with "Britons" or anyone who lives in a British dominion was not obvious to a reviewer in New Zealand's *Otago Daily Times* who refers to Rilla as an "American girl in wartime" ("Constant Reader" 2).

Unlike the Australian fiction discussed above, *Rilla* is focused on the "courage of ordinary Canadian girls and women" (Fisher 212), since Rilla Blythe stays at home on Prince Edward Island for the duration of the war. At the beginning of the novel, in contrast with the transnational girlhood ideal, Rilla is on the cusp of turning fifteen and has no ambition to attend college or to "be a housewifely, cookly creature" (Montgomery, *Rilla* 21). She has heard that "the years from fifteen to nineteen are the best years in a girl's life" and anticipates an immediate future of fun and pleasure (Montgomery, *Rilla* 20). She also has little sense of the implications of the potential war, stating that it "won't really matter much to us, will it?" and preferring to discuss her dresses instead (Montgomery, *Rilla* 22). Similarly, she does not understand the significance of Canada's place in the empire and questions its involvement in "England's battles" (Montgomery, *Rilla* 47). Both her brother Jem and Kenneth Ford, who initially cannot serve because of a broken ankle, explain to her Canada's connections to England and frame expectations of service in terms of family. Jem describes England as "the 'old grey mother of the northern sea'" and Canada as one of its "cubs" who must "pitch in tooth and claw if it comes to a family row" (Montgomery, *Rilla* 26).

Rilla gradually learns and embraces the place and role of girls during war time. She is made miserable by the thought that women "just had to sit and cry at home" (Montgomery, *Rilla* 47), though she is proud of the sight of Jem in his uniform answering "the call" of his country (Montgomery, *Rilla* 58). She reproduces a quotation from Sir Walter Scott's poem "The Lady of the Lake" in her diary, from a section in which women and old men are sent to shelter on an island in the middle of a lake in anticipation of an upcoming battle: "'He goes to do what I had done / Had Douglas' daughter been his son,' and [Rilla] was sure she meant it. If she were a boy of course she would go, too!" (Montgomery, *Rilla* 58).

Rilla is aware that, as a girl, she "can't do anything to win the war" but is determined to help at home (Montgomery, *Rilla* 70–1). Kristine Alexander observes that Canadian girls, like their mothers, were harnessed to support military efforts "through school, church, and a variety of voluntary organizations" (185). Rilla first joins her twin sisters, Nan and Di, in sewing sheets and bandages for the Red Cross and thus not only aids the war effort but begins to develop her poor domestic skills through "basting the hem of a sheet for the first time in her life" (Montgomery, *Rilla* 70). After Rilla's mother supplies the idea for coordinating a Junior Red Cross branch with girls in the area, Rilla resolves to take on the task as part of her aim to "be as *brave* and *heroic* and *unselfish* as [she] can possibly be" (Montgomery, *Rilla* 71). The ultimate way in which Rilla can contribute as a girl, and develop her femininity to suit her future domestic role, is by adopting a war baby until its soldier father, Jim Anderson, returns from the war. Rilla initially sees the Anderson baby as "an ugly midget with a red, distorted little face" but feels a sense of duty to bring it home because there is no one to care for it (Montgomery, *Rilla* 83). After some prompting from her father, she adopts the war baby as her own. Though Rilla has little maternal instinct and handles the baby "as if it were some kind of a small lizard, and a breakable lizard at that," she is dedicated to the task, "and there was not a cleaner, better-cared-for infant in Glen St. Mary" (Montgomery, *Rilla* 92). In her realization of the importance of her contribution to the war effort, Rilla practices the skills of the ideal woman and, quite literally, becomes the mother of the future generation of Canada.

Beginning as a frivolous young woman who spends too much money on a hat, Rilla has matured by the end of the novel into a thoughtful young woman who has willingly accepted the responsibilities of war time. Like Norah, Rilla finds the most difficult task to be waiting for the safe return of her brothers and friends: "If she were only a boy, speeding in khaki … to the western front! She had wished that in a burst of romance when Jem had gone, without, perhaps, really meaning it. She meant it now. There were moments when waiting at home, in safety and comfort, seemed an unendurable thing" (Montgomery, *Rilla* 195–6). Yet Montgomery's point is that the seemingly secondary role that girls and women occupied at home was essential to the war effort and, "equally importantly, to the continuation of a life of values and vision after the war" (Epperly 114). Like Norah and Brigid, Rilla realizes the importance of maintaining the home front while the boys are away at war.

Alongside these distinctly colonial texts, American series fiction featuring strong female protagonists engaged in war-time activities was also available in Canada, Australia, and New Zealand. The earliest of this fiction to depict the war was Margaret Vandercook's Red Cross Girls series, the first of which appeared in 1916.[4] In the first novel, *The Red Cross Girls in the British Trenches,* the four American protagonists travel to England to join the Red Cross and eventually travel to the front. In contrast, the "Outdoor Girls" are involved in more domestic activities as they support the war effort. The Outdoor Girls series, published by the Stratemeyer Syndicate under the pseudonym Laura Lee Hope, was published from 1913 to 1933. The first of the books in this series to feature war-time activities is *The Outdoor Girls in Army Service* (1918), which appeared late in the war, with seven volumes in the series preceding it. Three additional novels featuring the war were published between 1919 and 1921: *The Outdoor Girls at the Hostess House* (1919), *The Outdoor Girls at Bluff Point* (1920), and *The Outdoor Girls at Wild Rose Lodge* (1921). The war-time novels depict four girls running a hostess house and supporting the war effort in various ways. As Deirdre Johnson observes of the Syndicate's girls' series, in contrast to boys' "physical fortitude and courage in the face of danger, girls prove themselves through emotional stamina and perseverance" in stories in which they "aid the lost or heartsick, reuniting them with their families or bringing them into a circle of warm friends, and are rewarded by seeing their happiness" (118). While the girls' fiction is typically focused on the affective nature of their stories, it does occasionally depict female protagonists in more adventurous roles.

4 Although the series ran to ten novels, it appears that only the first four books were sold in Canada (Fisher 196).

Although critics tend to see girls' war fiction as being "kept in line with suitable sex-roles" (Hunt 198), the American series fiction sometimes depicted more active female contributions. The girlhood adventures of Grace Harlowe and her friends are depicted in a lengthy (1910–24) series written by Josephine Chase under the pseudonym of Jessie Graham Flower. In *Grace Harlowe Overseas* (1920), however, the war intrudes, and Grace joins a Red Cross unit and proceeds to have a series of adventures, including surviving the sinking of her ship and the bombing of her accommodation, foiling a German plot, being accused of being a spy, and delivering supplies to the front while being fired upon by German artillery. She performs her traditional feminine duty by comforting American soldiers while awaiting word of her husband's fate at the front.

These books were rarely reviewed and received only scant mention in the periodical press, potentially because of the poor reputation of series fiction. Although little mention is made of *Grace Harlowe Overseas* in Australian newspapers, advertisements for the earlier *Grace Harlowe's Second Year at Overton College* and *Grace Harlowe's Third Year at Overton College* appeared alongside listings for war-time fiction like Bruce's *From Billabong to London* and *Captain Jim* as well as Turner's *Brigid and the Cub* ("Maclellan and Co." 5). Similarly, in a letter to the children's page of Adelaide's *Daily Herald*, Nellie Miller writes that she is "reading a very nice book now, called 'The Outdoor Girls on Pine Island'" ("The Letter Box" 3). Although this book predates the war-time novels, it demonstrates that Australian girls had access to series fiction such as this, although these books were not typically reviewed or advertised extensively.

These girls' war-time fictions represent a diverse range of perspectives on how a girl might play a supportive, or even active, role at home or abroad during a time of global conflict. They also variously allow for the expression of, if not overall support for, anti-war sentiment through the measured representation of characters who are reluctant or unwilling to serve, as in *The Cub* and *Rilla of Ingleside.* In colonial-authored fiction, however, there is a fairly consistent model of girlhood service to the community and the war through nursing and the care of children, which is intimately tied to the maturation of girl protagonists. However, as we demonstrate in the following section, children's periodicals are less interested in the gendered nature of young people's contributions to the war effort, and are far more preoccupied with establishing the might of the British Empire and identifying the place of nations within that narrative of greatness.

The Great War in Children's Periodicals

Jane Potter suggests that "women's and girls' magazines published between 1914 and 1918 were sites of patriotic inculcation and fervour" (76). While there are no examples of colonial girls' magazines published during this period, educational magazines produced for both boys and girls in Australia and New Zealand displayed varying degrees of patriotism, but were deeply invested in war coverage and the British Empire. Rosie Kennedy has demonstrated that the British government, via the Board of Education, "recognised the unique opportunity it had to transmit its message into British homes through school children" (121). This message related to the population's need to "fight and work for the empire's survival" through supporting the war effort by fundraising, food rationing, and participation in auxiliary services (Kennedy 121). An important ideological role of such pedagogical publications was to ensure that children understood that they were an integral part of the nation and the British Empire, of which they should be proud.[5] This was also the case in the monthly, one-penny, Victorian *School Paper*, which was compulsory reading material in the Australian state's classrooms and published by the Education Department. An evolving sense of national pride in relation to the war was a feature of the combined papers for children in grades five and six, the final years of primary school, and grades seven and eight, the first years of secondary school, which means that ideologies of nationalism and imperialism were specifically targeted at children on the cusp of adulthood. Within this *Paper*, Australian participation is presented as critical to the success of the war effort. Articles on the latest battles, including maps of troop movements, sit alongside commemorations of fallen soldiers and requests that readers support the war by purchasing war bonds. As we discussed in chapter 3, and as the *School Paper* confirms, Australian identity was situated within the dual framework of nation and empire. However, the war served as a catalyst for an increasing emphasis on Australian identity and pride distinct from its relationship to empire, which developed alongside and began to challenge the existing metanarrative of imperial belonging.

---

5 Religious publications were not as universally supportive of the war. In the 1915 children's columns for the Australian *Catholic Press*, for example, the editor refers to the "terrible war" and asks for what benefit "thousands of brave men are being killed and maimed every week" ("Playmate" 42). He calls on child readers to pray, rather than to support the war effort through any practical means such as fundraising.

During the First World War, the *School Paper* increasingly reported on the status of the Australian soldiers and their performance in comparison with that of soldiers in the Second Boer War, in pieces taking a substantial place alongside articles that viewed the significance of the war through the perspective of Britain and the empire. A cover image from 1916 (see Figure 8.3) was adapted from a British recruiting poster and clearly demonstrates the roles of men on the front line, women in domestic and nursing work, and even a Boy Scout making a contribution. From the reports of England's minister for war to local updates, the abilities of Australian soldiers and the number of Australian casualties and Victoria Cross recipients were a major preoccupation in scores of articles in the *Paper*. For instance, in November 1916, the article "Testimony to the Judgment and Diligence of Australian Soldiers" distinguishes the nation's men from those of Britain and its other allies by proposing that Australians "have the qualities which are going to win this war – courage, judgment, and ability" (157). There was a clear importance in defining Australian identity positively, but doing so through emphasizing the contribution that Australian attributes could make to the British Empire.

In addition to the prevalence of war-related content, supplements of several additional pages were sometimes added for the purpose of conveying current war messages, such as letters from the director of education. In April 1916, Director Frank Tate's "Our Debt to Our Soldiers: An Open Letter to the Children of Victoria" makes clear several of the key ideas advanced throughout war time, including the emergence of Australian pride in the soldiers' actions:

> Every Australian has been filled with pride as he has read of the glorious deeds of our soldiers in Gallipoli; and, to-day, because of what they have done, the name of Australia stands high throughout the Empire, and, indeed, throughout the world. You children have read in your history of the great feats of arms which soldiers of our race have accomplished in the past, and you had, no doubt, the feeling that these men were far removed from you. But the Anzacs are men whom you knew when they were here amongst us, living their lives as ordinary, peace-loving citizens; they are your own brothers and cousins, your own fathers and uncles ... Every girl and boy should feel an inch taller when the thought comes, "These are my people who have made such a name." (2)

Tate's stirring account of the bravery of the students' relatives inserts Australians more prominently into heroic war narratives. The sacrifice of

EDUCATION DEPARTMENT, VICTORIA
(AUSTRALIA).

THE SCHOOL PAPER.

FOR GRADES VII. AND VIII. (1916).

No. 196.] [Registered at the General Post Office, Melbourne, for transmission by post as a newspaper.] MELBOURNE. Price 1d. [FEB. 1, 1916.

* RIGHT TO THE END.

Adapted from a recruiting poster, designed by Lt.-Gen. Sir R. S. S. Baden-Powell.]

HOW THE YEAR 1916 OPENED FOR THE BRITISH EMPIRE.

8.3 Cover. *The School Paper for Grades VII and VIII.* February 1916.

the Anzac soldiers, eleven thousand of whom were killed at Gallipoli in April 1915, became a defining event and mythology in the development of Australian and New Zealand national identity. The children themselves are called upon to play their part by denying themselves "visits to the picture shows and the lolly shops" to aid the war effort monetarily and thereby save the lives of Australian soldiers (Tate 4). In this pedagogic periodical, Victorian children were positioned to see all Australians, including themselves, as essential to saving lives and fostering national achievement that would invite the praise of Britain.

As we have shown, New Zealand imported a large number of books from other parts of the British Empire; most New Zealand authors published with overseas firms, and only a small number of children's books were published within the country before the 1930s. Yet, as we discussed in the previous chapter, each country established its own education system, which was supported by local educational content, such as several magazines intended for New Zealand school students. These included *Schoolmates: A Monthly Magazine for School and Home Reading* (1897–1906?), which was published in Dunedin and authorized by the New Zealand Department of Education, and *The Young New Zealander and Schools' Gazette* (1924–5?), published in Auckland. The most significant school magazine was the free monthly New Zealand *School Journal*, which was published in Wellington by the New Zealand Education Department from 1907 and continues to be published to this day. Some Australian states used the Victorian *School Paper* as a model, and so too did the New Zealand *School Journal*, which adopted the same design and lay-out as the Australian publication.

During the course of the war, the *School Journal* included general news about the progress of battles in Europe, but, as with the *School Paper*'s focus on Australian troops, the journal also showed particular interest in the contribution of New Zealand's soldiers to the international effort. Substantial articles were devoted to events such as "The Capture of German Samoa by the New Zealand Expeditionary Force" in October 1914, in which two ships from Wellington joined British and then Australian battleships to take possession of German Samoa, although "New Zealand's first overseas conquest" involved no actual combat (280). An extract from a letter written by New Zealander Captain Halsey to his brother in England was published as "H.M.S. 'New Zealand' in the North Sea Fight" in June 1915. The captain tells of the heroic efforts of the ship's men in sinking the German cruiser the *Blücher*. Intriguingly for emerging ideas about New Zealand identity, the motivating symbols carried aboard married Māori items with a flag bearing the Union Jack that had been purchased with funds raised by the women's branch of the Navy League in Timaru: "I had the Maori costume and the Maori *tiki*, and we flew out the silk ensign during the action" (159). The August 1916 article "H.M.S. 'New Zealand' at the Battle of Jutland" mentions and reproduces a photograph of a brass "Maori emblem" that sat on the ship's forward turret, representing "the carved head that the Maoris [*sic*] commonly placed at the prow of their war-canoes as an indication of the defiance with which they regarded their foes" (219). Captain Halsey, who captained the ship during the Battle of Jutland as well, reflects the magazine's understanding of New Zealand's war-time sacrifices as motivated by imperial identification and the sense of nation as a constitutive part of the broader British Empire: "We shall be spurred to greater efforts ... by knowing that we are representing not only the Empire, but a little circle inside it as well – that little million of New Zealand" (H.M.S. 217). As in the Victorian *School Paper*, pride in both nation and empire is encouraged.

When the outbreak of war was announced in the September 1914 issue of the New Zealand *School Journal*, the paper promoted an Education Department initiative in which children would contribute to a fund to enable the purchase of ambulance equipment ("War Notes" 251). While the fundraising was seen as part of a contribution to the empire, the article expresses a wish for New Zealand to be specifically identified and recognized as a constituent part. The fundraising scheme aimed to raise over two thousand pounds, in order for the gift to be "worthy of the children of the Dominion that has always been to the front in making sacrifices and affording assistance in times of the Empire's need" ("War Notes" 252). By October 1915, more than two thousand pounds was raised for the purchase of four motor ambulances for use in Egypt. In August of 1916, in a seven-page series of articles, the *School Journal* reported on how the ambulances were used at the front and described the Aotea Convalescent Home for New Zealand soldiers in Cairo. The paper emphasized that New Zealand children who had donated money ought to feel rewarded by the "generous appreciation" expressed by "their English, Canadian, and Australian cousins, at whose disposal the cars were freely placed whenever they had an influx of patients from Gallipoli" ("New Zealand Children's" 207). For New Zealand, the admiration of other dominions, in addition to that of the imperial centre, was crucially important.

The *School Paper* situates the heroism of New Zealand's soldiers alongside the bravery of combatants from other part of the empire, especially those from Australia, rather than placing sole importance on promoting the achievements of local men. An article on "Empire Day" in 1916, for example, mentions two New Zealand men who were awarded Victoria Cross medals, as well as the 32 New Zealand soldiers and nurses who lost their lives during the sinking of the transport ship the *Marquette* in the Aegean Sea in 1915, but also devotes substantial attention to an Australian Victoria Cross recipient and a heroic "Highland piper" (143). The reader is invited to take pride in the bravery of both New Zealand and Australian soldiers, united by their common work for the empire. An article by a naval nurse in 1916 begins with a poem about Anzacs by a New Zealander, "J. Mitchell, Oamaru, NZ," that describes those lost at Gallipoli as "our sons" and includes an illustration of the two dominions' flags entwined ("An Anzac" 154). The nurse describes both the Australians and the New Zealanders as "miracles of pluck and endurance" ("An Anzac" 158). She also conveys the personal excitement of "the experience of a lifetime" in caring for the wounded after Gallipoli ("An Anzac" 155), as well as the dutifulness of the nurses as they received the "desperately wounded men" and "cut away their blood-stained, muddy clothing" in order to tend to them ("An Anzac" 158).

Both Australasian school magazines detailed the importance of the contribution of those at home to the war effort, although there is a marked absence of actual children's experiences or voices in their pages. In contrast, newspaper children's correspondence columns often provide brief insight into their perception of the war, amid their other preoccupations. For instance, Marjorie Nolen wrote to the *Catholic Press* correspondence page in March 1915 to discuss her examinations and the price of tomatoes, and to note that some of her "school mates" have gone to the "terrible" war" ("My Post Bag" 42). The contribution of women at home to the war is also rarely discussed in Australasian school magazines, although one article in the New Zealand *School Journal* directly addressed the importance of women's labour for the chances of success in the war. It describes women's traditional work in making bandages and clothing and in fundraising, as well as the requirement, in the absence of forty thousand of New Zealand's men, to take on jobs such as working in munitions manufacturing, food production, essential services, and railways, as well managing farms and sheep stations ("Women in War"). As in the instance of children's participation in raising funds for ambulances, the fate of country and empire required every citizen, regardless of age or sex, to contribute: "It is not every woman that can send a son or a brother to the front, or make cartridges for the soldiers, or do men's work, but every woman can do a little towards beating the enemy" ("Women in War" 41). The contribution of women could be symbolic, as in their fundraising to purchase the ensign for the H.M.S. New Zealand, but also practical, as shown by the collection of garments they made for the men on board the ship to wear (see Figure 8.4). Women's sacrifices involve specific contributions, such as enabling family members to enlist or working outside the home, but they also revolve around the ideal of the home and maintaining the home front.

Unlike Australia and New Zealand, Canada had no such school magazines. Instead, children's war-time content came from Sunday-school magazines such as *The King's Own* and *Pleasant Hours* and from the children's pages in agricultural magazines such as the *Grain Growers' Guide* and in family magazines such as the *Family Herald and Weekly Star.*

Like the New Zealand *School Journal*, the *Grain Growers' Guide* emphasized the importance of girls' seeking out opportunities to help at home, rather than at the front. The changing roles on the farm during war time was a common theme in the magazine. Norah Lewis observes that "with large numbers of men in the military, women and children moved into positions in agriculture and industry previously held by men" (Lewis 202). These societal changes are reflected in the *Grain Growers' Guide*, with daughters replacing sons in the 24 July 1918 cover of "Taking Her Soldier Brother's Place." In the image, a girl sits on a tractor, preparing to plow the fields. A 1916 letter from twelve-year-old Edna Harcus to the children's page similarly reflects these changing circumstances. She writes that war "robs a country of its manhood, leaving in many cases only old men, women and children to the work at home" (Harcus 28). These images and letters promote a feminine ideal that emphasizes duty, patriotism, and courage. In the absence of their brothers and fathers, girls understood it was their responsibility to help the family in whatever ways they could, an ideal that was reinforced in girls' fiction of the period.

At the same time, Canada's proximity to the European theatre of war meant that its food production was an important contributor to British success. The 12 August 1915 *Grain Growers' Guide* cover proclaimed that "BRITISH IDEALS MUST TRIUMPH," and that Canada "must stand by Britain to the very limit of our resources" (1). This pro-war rhetoric was essential to convincing farmers with little personal investment in the war to do their utmost to contribute to the war effort. Eleven-year-old Violet Dimmick of Gilbert Plains, Manitoba, demonstrates that she is a farmer's daughter when she concludes her contribution by writing, "It is a good

8.4 "Women Packing Garments for Men of H.M.S. 'New Zealand.'" "Women in War," New Zealand *School Journal* (March 1916), 40.

thing to make [the price of] wheat go up" as a consequence of war-time demand ("Young Canada Club" 28).

In contrast to the children's pages found in the *Grain Growers' Guide*, some dedicated Canadian children's magazines were also published, such as the religious periodicals *The King's Own* (1900–25) and *Pleasant Hours* (1881–1929). In these magazines, girls were encouraged to see the war in ways that reinforced the necessity of duty and sacrifice. Fiction and correspondence in these publications reflect the magazines' engagement with the war and their efforts to show girls how they could contribute to the war effort.

In "At the Sign of the Maple Leaf," a 1917 short story published in *The King's Own*, Edith Doyle is dismayed to realize that "girls can't do anything for their country," at least nothing really worthwhile "like belonging to the army, and suffering hardship, and going into danger" (Allan 139). Edith can only conceive of her duties with the framework of male action at the front, but an injured soldier calls this idea "absurd" and explains that his wife is doing just as much for the country as any soldier in the army: "She is helping to make it a country worth saving" (Allan 139). Such texts occasionally needed to instruct girls as to how they could support the war effort, which they did by providing a realistic – if somewhat unlikely – example of how they could find opportunities to contribute. The girls' fiction appearing in the pages of these magazines during the war years is actively engaged in showing girls what they can do to help support the war effort and how their frustration at not being able to contribute to the fighting can be transformed into action. As Kristine Alexander explains, "Representations of these girls as innocent and dutiful daughters who were worth fighting for were central to the war-time efforts of numerous propagandists and cultural producers" (175). Women and children on the home front were the soldiers' inspiration, and girls on the home front were expected to uphold those values for which the soldiers fought.

In the correspondence sections of these religious periodicals, numerous examples of girls' war-time activities are described. These pieces show that girls are often involved in knitting and sewing, but they also articulate a strong requirement that all children act in ways appropriate for the country and, ultimately, the empire. Jessie A. Webb, aged 14, of Smithville, Ontario, explains that Canadian girls can best show their patriotism by "living to be a credit to their country, ... knitting socks, cuffs, scarves and caps for the soldiers, [and] by being kind to the poor families who have sent their fathers to the war" ("Our Mail Bag" 67). Girls are directed towards activities and behaviours that will help prepare them for their adult responsibilities as contributing members of the nation. As Kathlyn Cruse of North Vancouver, British Columbia, concludes, "Wouldn't it be great in future years to hear it recorded that the Canadian boys and girls at home had had a great part in the saving of our Great Empire" ("Our Mail Bag" 67). This correspondence shows how girls actively participated in the war effort in ways that contributed simultaneously to both national and imperial enterprises.

As we have shown, the informational articles appearing in magazines emphasize the admirable qualities of each country's soldiers and their bonds with other colonial fighters, alongside a widespread call to all children to support their country's contribution to the war effort. In the novels by Mary Grant Bruce, Ethel Turner, and L.M. Montgomery, representations of war time include highly gendered roles, where the children's unique colonial upbringing and qualities enable their success on an international stage, as in the Australian fiction, or at home, as in *Rilla of Ingleside.* The girls who participate in the war effort emerge from the experience as young women united through imperial and transnational ideals of femininity while also being independent within the nation. Their emergence into adulthood reflects transnational ideals of the colonial nations' own definition as independent in the post-war years. Nevertheless, their maturity into adulthood is designed to encourage their somewhat paradoxical development as both members of the empire and independent young colonials.

As the voices of young nations, Rilla, Norah, and Brigid tell a story of youth, adventure, and patriotism that is part of each country's mythology of nation building. Yet, the ideology of girlhood transcends this framework if we look beyond these national paradigms. The First World War was a "total war" that encompassed young men *and* young women from many nations, and consequently, these female protagonists are more than mere tools in the national propaganda to support the war effort. The similarities between girls of different nationalities are elided by closely associating femininity and colonial nationhood. The protagonists in these texts demonstrate the range of feminine models available to girl readers and suggest a range of possibilities for contributing to the war effort, from keeping the home fires burning to performing dangerous feats of heroism. While not all of these possibilities were equally likely, they offered heroic models of femininity that transcended national boundaries and encouraged girls to think of themselves as active participants in the war and also as transnational subjects.

CHAPTER NINE

Modernity and the Nation

But you must have a chance to grow and develop and be yourself. You must have the stimulus of association with great minds – the training that only a great city can give.

–L.M. Montgomery, *Emily Climbs* (1925)

In L.M. Montgomery's *Emily Climbs* (1925), the second book of the Emily of New Moon trilogy, writer and editor Janet Royal tells Emily that she must move to New York to become a successful writer. The metropolis offers opportunities and ideas that are unheard of in Emily's rural Prince Edward Island, but Emily rejects the modernity of the big city, instead preferring to remain connected to the land of her birth and her ancestors. This tension between the urban and the rural is central to colonial girls' experiences of modernity in fiction, and is often resolved through a retreat to the country. These colonial girls reflect a distinct conception of modernity that manifests itself in both urban and rural spaces and in ways that demonstrate their alignment with shifting expectations of women's freedom. Yet the agency of the modern colonial girl nevertheless remains the subject of intense scrutiny in the periodical press. Colonial girls' print culture can be situated in a complex engagement with modernity that seemingly supports some of its capitalist and consumer objectives while also rejecting its sexualization of girlhood.

In her final chapter of *The New Girl*, discussing the modernity of British girlhood after World War I, Sally Mitchell explains that girls' culture after 1920 was "less open, less fluid, less promising than the new culture of the nineteenth century's final decades" (188). Although our goal in this chapter is not to provide a comparison to British girls' print culture,

Mitchell's conclusions provide a starting point for our discussion of modernity in Australian, New Zealand, and Canadian girls' print culture after the turn of the twentieth century. The colonial girl who appears in these texts is modern, casually employing new technology and often wearing the latest fashions as she is inducted into twentieth-century consumer culture. She is also much more physically active, no longer content "to be docile, obedient, self-sacrificing and kind" like the British girl (Mitchell 172). Yet this colonial girl can be modern only in certain limited ways that are constrained by anxieties over the future of girlhood for the nation. Since references to nationality – and to "types" of Canadian, Australian, and New Zealand girls – had declined in girls' print culture, as had explicit references to the empire, the modern colonial girl is represented as a transnational figure. These modern girls are presented with some limited freedoms while also shown retreating from some of the more exciting possibilities for girls' futures offered by universal suffrage, new employment opportunities that appeared during World War I, and the international women's associations that emerged in the post-war period. Instead, the modern colonial girl character tends to remain inscribed within traditional colonial models of femininity emphasizing duty, work, education, family, and sacrifice.

Understandings of the modern colonial girl are framed by technological, industrial, cultural, and aesthetic shifts of the nineteenth and early twentieth centuries. Yet we must also recognize that girls encountered these changes in distinct ways enabled by and produced through their identities as white, middle-class girls, but also made possible by their "various and overlapping identities and practices" as consumers, daughters, workers, activists, and readers (Felski 21). Owing especially to the First World War, in which the traditional expectations of girls shifted substantially, the modern girl was increasingly concerned with asserting her independence. The ways in which she defined her modernity varied, since girls' experiences of both technological and social change were characterized by "discontinuities, reversals and unevenness" (Parkins 7). Girls encountered and engaged with modernity at different times and in different ways.

Modernity is the product of "scientific and technological innovation, the industrialization of production, rapid urbanization, an ever expanding capitalist market [and] the development of the nation state" (Felski 13). Yet it also incorporates aspects of the modernist aesthetic and a sense of dislocation and ambiguity that produces a distinction "between traditional societies ... and a modern secularized universe predicated upon an individuated and self-conscious subjectivity" (Felski 13). The idea of the modern is produced by and through a rupture with the past and is often experienced through the act of moving from the rural to the urban. Such movement brings attention to the technological advancements, expanding urbanization, and consumerism found in cities. Yet Wendy Parkins argues that "if representations of movement from the country to the city and back again form part of the complex response to modernity, then attention must also be paid to women's mobility across and between villages, towns, suburbs and rural landscapes" (10). The liberation made possible in and through the city is certainly one facet of female modernity, but this modern condition is also made possible through women writers' exploration of "women's agency within as well as beyond the domestic" (Parkins 11). As we will show, female protagonists in colonial girls' fiction demonstrate their modernity in both urban and rural, as well as public and private, spheres.

Colonial girls' print culture can be situated within a complex engagement with modernity that seemingly supports some of its capitalist and consumer objectives while also rejecting the sexualization of girlhood and demonstrating a pervasive anxiety about its manifestations. In the introduction to *Modern Girl around the World: Consumption, Modernity, and Globalization* (2008), the authors argue that the defining characteristics of "modern girls" in the first half of the twentieth century were "their use of specific commodities," particularly cosmetics, and "their explicit eroticism" (Weinbaum et al. 1). Moreover, these modern girls "appear to disregard roles of dutiful daughter, wife, and mother" (Weinbaum et al. 1). While the type of modern girl they define is rarely, if ever, apparent in the girls' print culture we discuss in this book, this approach to understanding and making visible the modern girl is pertinent to our discussion. The authors of *Modern Girl around the World* explain that their approach of "connective comparison" – that is, the positioning of "specific local developments *in conversation with* those occurring elsewhere in the world" (4) – highlights "the inchoate manner in which things understood to be local come into being through complex global dynamics" (4). The transnationalism of modern colonial girlhood in girls' print culture reflects both the global processes of capitalism and consumption and local reactions against this cosmopolitanism.

The Modern Girl in the Colonial Press

Although concern about the modern girl dates back to at least the 1860s, when Eliza Lynn Linton launched her famous critique against the "Girl of the Period" for being too forward and fashionable, the concern about the modern girl takes on new life in the period following the First World War.[1] Similar concerns about the modern girl appear almost simultaneously in Canadian, Australian, and New Zealand newspapers. A heated exchange followed the report of a *Toronto Daily Star* interview given in 1921 by the Hon Mr Ralph Smith, a minister in the British Columbia legislature. Smith observed that "the average girl of to-day is in advance of the girl of fifty years ago. She is better educated," with "a different viewpoint and wider vision than the girl of years ago, and her experience in the world outside ... helps her to appreciate public welfare problems" ("Prefers" 12). In this perspective, embracing modern opportunities does not make women unfit for home life. In contrast, Smith asserts, "The woman who takes part in the affairs of the country means more to her home and consequently to the nation" ("Prefers" 12). Smith is here using arguments employed elsewhere in British and colonial women's rights movements to advocate for better education for girls.

This article resulted in a response from an "Old-Timer" on 20 April 1921, in which he critiques the "girl of today." She may have a wider view, he admits, but this view is composed of "movies, theatres, dance halls, bridge parties, extravagant and immodest dressing, as scant as can be, and to be well painted" ("Old-Timer" 10). He rejects Smith's claim of better education by declaring that girls will read "the most slangy and vulgar novel they can find" ("Old-Timer" 10). In addition, he asserts that they have poor health and fail to regularly attend church. They are, in every way, he claims, a poor substitute for girls of fifty years ago. "Old-Timer's" response is clear evidence of the ways in which Canadian girls of this period were more modern than girls of the past.

Other readers were unwilling to accept this criticism. "Old-Timer's" letter prompted a spirited defence by "A Modern Girl," who admits that there are "painted, slangy, loud, indecently-clothed girls in our present scheme of things, but these are by no means in predominance" ("Miss Modern" 10). She claims that "the Victorian idea – that all girls should prepare only for a future of wifehood and motherhood – has partially

---

1 A search on the term "modern girl" in Trove, a database of Australian newspapers from 1803 to 1954, reveals 1,570 references between 1900 and 1909, 3,014 references between 1910 and 1919, and 9,420 references between 1920 and 1929, with a peak of 10,352 references between 1930 and 1939. The number of references plummeted to just 2,048 between 1940 and 1949, suggesting much less concern about the modern girl during this period.

disappeared" ("Miss Modern" 10). Moreover, alongside the "slangy, extravagant" girls of today are "V.A.D.s, ambulance drivers and social service workers" ("Miss Modern" 10). She signals the different employment opportunities available to the modern girl in 1920s Canada as well as the rupture with the past. These changing attitudes towards girlhood are accompanied, in the "Modern Girl's" view, by significant advances in women's contributions to the community and the nation:

> Perhaps movies and dance halls encourage the feeling of independence and resourcefulness that the girls of to-day have acquired. Independence and resourcefulness are fine things for a girl to carry into life. They are necessary factors in the great human instinct of keeping up with the times, and who shall judge whether or not in the long run the modern girl is not making her life the most worth while? ("Miss Modern" 10)[2]

She connects the new experiences of girlhood with ideas of independence that typify modernity. The changing nature of colonial girls' culture is a response to shifting social, political, economic, and cultural conditions in white settler colonies in the early twentieth century.

In Australian newspapers, women's work and its potential to destabilize the ideal of marriage and maternity is a dominant concern. For example, a 1910 article titled "The Modern Girl," which appeared in *The Horsham Times*, explains that

> The girl of the future can still be tender, gentle, affectionate; she need not lose any of the beautiful qualities of her grandmother. She can be loving and lovable, almost an angel in beauty and manner; yet these divine attributes need not debar her from making her way in life, fighting to hold her own. (7)

The modern Australian girl must be educated to deal with everyday realities and concerns, while still retaining a connection to the past. She

2 This discussion continued, with another response from a woman of fifty, L.A.B., who blames the modern, slangy, uncouth girl on her mother and grandmother, wondering, "Who was it that did not bring these girls up properly, that didn't demand obedience, that did not insist on proper hours and proper dressing?" ("Be Fair" 10). The "Old-Timer" responded to both critics on 30 April 1921, reasserting that the modern girl pales in comparison to the girl of fifty years ago ("Critics" 13).

should keep the "beautiful qualities" of her grandmother and remain the "angel" in the house, an echo of Coventry Patmore's poem "The Angel in the House" (1854), which valorizes the domestic qualities of femininity. The author of this article sees no contradiction in extolling the tender, gentle, affectionate qualities of the modern girl while also accepting her need to "fight" in modern society for employment and rights. Yet this modern girl "must not be sent into the world with her eyes shut; she should know and see human nature as it is, be able to hold her own" ("The Modern Girl" [1910] 7). That she should have her eyes open and recognize human flaws is likely an allusion to structural inequalities faced by women in terms of property rights, suffrage, and employment and education opportunities, and to the need to make informed decisions. According to the *West Gippsland Gazette*, the modern girl, "so far as she is typical, is not a solitary and isolated product of a single cause" ("The Modern Girl" [1911] 6). Like modernity itself, the modern girl is the product of multiple, interconnected cultural, political, and economic structures. Given that this article was published in 1911, well before the start of the war, the concern about the modern girl cannot be exclusively attributed to war-time social and economic changes.

According to "The Undomesticated Modern Girl," appearing on 23 August 1912 in the *Telegraph*, employment in an office actually enables marriage. The article argues that a girl's school or college life "has not prepared her for settling down quietly at home" and that she has "much spare time which might be more profitably employed" ("Undomesticated" 2). She turns to the office because it offers a chance to be "part of the active business world" ("Undomesticated" 2). By the time a girl has been at office work for five or six years, "she ha[s] probably been in several offices, knows her work, and the peculiarities of managers no longer give rise to astonishment and indignation in her" ("Undomesticated" 2). Although this girl "probably cannot cook and knows little of house work, ... the thought of marriage does not alarm her," because it can be regarded simply as a "new position" ("Undomesticated" 2). "It is impossible," according to the article, "to say of how much value the years of office work are to the office girl as married woman" ("Undomesticated" 2), because this experience means she will be able to take intelligent interest in her husband's business. A similar sentiment appears in the *Auckland Star* on 30 April 1910, in an article asserting that business knowledge will help make the modern girl "a more competent housekeeper" ("Over the Tea-Cups" 16).[3] At the same time, the article reassures the reader that "there is no likelihood of the normal girl going to extremes and preferring a business career to a happy marriage. Her business ability and success in business will never turn her from her special vocation" ("Undomesticated" 2). Although the modern girl can participate in new employment opportunities, she remains dedicated to her role as a wife and mother. Moreover, this new attitude towards work enables her to be more successful in her marriage.

Articles appearing after the war sometimes refer to the new attitudes it enabled. As Birgitte Søland observes of western Europe in the decade following the First World War, new educational and employment opportunities as well as burgeoning feminist and suffrage movements had transformed the modern feminine ideal: "Collectively, these changes all seemed to liberate women from conventional ties and obligations" (4). Yet "many contemporaries worried about the emergence of a 'new' type of woman, who rejected Victorian concepts of domesticity and instead threw herself into a broad range of public activities previously deemed incompatible with proper womanhood" (Søland 4). For instance, in a 1919 article, originally from the *London Daily Chronicle* and reprinted in *The Brisbane Telegraph*, a modern girl riding a motor bicycle pulls up in front of a cigarette shop. She is "just a modern girl – that's all; perhaps some people might say I was very modern, but that's all nonsense. I'm half a product of the war – half a sign of the times. I did my bit during the war. I've won my freedom – my emancipation … And I've earned my right to smoke cigarettes" ("Modern Girl" [1919] 3). This modern girl is content with signifiers of her modernity – her clothes, the motorbike, and the cigarettes – and unlike in the Canadian correspondence from "Miss Modern," she makes no attempt to defend herself. She is to be accepted as she is.

The tension between present and past that appeared in the Canadian and Australian press also appeared in New Zealand. One example was inspired by British author Ella Hepworth Dixon, a well-known New Woman novelist.[4] In 1910, the *Marlborough Express* included an article

3 This article on "Girls and the Business Faculty" was reprinted in its entirely in the "Business Life" section of the *New Zealand Herald* on 4 May 1910 and printed in a slightly revised form as "A Useful Faculty" on 18 May 1910 in the same section of this newspaper.

4 Dixon's novel *The Story of a Modern Woman* (1894) is a semi-autobiographical story of a woman who is forced to earn her living as a novelist and journalist.

on "The Modern Girl: Manifestations of Feminine Independence," which summarizes Dixon's opinion of the modern girl. She is viewed with alarm by those who fear her "amazing mental and physical developments," yet she remains "genial," "tolerant," and "efficient" ("The Modern Girl: Manifestations" 3). Rejecting the "slipshod training, the amateur methods of the Victorian daughter," the modern girl brings "an enthusiasm and power of concentration" to any task before her ("The Modern Girl: Manifestations" 3). Less than a month later, in the *Observer*, "Myra" reprinted Dixon's article on the "Pluck of the Modern Woman," in which Dixon asserts that the "foolish little bore" of the past, who had to be "helped over stiles, ... was mortally frightened of cows, and ... did not know one end of a gun from the other, hardly exists nowadays" (8). She has been replaced by "the handy girl of modern days," who drives and maintains her own car. She also "swims the channel," "scales the peaks," "goes big-game shooting," "sails her own yacht," and skis "down the precipitous sides of mountains" ("Myra" 8). Her pluck "is indeed one of the most hopeful of all the many signs of a society in a state of change" ("Myra" 8). The decision by the New Zealand press to republish Dixon's article reflects the country's concerns about modernity and girlhood. In this view, the modern girl has been liberated from nineteenth-century constraints on femininity and has shown herself to be capable and competent.

The Modern Girl in Girls' Literature

The girl appearing in colonial girls' periodicals signals few anxieties about modernity and girls' roles within the modern world. Instead, presumably because colonial girls' print culture was intended to appeal to girls of the period, the modern girl appears to be a *fait accompli.* Texts echoing old-fashioned values and ideals would be unlikely to attract readers. Instead, the girl these works depict is distinctly modern based on her appearance and the events in which she participates. The inaugural *Young New Zealander and Schools' Gazette*[5] on 11 September 1924 includes an article about "Girls at Play" that discusses exhibition

5 The magazine, published by Auckland's Edwin Sayes, was short lived in this format. In April 1926 (vol. 2, no. 19), it became *The Young New Zealander* and was incorporated with *New Zealand Woman and Home,* which ceased publication with vol. 3, no. 34 (July 1927) (*Union List* 443). The magazine itself suggested that it was intended "for secondary and primary pupils."

9.1 Advertisement for Petone Bathing Costumes. *The Young New Zealander and Schools' Gazette* 11 September 1924: 33.

matches between representatives of north and south Wellington schools. The names of all the players are listed, as well as the results of the games. The ideal of the healthy, active girl in this article is supported by an accompanying advertisement for Petone bathing costumes (see Figure 9.1). The ad depicts a girl on water skis in the ocean with a sailboat in the background. With short hair tied with a bow, she wears a form-fitting bathing costume as she leans back to keep herself upright. This strong, yet feminine, figure is an exemplar of the new, sporty, active girls, who participated in the "very enjoyable and instructive" school basketball games ("Girls at Play" 33).

This periodical evidently felt that girl readers would be attracted to fashion advertising. In the same issue, an advertisement for James Adams & Co explains that "KNOWING THE SECRET OF BEING WELL DRESSED during her College days, means much to the Modern Young Lady" ("James Adams" 42). The ad explains that young ladies who attend college "are setting a standard in College Dress quite unknown during former days" ("James Adams" 42). The modern New Zealand girl is pursuing an education while also remaining fashionable.

This same concern with fashion appears in colonial girls' fiction. In Esther Glen's *Robin of Maoriland* (1929), Clem, at seventeen, is the oldest of six. The narrator explains that this New Zealand girl embodies the universal ideal, since "she was like any other girl in any other part of the world" (11). Clem has some sewing skills – she is "really clever with her needle" (Glen, *Robin* 100) – and she regularly remakes dresses to keep them modern. In one case, she decides not to go to a party because the family finances mean that she would have to wear a dress that she has worn previously. Her hard-working mother is saddened by this: "she did so love to see her girls pretty and well dressed, and longed to give them the little luxuries and pleasures which their friends enjoyed" (Glen, *Robin* 88). With the arrival of an unexpected gift of a new dress and shoes, Clem happily attends the party. This concern with fashion and modernity is attributed to older girls like Clem; her younger sisters are not invited to the event. Moreover, the younger girls are unable to operate in this sphere. When thirteen-year-old Robin attempts to make a fashionable Jacquinette, her sewing skills are so inadequate that the jacket is unrecognizable.

Clem's modernity manifests itself through her attitude towards work. She has left school and is presently helping her mother at home with domestic chores, "since help in New Zealand is hard to obtain, and Father would not hear of her starting yet on the journalistic career upon which she had set her heart" (Glen, *Robin* 20). When Clem meets a newspaper editor at a party, however, she unabashedly declares her interest in working for his paper, and he provides some cautious support, explaining that "if she studied hard, practiced her shorthand, and wrote at all times, perhaps ... there might be an opening on his paper one day in the future" (Glen, *Robin* 109). At the same time, her popularity means that she is frequently invited out to play tennis and golf and attend garden parties, which means that her mother does most of the domestic work alone, eventually becoming ill. As with so many other girls' stories, girls are often punished when their outside interests mean that they ignore their domestic duties. In this case, however, Clem's tearful plea to her mother results in her recovery.

As it does in *Robin of Maoriland*, fashion operates as a signifier for modernity in *Golden Fiddles* (1928), but modern consumer culture is ultimately proved to be unsatisfactory. Given Mary Grant Bruce's focus on rural Australia and the land (as we see in the Billabong series), the critique of the urban and consumer culture is unsurprising. In this novel, a very poor farming family comes into a huge inheritance that enables them to seemingly transcend class boundaries. The family is generally happy on the farm – raising their own food and enjoying a successful day at a local fairground where they display their agricultural and animal-husbandry skills – except for the father, who is constantly worried about how he will support his family. As Kitty explains to her mother, she is happy to work hard: "I'll go off and earn my own living when I'm twenty-one ... I wouldn't mind being poor ... But I'd like to be poor cheerfully" (Bruce, *Golden* 11). When Mrs Balfour inherits £80,000, they sell the farm and move to Melbourne, no longer needing to work to support themselves.

The children are amazed at the modern technology available in the city, such as lifts and vacuums. Moreover, their fortune means that the consumerist features of modernity are now easily available to them. Mrs Balfour enables their behaviour, as she has fond recollections of living in the city. Yet the move to the city, and the associated focus on consumption, are corrupting influences, especially for Kitty, who becomes obsessed with being fashionable. She complains about how their house has been decorated for a party, finding it insufficiently innovative: "One must have something new if one is to stand out at all" (Bruce, *Golden* 161). Mrs Balfour remarks that she sees herself as "the ancient mother of a modern young girl" (Bruce, *Golden* 169), but this modernity is explicitly critiqued by Kitty's younger brother Bob, who – of all the children – is least influenced by the trappings of modernity. He describes Kitty as "all frills" and without "as much sense as she used to have" (Bruce, *Golden* 189). Indeed, she and her brother Norman are both described as "professional idlers" (Bruce, *Golden* 166). Kitty eventually becomes "tired" and "impatient" in Melbourne as she wearies of the "ceaseless chatter" at parties and yearns for something more satisfying (Bruce, *Golden* 157). In the frontispiece of the novel (see Figure 9.2), Kitty leans on the arm of a chair and cries, while her sister Elsa tries to comfort her. The luxurious trappings of modern life are evident in the room she inhabits, with its high ceilings, ornate paintings, and vase with flowers, and in the book

9.2 Frontispiece. Illust. J. Dewar Mills. Mary Grant Bruce, *Golden Fiddles* (London: Ward, Lock & Co., 1928).

beside her. Her unhappiness can be directly attributed to the life of luxury that this room signifies.

The modernity of the city is independently rejected by three of the four children, who decide that they should return to the country – although this time with enough money to be able to outsource some of the hardest work – and become self-sufficient once again. Kitty observes that although it was "a hard life," they were "pretty happy," even "happier then than we are now, when we've got everything we ever longed for" (Bruce, *Golden* 237). Her sister Elsa attributes this happiness to having a purpose: "we all need work, more or less" (Bruce, *Golden* 238). The modernity of Melbourne life has rendered them idle, or rather working hard at socializing, a task that is largely without satisfaction or value. The conclusion of the novel demonstrates that work is important, and the advantages of the modern, urban life must be incorporated within work that adds value. This theme is echoed in other Australian fiction of the period, in which, as Graeme Turner explains, "nature ... not only offer[s] a Romantic retreat from society; it offers also a withdrawal from the political, socio-economic realities of existence" (36). In *Golden Fiddles*, girls (and children more generally) are best situated within the natural realm, away from the temptations of modernity.

The same concern about the corrupting influence of the modern is apparent in Nellie McClung's Pearl Watson trilogy, which began with the publication of *Sowing Seeds in Danny* in 1908. In the second novel, *The Second Chance* (1910), Pearl acknowledges that living in an urban centre is a bad influence on her brothers. She proposes to her father that they move out to a farm so the boys will have more to do, even though this means Pearl will have to sacrifice her education. The city offers Pearl the opportunity to attend school, but the temptation for the boys is much less wholesome. Pearl fears they will get into trouble and will not grow into honourable men, so she sacrifices her desires to help the family. This traditional feminine ideal of sacrifice is consistent with that depicted in some other colonial texts appearing in the early 1900s, which tend to continue to exhibit ideals from the previous century. By the 1920s and 1930s, this ideal had shifted. The modern colonial girl in these texts is, as Mitchell suggests about British girls, less constrained by the realities of the nineteenth century. Instead, she is freer to pursue things that she feels are important.

Although the final novel in the trilogy, *Purple Springs* (1921), undoubtedly reflects McClung's own personal experiences, it also demonstrates Pearl's engagement with the significant political and social issues of the day. Reflecting McClung's own interest in women's suffrage, Pearl attends school in Winnipeg in order to obtain her teaching certificate and supports the campaign for provincial women's suffrage. Although the city offers Pearl an education and an increasing confidence in her ability to speak to her country neighbours in an engaging and persuasive manner, her position in the modern world is not a concern. She moves easily between the rural and the urban, and both experiences contribute to her development into a successful, accomplished young woman. Unlike in other narratives where the influence of the city is a major concern, Pearl's family is not worried about her absence from home. Pearl returns to the country and demonstrates her value as a teacher and a member of the community. This lack of concern is not a retreat from the modern, as it is in *Golden Fiddles,* but rather an acceptance of the role of the modern in obtaining women's rights. In light of rural problems like alcoholism and gambling, women are helpful contributors to the twentieth-century prairie community and play an important role in the progress of the nation, a role enabled by their active participation in local, provincial, and national politics.

The Pearl Watson trilogy is ultimately a romance, similar to the trajectory of the Anne of Green Gables series. Ken Gelder and Rachael Weaver suggest that the colonial romance provided "a crucial site for the struggle over the model of womanhood that seemed to best express the aspirations of an emergent nation" (2). In *Purple Springs,* Pearl eventually reconciles with the doctor, Horace Clay, who has refused to marry her because of his illness. He does not want Pearl to be hindered by a chronically ill husband: "You have ambition, brains – something about you that will carry you far" (McClung, *Purple* 53). As an educated, Christian, and modern figure of twentieth-century femininity, Pearl is the "epitome of the feminist figure of the mother of the race" (Devereux, *Growing* 64). She is transformed from the uneducated maternal figure at the beginning of the series into a feminist figure for whom marriage, maternity, and women's rights become interconnected.

Published only two years after *Purple Springs,* L.M. Montgomery's Emily of New Moon trilogy introduces a less obviously modern protagonist in the figure of the eponymous Emily, who is raised by her relatives after her father's death. She spends almost all of her time in New Moon and its surrounds, leaving only for occasional visits to other relatives and for her secondary-school education in Shrewsbury. In Joe Sutliff Sanders's discussion of orphan girls' fiction, he describes the Emily trilogy as part of a "nostalgic, sentimental orphan girl genre," which "gave way to stories about more modern, more urban girls" (141). Despite the absence of a modern setting, however, Emily's attitudes towards her writing and romance signal the ways in which she can be seen as a modern figure.

Emily's passion for writing is one of the strongest signals of her modernity throughout the series. She is determined "to climb the Alpine Path to the very top, 'And write upon its shining scroll / A woman's humble name'" (*Emily Climbs* 39). Emily's writerly ambitions are the source of much conflict with her aunts and her fiancé, Dean. When Aunt Elizabeth insists that she stop writing for the three years she is at Shrewsbury, she passionately explains, "I *can't* help writing ... It's in my blood .... I *do* want an education ... but I can't give up my writing to get it" (*Emily Climbs* 79). She is fiercely determined to continue writing, although she eventually agrees to forgo fiction and write only true stories while she is away. For Emily, not only is writing a vocation that will enable her to support herself but it also serves as an outlet for her imagination. Antoinette Burton has described the "incompleteness" and "precarious vulnerability" of colonial modernities that have the capacity, "as contingent and highly unstable systems of power, to interrupt, if not thwart, modernizing regimes" ("Introduction" 1). Emily's insistence on the necessity and validity of her writing is a marker of modernity, especially in old-fashioned New Moon.

Her "Alpine Path" to success is lengthy and erratic, with numerous missteps along the way. Nonetheless, she pursues her goal in New Moon even as her friends leave for big cities like Montréal for further education and opportunities. Emily, too, has an opportunity to move to New York and make her name in the publishing world. Janet Royal, a writer from Prince Edward Island who has made the move, tries to convince Emily that she can reach the peak of her achievement only by opening herself to the modernity of the city. Emily rejects this notion and eventually writes a novel whose success is based on her rural connections. As she explains, "I may not succeed here – but, if not, I wouldn't succeed in New York either. Some fountain of living water would dry up my soul if I left the land I love" (*Emily Climbs* 300). Unlike in some of the other fiction discussed in this chapter, Emily's rejection of modern life is not a retreat. Instead, she declares her independence by resisting the lure of the city and defining her modernity within a rural environment.

The romantic plot of the trilogy is a further sign of Emily's modernity. Emily has a series of suitors but refuses them all, despite her family's belief that some of them would have been appropriate husbands. She rejects her friend Perry's many proposals knowing that they do not love each other.

As she explains, "he doesn't happen to be the type I fancy" (*Emily Climbs* 234). Her family is astonished at her clear-headed discussion of marriage and love: "Could *this* be Emily – this tall young woman coolly giving her reasons for refusing an offer of marriage – and talking about the 'types' she fancied?" (*Emily Climbs* 234). Emily has a choice about whom to marry, or even whether to marry at all, a key sign of her independence. Only Dean's proposal is accepted, but his love demands that she sacrifice her writing, a relinquishment that he facilitates by telling her that her first novel is merely a "pretty little story" (*Emily's Quest* 74). Emily later discovers that he lied to her about his impression of the book because she loved it more than him. Although Emily is upset about this betrayal, she also feels a curious sense of liberation: "Something has happened – she was really free – free from remorse, shame, regret" (*Emily's Quest* 135). Although she yearns to be with her old school friend Teddy, to whom she feels she "belongs" (*Emily's Quest* 131), she is also happy to be free from romantic entanglements that limit her autonomy. The novel concludes with her engagement to Teddy, and everyone in New Moon is pleased. Emily, too, knows that this relationship will not be at the expense of her writing.

In contrast to the feminist ideals appearing in the trilogies featuring Pearl and Emily, Isabel Maud Peacocke's *Robin of the Round House* (1918) presents a more traditional New Zealand model of femininity. Two cousins, Sylvia and Una, live together in Auckland while trying to eke out a living. Una's health is not especially good, and Sylvia, a typist and clerk in a business office, struggles to keep them afloat. The modern trappings of the city provide employment for the girls, yet this novel – like *Golden Fiddles* – presents the rural environment as a place for health and happiness. Una's mother insists that the girls be able to support themselves and equips them "for the struggle with a sound commercial training, though secretly deploring the necessity and thought of her two pretty, high-bred girls tied to an office stool and the dry routine of a business career" (Peacocke, *Robin* 14). The unexpected inheritance of a small house and farm in the country provide a change that proves instrumental to both girls. By reading, Sylvia ably learns everything she needs to know to make the farm a financial success. Sylvia knows it will require "work, real hard work for us both," but she readily accepts the challenge: "I'll get books on poultry and bee farming and study up" (Peacocke, *Robin* 29). A nearby neighbour also provides some practical advice, but the girls never struggle with this new-found work. Instead, they leave behind the drudgery of office work and a meager wage for the sustainable farm that provides them with most of their basic needs.

Like Pearl, these girls, especially Sylvia, also perform the maternal role when they adopt an orphan from a nearby orphanage. Although the caregiver at the orphanage has good intentions, she is clearly unable to cope with the demands of Robin, a young boy who has arrived at the orphanage under mysterious circumstances. Sylvia is determined to adopt the boy despite having no practical experience with children. She is instinctively maternal, as she explains to Una:

> I don't pretend to understand children – I have never cared for children as you do. I am doubtful, inexperienced, all at sea, where they are concerned, but if a dog had come to me in such pitiful distress as made that little boy tremble and cling to me, I could not have refused him food and shelter and a home, and much less could I refuse a child. (Peacocke, *Robin* 106)

The Round House, as the farm is called, is an ideal environment in which to raise children. The illustration accompanying the chapter about Robin's adoption (Figure 9.3) emphasizes the mother–son relationship. Against a dark background, the candle Sylvia holds casts a warm glow over her as she gazes at Robin, who clings to her and appears content in her arms. Sylvia and Robin are universal signifiers for the maternal role and the importance of raising children. Sylvia's new occupation means that she has the time and ability to consider the welfare of others, especially children. She is able to become a mother without being married herself.

The radical potential of this modern girl is curtailed through her romantic relationship with her former employer, Philip Darrel. This ultimately results in the creation of a new family when Philip discovers that Robin is his long-lost son. The natural conclusion, where Sylvia and Philip marry and eventually have children of their own, is foregone. Sylvia has demonstrated her feminine qualities of domesticity and caregiving through her successes at the farm, and, upon her marriage, she returns to the city. The Round House becomes a weekend retreat from the modern world inhabited by Philip. The world in this novel is divided along clearly gendered lines, with the masculine modern sphere strictly separated from the feminine domestic one. Sylvia happily returns to the city in all its modernity because she is accompanied by her husband and her son. Without them, the modern world is too challenging and unhealthy for a young woman to inhabit successfully, a striking difference from the earlier bushman myth that foregrounded the depiction of men in rural settings.

9.3 "Bed-time, sleepy boy!" Illust. J. Macfarlane. Isabel Maud Peacocke, *Robin of the Round House* (London: Ward, Lock & Co., 1918).

The rural environment is similarly valorized in Phillis Garrard's Hilda series, where examples of female modernity are strongly critiqued. On one of her adventures, Hilda, a sensible, capable girl, encounters Cynthia Norton, a quintessentially modern girl who is fashionably dressed and who, Hilda later discovers, has jilted a man she loved because he was poor. In her oblique conversation with Hilda, Cynthia declares that she wishes she could travel back in time: "But no, one must always go on – to get older, further away, more disillusioned, more bored, more bewildered. It is – unkind" (Garrard, *Hilda* 39). This modern girl lacks the connection to the land and the simple pleasures of "games and picnics and swimming" as well as riding and gathering food (Garrard, *Hilda* 37). Consequently, she has made poor decisions that have hurt others. Hilda's father, the moral centre of the novel and "a being apart" (Garrard, *Hilda* 57), criticizes Cynthia's actions and calls her spoiled. Hilda, and the implied reader, understands that Cynthia's behaviour is inappropriate for the modern colonial girl.

Yet Hilda is not a traditional, conservative model of femininity. She has some domestic skills, but unlike Norah in the Billabong series, who learns at the hearth of the family housekeeper, Hilda spends little time performing domestic chores for her family. Instead, as we briefly discussed in chapter 3, she sees herself as part of the British Empire. She also adopts egalitarian principles that are evident when she gives a schoolmate, Lizzie, a ride home. She discovers that Lizzie's family is poor and that Lizzie spends much of her time outside school hours caring for her brothers and sisters. In this bucolic setting, the novels in the series are seemingly removed from the realities of everyday life. However, Garrard includes some political context, and also questions traditional British expectations that girls should attend private boarding-schools. As Hilda explains to a new student who comes from England, "this is a democratic country. And when we say public schools here we *mean* public – where everyone has a chance" (Garrard, *Hilda* 168). She also rejects boarding-schools as "mushy on account of there being no boys in them" (Garrard, *Doings* 53), echoing sentiments expressed earlier, in *Hilda at School*, that "it's much sensibler and jollier for boys and girls to go to school together" (141). Hilda's consciousness of her democratic principles foregrounds a belief common in New Zealand during the nineteenth and early twentieth centuries: that New Zealand was a "social laboratory" where "experimental, progressive policies were implemented for the western world to watch and emulate" (Nolan 113). Even if this concept of New Zealand nationhood draws, as Nolan observes, on "a rich amalgam of truth and myth" (127), it is incorporated into Garrard's depiction of Hilda and her vision of herself as a New Zealander.

Although some examples of modern technology are present, such as the telephone, in general, the series is removed from many aspects of modernity. Priscilla, a new girl, finds Hilda to be "realer" than any other girls she knows, in part because of her connection to the land. Priscilla is cosmopolitan, having lived in France, England, Argentina, and the United States. Her father wants her to be a "citizen of the world, not just of one country" (Garrard, *Doings* 151), yet Priscilla laments her lack of connection to "a native land" (Garrard, *Doings* 175). Hilda and her friends are "something real" while Priscilla is a "mixture" (Garrard, *Doings* 176). Hilda's strong sense of place is an important factor in her identity. In the final chapters of *Doings of Hilda*, she succumbs to "Spring Fever" and takes a day off from school, instead spending time feeding the new lambs, planting sweet pea and radish seeds, mowing the lawn, feeding the horses, and going for the first swim of the season. The day ends, after a game of moonlit hide-and-seek with Mary and Priscilla, with Hilda in bed: "She sighed and stretched luxuriously in vast and utter contentment," feeling "a little guilty at being so disgracefully happy" (Garrard, *Doings* 207). For Hilda, nothing is more satisfying that spending a gorgeous day enjoying the natural world.

The model of modern colonial girlhood in *Doings of Hilda* is rather divorced from most symbols of modernity. Indeed, as the headmaster remarks, "on the whole, you girls have a very free, independent time of it" (Garrard, *Doings* 60). Yet anxieties about the modern girl appear in many texts from the 1920s and 1930s. Angela Woollacott explains that although Australian women, largely because of their earlier access to universal (white) suffrage, saw themselves as distinctly modern in comparison to their British and Canadian counterparts, this modernity rarely makes it into girls' fiction of the period, which tends to be quite conservative. In particular, the modern colonial girl appearing in this Canadian, Australian, and New Zealand fiction is overwhelmingly white and middle class, which contributes to her function as a transnational figure.

In *The Four of Us: New Zealand School-Girls' Story* (1935), Olga P. Meyer explains that she has attempted to produce the "school 'atmosphere' … where imaginary characters face the vicissitudes of the all-important period of their school-life" (n.p.). As in many of these colonial school stories, the overarching narrative is mainly one of interlinked stories about school life, but here technology is depicted as integral to modern life. Mary Martin travels by car to get to the school:

> a big, well-travelled car slid smoothly round the corner from Devon Street, and after a brisk run up Mangorei Road turned in at the main entrance of Scotlands. With a sigh of relief after a long journey, the car came to a standstill at the rear of a line of motors already on the circular drive ... Mary Martin alighted from one side, while her mother, who had been driving, stepped out from the other. (Meyer 9)

Cars are evidently the common form of transportation for these schoolgirls, and significantly, Mary's mother – rather than her father – is the driver. Interestingly, her father does not see her off. Instead, the modern mother transports her modern daughter to school.

The school is distinctly, and unusually, modern in its approach to race, as well, providing a rare exception to the whiteness of modern colonial girlhood in other books. Although one of Hilda's schoolmates, Tom, is Māori, he is an occasional figure of fun and stereotype: "with true Maori calm and good sense [Tom] had begun to doze in his seat at the end of the room" (Garrard, *Doings* 58). Race is employed differently in *The Four of Us*, however, when one of the four girls in the club, Huia, is explicitly identified as Māori. She boards at school, thereby signalling her family's wealth, and explains that, although she "belongs" to North Auckland (Meyer 49), she is living with an aunt in Taranaki until she goes to university. Higher education is explicitly identified as one of her goals, while her other friends are not described as having such lofty ambitions. Indeed, Mary's concern is that she has no special abilities, while Huia is an accomplished musician. Her ancestor – she is "the great-great-granddaughter of the Ngapuhi chief, Kawaiti; about whom you read in history books" (Meyer 49) – is a source of pride for her friends, and their teacher has just been reading about him in a history book. In this way, Huia is marked out as exceptional within Māori and white settler culture, yet her uncontroversial inclusion in the narrative signals a new conception of modernity in which Māori girls have a place in the modern colonial world.

The photo of a young Māori girl that appears in the 15 January 1925 issue of *The Young New Zealander and Schools' Gazette* (see Figure 9.4) provides a sharp contrast to this modern conception of race. The girl wears a cloak of feather quills – a sign of aristocratic birth – over one shoulder, with one arm bare. She looks off to the right, not directly at the camera, and her tousled hair suggests her uncivilized nature. The caption, reading "I'se a young New Zealander, too!" simultaneously includes this young girl as part of modern New Zealand and excludes her because she

9.4 "I'se a young New Zealander, too!" *The Young New Zealander and Schools' Gazette* 15 January 1925: 48.

lacks the requisite knowledge of proper English. In Woollacott's discussion of white colonialism, she explains that "Western modernity must be viewed as having been created in a symbiotic relationship with its racially constructed others, and that racial hierarchies, including whiteness as a racial identity, have been integrally constitutive of modernity" ("White Colonialism" 49). The difference between the girl wearing the Petone bathing costume and the young Māori girl is striking. Appearing in the same magazine only months apart, they present a distinct view of modern colonial girlhood in which the white girl is modern and civilized while the Māori girl is younger, less cultured, and tied to the past through her native dress.

Racial categories also appear in *The Canadian Girl*, a United Church of Canada publication beginning in 1930.[6] The Canadian girl defined in the magazine is both white and modern, as images such as the one accompanying the Rev J.R.P. Sclater's article "The Dew on the Grass" in the 4 January 1930 issue reflect (see Figure 9.5). In this image, a girl wears skis and stands with a young man. She is not alone, and her presence is contained by expectations of heteronormativity and eventual marriage. Yet her short hair is tucked in a warm hat, and her knee-length skirt swings forward, suggesting movement and action. This healthy, outdoor girl looks as if she is about to push off on her poles and ski away.

The accompanying article's concerns about the modern girl reflect those appearing elsewhere in the press. Sclater directly addresses the girl of today and signals her difference from girls of the past: "The things you say and the way you say them; the clothes you wear and the clothes you do not wear; the freedom you demand ... are not quite what we were used to in our young days" (Sclater, "Dew" 4). The changes in the modern girl are improvements, he argues, and the "fine, vigorous, athletic comrade of to-day has nothing to regret" (Sclater, "Dew" 4). Sclater's one concern is related to what he calls keeping "the dew on the grass," maintaining the "stainless kind of quality" that comes from being "pure of heart" (Sclater, "Dew" 4). The purity and virtue of the girl of today remains crucial. As he explains, "It is possible to be free and coarsened;

6 *The Canadian Girl* emerged out of the Methodist publication *Pleasant Hours*, which had the subtitle of "a publication for Canadian girls" beginning in 1926, after the merge of the Methodist and Presbyterian churches. The Presbyterian publication *The King's Own* (1900–25) became the official boys' magazine at that time. Prior to this gender differentiation, each publication attempted to appeal to both boys and girls, occasionally reprinting materials from the other magazine.

9.5 J.R.P. Sclater, "The Dew on the Grass," *The Canadian Girl* 4 January 1930: 4.

modern and slightly shop-soiled" (Sclater, "Dew" 4). The modern Canadian girl must maintain the virtuous ideals of the past if she is to marry successfully and be of value in the modern world.

Elsewhere in *The Canadian Girl*, and in similar to the depictions of the normative Anglo-Saxon ideal in *The Young New Zealander and Schools' Gazette*, girls in different racial categories are figured as "other." Sclater observes in "He Shall Have Dominion Also from Sea to Sea" that the wonder of Canada is more obvious to new Canadians who are not used to it. He explains that, in Canada, "there is coming to be a new race of men: and it depends on how we, who are of British stock, behave ourselves now, whether that new man is to be great or not" (Sclater, "He" n.p.). Sclater defines his girl readers as being of British ancestry when he uses "we." Those who do not come from this background are highlighted through the inclusion of a photograph of a group of Japanese members of Canadian Girls in Training (CGIT) based in New Westminster, British Columbia. The CGIT program was launched by the United Church to respond to the growing influence of girls' associations like the YWCA and the Girl Guides, which the Church felt were too American in their orientation. The CGIT program was designed to encourage girls in their duty to God and nation. The photograph includes ten Japanese girls organized around the Caucasian leader, Miss Margaret Ryan. The brief description below the photo explains that they are the "only group" of Japanese girls in Canada organized as a CGIT group and that they are "doing excellent work" ("Wohelo" n.p.). Their difference is made visible through the inclusion of the photograph and highlighted in the concluding paragraph of Sclater's article:

> But the bed-rock of it all is Britain and British ideals. It has been Britons who have laid the foundations; Britons who have tamed Nature to their uses; Britons who have framed the laws; Britons who have won and kept the freedoms where with these, our new friends, are free. So as you look forward to the future, hold fast to the past. Lose nothing of character, or steadiness, of love, of truth, and of the fear of God that our fathers have handed to us as our noblest inheritance; and we and they together may go forward to a noble future in a noble land." ("He" n.p.)

Although the idea behind the CGIT organization is to provide a model of universal Canadian girlhood, this model is differentiated based on race and clearly privileges girls of British ancestry. This is reminiscent of Lake and Reynolds's study, which we discussed in chapter 6 and which points out that Australia, Canada, and New Zealand regarded themselves as "white nations" under the aegis of the British Colonial Office.

At the same time, however, *Pleasant Hours* and *The Canadian Girl* attempt to reflect the universal experience of Canadian girlhood regardless of racial background. The 8 June 1935 article in the latter publication on "The Teen-Age Girl in Canada" by Evelyn Craw explores what the United Church was doing for teenage girls in Canada at the time. Once again, the photographs – this time, one of a CGIT group at an "Indian Mission" in Ahousaht, British Columbia, and another from a Ukrainian mission in Winnipeg – emphasize the exoticism of these groups of non-British ancestry. Yet the text focuses on the extent to which the Church attempted to be multicultural and universal in its orientation. With over 2,500 registered CGIT groups and an average of twelve girls in each group, CGIT leaders served over thirty thousand girls (Craw, "Teen-Age" 178). The United Church was focused on being the "Church of All Nations"; Craw explains that "the Sunday School classes and CGIT groups help the New Canadian girl to learn Canadian ways, and to form friendships with other girls" ("Teen-Age" 178). While learning to be Canadian is seen as important, so is retaining her culture; the Church of All Nations' annual festival "encourages a girl to be proud of her own racial heritage" (Craw, "Teen-Age" 179). It seems unlikely that this support for racial heritage extends to what Craw calls the "first Canadians" ("Teen-Age" 179). In her discussion of the girls on the "Indian Reserve," she explains that there are thirteen "fine" residential schools, at which girls receive instruction in academic subjects and "also make progress in learning to bake bread, make butter, sew their own clothes and, in general, master the art of housekeeping" (Craw, "Teen-Age" 179). The assumption is that these Indigenous girls lack the innate ability and knowledge to care for their homes because they come from non-British backgrounds. They must be educated in British norms of domesticity to fulfil their roles in the modern Canadian world.

In stark contrast to this discussion of residential schooling is a poem in *Pleasant Hours*, "To a Little Eskimo," by Bessie M. Chadwick. Accompanying the poem is a photo (Figure 9.6) of a young girl with dark hair and eyes, wearing a heavy fur coat along with hood, mittens, and warm boots. She has a slight smile on her face and looks directly at the camera. Unlike other images of Indigeneity, where the figures are often coded as poor, disadvantaged, and uncivilized by their attire, this girl is exotic. But the poem uses a first-person narrator to explain that "I know a little child who played about / The frozen doorway on an igloo, found / In some

9.6 Bessie Chadwick, "To a Little Eskimo," *Pleasant Hours: A Paper for Canadian Girls* 30 October 1926: 175.

wild northern land" (Chadwick 175). The intimacy of the narrator lends authenticity to the description of the little girl who plays on icebergs and enjoys the aurora borealis in the dark winter sky. She is privy to different knowledge, based on her natural environment, for it "told her things" about the life of the polar bear and the "gray, creeping seals along the distant shore" (Chadwick 175). When the unnamed "they" remove the girl to "a southern land," the narrator explains that the "poor little Iceland bloom transplanted far / From all her childish heart had deemed most dear" was uncomplaining, for "no one ever saw her shed a tear" (Chadwick 175). The stark ending of the poem, "But in a little year she drooped and died," speaks to the negative consequences of removing a child from everything she loves and holds "most dear" (Chadwick 175).

The poem is an obvious nod to the practice of residential schooling, in which, beginning with the Indian Act of 1876 and lasting into the late twentieth century, Inuit, Métis, and First Nations children were forcibly removed from their homes and sent to board at schools. The poem is uncompromising in its conclusion. The well-meaning people who give her new toys fail to understand why she, who played with things from nature, such as "a bit of reindeer moss" and a "bone carved ... into human form" (Chadwick 175), does not play with them. The narrator understands that this young child should remain in her "wild northern land" (Chadwick 175). Although Chadwick does not incorporate the "little Eskimo" within the ideal of Canadian girlhood, her unwillingness to sacrifice the girl to this ideal is unusual in the magazine, which otherwise privileges whiteness and modernity.

Although Indigenous girls cannot fit within the framework of girlhood employed in *Pleasant Hours* and *The Canadian Girl*, it was clear that Canadian girlhood could and should be inclusive, especially in relation to the magazine's Christian framework. Evelyn Craw's metaphor of Canada as a mixing bowl in a 26 November 1927 article has two dimensions. First, she explains that "to Canada's mixing bowl each province gladly brings its own particular gift of forest and field, mine and river, farm and city" (Craw, "Canadian" 190). The diverse and expansive nature of Canada's geography results in a variety of different people coming together to form the nation. However, Craw continues, "our young nation is a mixing bowl not only for many provinces but also for many races, and every race will make its own particular contribution be it for weal or woe" (Craw, "Canadian" 190). Given the rapid influx of immigrants into Canada, at a rate of three thousand a week in September 1927, and the declining proportion of immigrants from the British Isles, Craw asserts the importance of incorporating the "strangers within our gates" into the idea of the nation (Craw, "Canadian" 190). Significantly, however, Indigenous peoples are not seen as part of Canada's mixing bowl. They receive no specific mention at all. Of far greater concern is the treatment of the influx of eastern-European and Asian immigrants.

Although this article encourages all Canadian girls to be part of the "beautiful Miss Canada" who emerges from the mixing bowl, Craw still explicitly privileges whiteness, which Lake and Reynolds describe as "a paradoxical politics, at once transnational in its inspiration and identifications but nationalist in its methods and goals" (4). Edith, a girl from western Canada, which was considered less cosmopolitan and less modern, visits Ruth in the east and discusses the "hordes" of foreigners in her city. She is happy that she does not have to "run into them often because we keep them down in their end of the city" (Craw, "Canadian" 190). Ruth wonders whether these immigrants can "ever become real Canadians, alone, ... in their end of ... town," for they are "here to stay, a part of Canada, and they are too big a factor to ignore. If they don't make good Canadians they will make bad ones" (Craw, "Canadian" 190). The eastern-Canadian girl is more open-minded and knowledgeable about the future of Canada, while the girl from the west is more racist and isolationist. Yet, as the article suggests, these ignorant girls can be better educated to contribute to Canada's future by welcoming these foreigners and helping them adapt.

This nascent stage of Canada's multiculturalism is not reflected in girls' print culture in Australia and New Zealand, although the New Zealand texts are somewhat more accepting of Māori influence. Attitudes towards race are one of the significant differences between the three countries, even though they all privilege whiteness. Indeed, by the 1920s and 1930s, the colonial girl has become a distinctly modern figure who embraces the advances of the twentieth century in terms of her freedom to pursue work of her own, to be self-supporting, and to adopt new fashions that reflect her identity as a modern girl. She takes advantage of new conveniences and is no longer as constrained by nineteenth-century conceptions of femininity that demand duty and sacrifice, although vestiges of these values occasionally find their way into these modern texts.

Yet the modern girl is often happiest away from the trappings of civilization, thus harkening back to the myth of the bush or the natural world as a place for an ideal model of femininity. As we have seen in other chapters, texts written and published prior to 1900 sometimes depict the reality of settler colonial life as at odds with these nostalgic or romanticized representations. What remains in these modern texts is the importance of marriage and modernity, particularly in those for older girls. Texts for young girls highlight the distinctiveness of a girl's life prior to her entry into the world of romance. For younger girls, modern girlhood is a world separate from the concerns of adulthood. The modern girl in colonial girls' print culture is not sexualized in the way that adult women are, even as she uses fashion as a symbol of contemporary life. In Canada, Australia, and New Zealand, she may look modern, and she may exhibit aspects of transnational modernity, but she remains valued for her prospective contributions to the future as a wife and mother.

CHAPTER TEN

Conclusion

The real and represented girls who fill the pages of this book originate from diverse national and class origins. Among their number, a few non-white girls appear, always depicted through the lens of white authors for whom European culture is normative. Charles Welsh's 1884 survey of girls' reading canvassed the opinions of over a thousand British girls aged between eleven and nineteen; most of the magazines, annuals, and novels we have discussed feature protagonists whose ages fall within a similar range, implying readers of around the same age. At the upper end of the age spectrum, texts read by girls shaded into texts that adult women also read, including popular novels, which girls borrowed from the circulating libraries established in Britain and the colonies during the nineteenth century and into the twentieth. While recognizing the porous nature of texts produced for adults and read by girls, we have focused on texts produced specifically for girls between 1840 and 1940, when the field of children's literature emerged as a significant component of the book publishing industry.

Across this century of publications for and about girls, changing values and cultural norms shaped models of girlhood and moral and ethical principles. The title of our book, *From Colonial to Modern,* signals the temporal spread of our project, but we do not subscribe to a teleological model of literary history. It is not the case that the texts we discuss plot a steady pathway from one phase to another, for instance, from oppression to emancipation or from colonial typologies of race to more enlightened views. Michel Foucault, reflecting on the connections between truth and fiction in his interview on *The History of Sexuality,* says, "The possibility exists for fiction to function in truth, for a fictional discourse to induce effects of truth" (*Power/Knowledge* 193). But truth is not a simple or static entity, since it is "linked in a circular relation with systems of power which produce and sustain it, and to effects of power which it induces and which extend it" (*Power/Knowledge* 133). It follows that the versions of truth presented in texts for girls hinge upon a multitude of circumstances and cultural practices as well as the dispositions and experiences of authors. While we have often noted the existence and influence of what Foucault refers to as regimes of truth, we also identify moments of resistance, tangles of inconsistency, and expressions of anxiety concerning the truth about girls, their location in society, and the futures imagined for them. Strands of ideation and imagery persist through the cavalcade of texts we have read and discussed, notably, the close attention paid to girls' bodies, the significance of spatiality in the formation of girls' characters, and the sense of futurity associated with girls imagined as citizens of new societies and mothers of future citizens. By way of conclusion, we tease out these strands of meaning and their intersections with the topics we address in the book's nine previous chapters.

Girls' Bodies, Colonial to Modern

In the texts we discuss, girls' bodies are inscribed with cultural meanings and model to readers values about femininity and the place of girls and women in society. Whether authors resided in the colonial cultures they described or were armchair travellers relying on second-hand information about life in the colonies, they routinely compared the bodies, deportment, and practices of British girls with those of their colonial sisters. The most pervasive feature of such comparisons is the assumption that colonial girls enjoy more physical freedom than British girls do, engage more actively in outdoor activities, and are charged with more responsibilities in households and farming properties. Over and over again colonial girls are attributed with energy, good health, and high spirits, qualities that claim a nexus between new nations and their inhabitants, distinguishing the Old World from the New. When Ethel Turner carves out an Antipodean setting that distinguishes Britain from Australia in *Seven Little Australians,* she links the natural world with the "naughtiness" of Australian children: "There is a lurking sparkle of joyousness and rebellion and mischief in nature here, and therefore in children" (10). Judy's body is imprinted with this joyousness, rebellion, and mischief, since she is the ringleader of the seven, having "quicksilver instead of blood" in her veins (15). But Judy also epitomizes the dangers that crowd around the figure of the wild, rebellious girl, and her death precludes the possibility that such a wild girl might grow into a refractory woman.[1]

The example of Judy points to one of the liveliest tensions that surround depictions of girls' bodies between 1840 and 1940. On the one hand, narratives are replete with approving descriptions of energetic, independent Australian, Canadian, and New Zealand girls; on the other, girl readers are warned against transgressing social and cultural norms. Indeed, it seems that colonial girls' bodies are themselves transgressive, and they reach physical maturity earlier than British girls: the Australian girl is, for instance, described as "blooming and buxom" with a "full" figure ("Our Australian Cousin" 44). Such coded references to girls' sexuality sketch a connection between the comparative freedom enjoyed by colonial girls and the sexual dangers that lurk within colonial Edens. Relatively few Indigenous girls feature in nineteenth-century and early twentieth-century texts, and those who do frequently succumb to sad deaths involving suicide or murder. The explanation proposed in *A Mother's Offering to Her Children* and other texts we discuss is that Indigenous bodies manifest an excess of sexuality evident in the "unrestrained passions" that characterize Indigenous girls (Barton 197). These monitory narratives position white girl readers to give assent to the binary distinction between white and non-white races, and to appreciate their own good fortune as girls who by virtue of their whiteness are exempt from the uncontrollable sexual desires of non-white girls.

The clothing worn, created, and purchased by girls functions in texts as markers of class, race, age, and temperament. When Anne Shirley arrives in Avonlea at the beginning of *Anne of Green Gables*, she wears what the orphanage has issued her, "a very short, very tight, very ugly dress of yellowish-gray wincey [and] a faded brown sailor hat" (63). Her gradual incorporation into the Cuthbert household and the society of Avonlea is marked by a gradation of clothes: at first, the plain but "good, sensible, serviceable dresses" that Marilla makes for her (124); next, the fashionable dress, adorned with puffed sleeves, which Matthew, conscious of her difference from the other Avonlea girls, gives her for Christmas; and finally, Marilla's subsequent production of

1 In his essay "The Return of Judy," Richard Rossiter argues that the death of Judy avoids a problem of representation, since "there is no place for the rebellious, highly individualized character in the Australia of this period" (64).

similarly stylish clothing. These changes signify both Anne's progress as the adopted daughter of the household and Marilla and Matthew's induction into something like parenthood. Girls' clothes more broadly signify distinctions between British and Australian practices and fashions, between local and transnational formulations of femininity, and between concepts of modernity. The most striking contrasts in regards to clothing are not those between British and colonial girls, or between girls of different nations, but between white and non-white girls. When Indigenous girls adopt styles of dress similar to those of non-Indigenous girls, they expose their incapacity to behave like white girls; when they wear "native" clothing, they are marked as exotic or inferior. In either case, their clothing locates them as other to white society and its norms.

Bodily activities loom large in many of the texts we discuss. A few texts depict girls, such as Maudie in Marchant's *A Heroine of the Sea* and Shenac in *Shenac's Work at Home,* who undertake strenuous physical work, Maudie by fishing to support her family and Shenac by toiling in the fields of the family farm. But these narratives expose cultural anxieties about girls' bodies once they move beyond the domestic sphere. What Foucault refers to as the "disciplinary gaze" that maintains control over bodies is not so easily achieved when girls' work takes them outside the home (*Discipline and Punish* 174). Both Maudie and Shenac are eventually restored to domestic settings where they are subjected to styles of discipline that produce "subjected and practiced bodies, 'docile' bodies" (Foucault, *Discipline and Punish* 138). These bodies, carrying out activities coded as feminine, become suitable subjects for marriage. Both girls are rewarded for their docility, Shenac by marrying a minister and Maudie through her transformation into a "gracious and noble woman" whose domestic skills demonstrate her fitness for marriage (Marchant, *Heroine* 220). The energy and freedom attributed to Australian, Canadian, and New Zealand girls manifest most often in the recreational pursuits and adventures that are part of many novels. Girls ride horses and bicycles, walk for miles, attend dances, and play various sports. There are, however, limitations on these freedoms; even the modern girls of twentieth-century fiction are subject to the "normalizing judgement" of society, which establishes norms and hold girls to them (Foucault, *Discipline and Punish* 183). Chief among these norms as they relate to girls' bodies is the expectation that marriage and childbearing are the destiny of transnational girls, from colonial to modern.

Spatiality and Girls

The significances attributed to spatiality in colonial texts for girls are imbricated with the geographies of settlement and occupation, the emergence of national identities, and conceptions of the place of girls and women in colonial settings. Although in Australia, Canada, and New Zealand settler populations were located predominantly in developing towns and cities, myths of nationhood in each colony centred upon natural landscapes that became iconic national symbols. In Canada, the locus of identity was the northern wilderness celebrated by the influential artists known as the Group of Seven.[2] Australian mythologies revolved around the bush, the term used in the vernacular to refer to rural and remote regions; in New Zealand, the rugged, mountainous stretches of the South Island defined the nation's self-representation as a pioneer nation. Colonial girl characters who feature in such locations are typically located in domestic settings, such as family homes on pastoral properties. From these homes, boys and men depart to undertake heroic adventures, while girls and women play ancillary roles: cooks, nurses, educators, and admiring witnesses of masculine courage and enterprise. But as books by authors living in Australia, Canada, and New Zealand took precedence in their respective nations' markets over those by British authors, the qualities of energy and independence associated with colonial girls increasingly played out in narratives set in rural locations. These girls – among them Anne Shirley, Norah Linton of the Billabong books, and the Malcolm girls in *Six Little New Zealanders* – feature in narratives that plot girls' development as individuals and as citizens through their engagement with iconic national settings.

Six Little New Zealanders incorporates a trope common in settler society fiction: characters from towns or cities are relocated to rural settings, where they must prove that they are more than pampered, effete city dwellers. Ngaire Malcolm, the first-person narrator of the novel, travels with her five siblings from their home in Auckland to Kamahi, a sheep station in the South Island owned by their two uncles, while their parents visit Britain (referred to as "home") so that their mother can access medical treatment. Kamahi, with its mountainous terrain, river, and

2 Working between 1920 and 1933, the original Group of Seven – Franklin Carmichael, Lawren Harris, A.Y. Jackson, Frank Johnston, Arthur Lismer, J.E.H. MacDonald, and Frederick Varley – produced landscapes notable for their romanticized depictions of the vast expanses of Canada, notably devoid of their Indigenous inhabitants.

luxurious vegetation, offers physical and psychological challenges that both test Ngaire's character and shape her identity as a New Zealand girl. The remote setting constitutes a metonym for the nation, evoking its history and asserting its identity. Ngaire's explorations of the countryside around Kamahi disclose pioneer narratives: the empty house once inhabited by a family, the Morrisons, whose children died of a fever, far from medical assistance, and the flooded river that claimed the life of a young woman who attempted to ford it on her horse. The presence of Māori in the landscape is symbolized through a fraught episode in which Tairoa, a Māori employee at the station, goes "raving mad" when teased by the Malcolm boys and their friends (Glen, *Six* 79). The narrative contrives, however, to pass over this allusion to histories of conflict and warfare, attributing high courage to Ngaire and her sister, who encounter Tairoa and calm him down. The episode thus inserts Ngaire in a lineage of brave pioneer girls and women.

While the narrative lingers on the historical associations of the rural setting, *Six Little New Zealanders* also positions its readers to admire and value the beauty of the landscape, frequently described in rhapsodic tones, such as in Ngaire's description of the station: "Beyond the river lay the bush-clad hills, and beyond these again the wonderful snow-capped mountains, where the sun sank to rest every night, piercing the soft grey mists" (Glen, *Six* 33). The novel ends with the return of Mr and Mrs Malcolm and the family's departure from Kamahi. But the narrative's closure foregrounds the durability of Ngaire's alignment with Kamahi and the bush: Mr Malcolm obtains a position in Christchurch, close enough for Ngaire to spend her holidays with the uncles. The transnational commonalities of early twentieth-century texts for girls are nowhere more obvious than in their celebratory depictions of natural environments: in *Anne of Green Gables* and *A Little Bush Maid,* Anne Shirley and Norah Linton respectively similarly delight in landscapes where reminders of Indigenous displacement are muted or absent.

Raymond Williams observes that the city in twentieth-century British literature is "not only … a form of modern life; it is the physical embodiment of a decisive modern consciousness" (239). The country, in contrast, is often imagined as an idealized state, associated with the past and endowed with qualities that constitute an antidote to modernity. While Williams's analysis focuses squarely on the British context, it chimes with depictions of the city in many of the twentieth-century texts we have discussed. When characters like Montgomery's Emily and Bruce's Kitty move between country and city, their formation as modern girls is often tinged with cultural anxieties about the dangers of the city, and their return to the country constitutes a recuperation of qualities associated with an idealized rural past: stability, security, and simplicity of life. These qualities are readily folded into conceptions of national identity that celebrate settler projects involved with "discovering" and "settling" the land.

In colonial texts, Indigenous girls are commonly linked with the natural environment and attributed with intimate knowledge of the survival skills required to prosper in it. Thus Waihoura in Kingston's *Waihoura* and Indiana in *Canadian Crusoes* are adept at navigating difficult terrains and gathering food to sustain the settler families with whom they travel through the country. In twentieth-century texts, Indigenous girls are absent from rural settings where settlers have established gardens, orchards and farms based on European models. The few texts for younger readers that locate Indigenous girls in places coded as wild or only partially settled – such as Grey Owl's *The Adventures of Sajo and Her Beaver People,* Davison's *Children of the Dark People,* and Gunn's *The Little Black Princess* – proceed from the supposition that the peoples and cultures from which these young girls originate are destined to disappear, being incapable of survival in the modern age. The places where Ngaire, Anne, and Norah develop as citizens of young nations are largely empty of Indigenous presence. Rather, these girls are the new natives, identifying with landscapes used, defined, and named by settler populations.

Transnational Girls and Futurity

Children's literature as a field is powerfully invested in the future: children's books construct characters who typically progress from one state to another, for instance, from childhood to adulthood, or from a position of insecurity to one of enhanced well-being. Narratives close with scenes that encourage young readers to imagine characters inhabiting social worlds that stretch beyond the end of the books and into the future. In addition to this general tendency in books for the young, Australian, Canadian, and New Zealand texts for and about girls between 1840 and 1940 take up cultural agendas that shape their perspectives of girls' future lives as women and citizens of settler societies. Thus many nineteenth-century texts promoted the virtues of migration for girls, pointing to the advantages that lay in the colonies in comparison with overcrowded Britain, such as enhanced marriage prospects and better health. By the turn of the twentieth century, writers in Britain and the former colonies were keenly interested in girlhood, responding to feminist and suffragette movements that sought to wrest power from entrenched masculine interests. These concerns find their way into texts where girls negotiate models of femininity that incorporate education and paid employment as well as family obligations.

As we have noted, the symbolism of mother and child is frequently marshalled in colonial discourses to signify relations between Britain (the "mother country") and her colonies. Girls and women are accorded high importance in settler societies since their roles (present and future) as wives and mothers are central to the formation and survival of new nations. This emphasis on maternity colours depictions of colonial girls, whether they are immigrants to the colonies or born into colonial societies. A striking feature of many of the texts we discuss is that, in many cases, mother figures are dead, absent, or incapable of carrying out their maternal duties. This trope functions as a plot device that places girls in positions where they must carry out roles that mothers might be expected to fill, such as homemaking and taking care of younger siblings. But the absence of mothers also enables depictions of specifically colonial models of motherhood. Norah Linton's progress from "little bush maid" to mother in the Billabong series foregrounds Norah's energy and her love of the physical activities associated with station life. The series calls on her lack of a mother to normalize a model of femininity that involves "masculine" pursuits, such as droving cattle, as well as the conventionally feminine skills associated with the family home. Norah's mother died in childbirth and is present only as a hazy memory, associated with the climbing plants she trained on the verandas at the Billabong station, and the music she loved to play. These associations speak to a version of motherhood centred on homemaking and are consigned to the past; in contrast, Norah's upbringing involves her doing "pretty well whatever she wanted – which meant that she had lived out of doors" (Bruce, *Little* 12). This account of Norah's childhood looks to a future where she will become a woman and mother quite different from her own mother, even as the novel emphasizes what mother and daughter have in common: a love of music and gardens.

At the other end of the scale of absent mothers, Peacocke's *Brenda and the Babes* involves a neglectful mother whose eldest daughter, the eponymous Brenda, is obliged to care for her young siblings while her mother writes romances. This scenario positions readers to sympathize with Brenda when she criticizes her mother for neglecting her duties as a mother, projecting a future in which Brenda, having learned from the negative example at home, will embrace a traditional maternal role when she herself becomes a wife and mother. Just as *Brenda and the Babes* discloses a marked unease about women who prioritize their occupations over their maternal obligations, many texts of the early twentieth century seek to persuade readers to close their ears to the seductive messages of modernity with their siren songs of women's independence and autonomy.

In line with depictions of Indigenous peoples in colonial texts more generally, texts for girls almost always consign Indigenous girls to a past time incompatible with modernity. The "doomed race" theory, which assumed that non-white populations would inevitably yield to settler populations, informed texts for girls until well into the twentieth century, investing depictions of Indigenous girls with an aura of hopelessness and gloom. The figure of Wanda in *The Algonquin Maiden* is a paradigmatic instance of this style of representation, and her suicide functions as a signifier of her incapacity to survive in a world dominated by European settlers. Indiana, in *Canadian Crusoes,* constitutes a curious exception, since, at the end of the novel, she marries the young settler Hector. Presented as something of an afterthought, the novel's description of their wedding attributes agency to Hector, who "presented at the baptismal font as a candidate for baptism, the Indian girl, and then received at the altar his newly baptized bride" (Traill 350), while "the Indian girl" is marshalled into place, her future as a settler's wife hanging in the air. The spectre of miscegenation hovers over the few Indigenous girls who feature in twentieth-century texts, most of which adopt an elegiac tone to depict the inevitable disappearance of Indigenous cultures and people.

We began this book by observing that a culture's beliefs and values can readily be discerned in its texts for the young. In the twenty-first century, girls are scrutinized, judged, and worried over; their clothes, behaviour, and attitudes are subjected to surveillance by adults, and moral panics frequently erupt over aspects of girls' experience. It is clear from our discussions of texts and cultural contexts that girlhood similarly constituted a site of cultural anxiety in Britain, Australia, Canada, and New Zealand between 1840 and 1940. During this period, transnational texts for girls circulated across settler societies, positioning young readers to align with protagonists who modelled behaviour seen as desirable in girls who were to participate in the formation of new nations. In the main, these texts promote relatively conservative views of femininity, imagining girls as future wives and mothers and custodians of cultural values. But the girls who appear as protagonists in these texts often evade and circumvent surveillance, act autonomously, and resist authoritarian orders, as if gesturing towards other possibilities, other ways of being girls. Foucault argues that "one should not assume a massive and primal condition of domination, a binary structure with 'dominators' on one side and 'dominated' on the other" (*Power/Knowledge* 142). The fictive girls we have discussed in this book do not generally wield power; but neither are they powerless, since the fiction in which they appear is informed by the tensions, anxieties, and anomalies of transnational societies.

Bibliography

Primary Texts

Adam, G. Mercer, and A. Ethelwyn Wetherald. *An Algonquin Maiden: A Romance of the Early Days of Upper Canada.* London: Sampson Low, Marston, Searle & Rivington, 1887.

A.F.M. "An Australian Girl." *Argus* 11 Feb. 1899: 10.

Allan, Elizabeth Preston. "At the Sign of the Maple Leaf." *The King's Own* 1 Sept. 1917: 139.

"Anne's Daughter." Rev. of *Rilla of Ingleside* by L.M. Montgomery. *The Mail* 7 Jan. 1922: 10.

"Announcements of English Publishers." *Bookseller and Stationer* 16.9 (Sept. 1900): 12–16.

"An Anzac in a Hospital Ship by a Nurse." *School Journal* (June 1916): 154–9.

"Aunt Tabitha." "The Australian Girl." *Argus* 8 Feb. 1899: 8.

– "The Australian Girl." *Argus* 15 Feb. 1899: 5.

Aylmer, J.E. *Distant Homes; or, The Graham Family in New Zealand.* London: Griffith and Farran, 1862.

Barnicoat, Constance A. "The Reading of the Colonial Girl." *Nineteenth Century and After* 60 (1906): 939–50.

[Barton, Charlotte]. *A Mother's Offering to Her Children by a Lady Long Resident in New South Wales.* 1841. Sydney: Jacaranda Press, 1979.

"'Be Fair, Old Timer,' Says Woman of Fifty." *Toronto Daily Star* 26 Apr. 1921: 10.

Bennett, Ethel Hume. *Judy of York Hill.* Boston: Houghton Mifflin Co., 1922.

"A Book List for Young People." *The Register* 15 Dec. 1923: 4.

"Book Notices." *Otago Daily Times* 13 Feb. 1904: 8.

"Books and Periodicals." *Bookseller and Stationer* 16.12 (Dec. 1900): 5–14.

"Books and Publications: Christmas Reviews." *New Zealand Herald* 15 Dec. 1906: 5.

"Books by Australian Authors." *Kapunda Herald* 29 Aug. 1913: 4.
"The Books Girls Read." *Sydney Morning Herald* 7 Jan. 1878: 3.
Bowman, Anne. *The Kangaroo Hunters.* London: Routledge, 1859.
"Boyet." "Ways of the World." *The Australasian* 11 Feb. 1899: 44.
"British Empire League." *Taranaki Herald* 31 Mar. 1909: 7.
"British Ideals Must Triumph." *Grain Growers' Guide* 12 Aug. 1915: 1.
Bruce, Mary Grant. *Captain Jim.* London: Ward, Lock & Co., 1919.
– *From Billabong to London.* London: Ward, Lock & Co., 1915.
– *Golden Fiddles.* London: Ward, Lock & Co., 1928.
– *Jim and Wally.* London: Ward, Lock & Co., 1916.
– *A Little Bush Maid.* 1910. London and Melbourne: Ward, Lock & Co., 1967.
"The Capture of German Samoa by the New Zealand Expeditionary Force." *School Journal* (Oct. 1914): 274–80.
Census of England and Wales 1871, General Report: "Population." 1873. *A Vision of Britain through Time.* Web. 12 March 2016. <http://www.visionofbritain.org.uk/census/EW1871GEN/3?show=ALL>.
Chadwick, Bessie M. "To a Little Eskimo." *Pleasant Hours: A Paper for Canadian Girls* 30 Oct. 1926: 175.
"Children's Corner." *Daily Mercury* 13 Jan. 1945: 5.
"Christmas Gift Books." *The Australasian* 10 Dec. 1927: 8.
"Christmas Presents." *Evening Star* 8 Jan. 1887: 1.
"Close of Women's Institutes Convention." *Charlottetown Guardian* 8 Nov. 1919: 1.
"Constant Reader." *Otago Daily Times* 14 Jan. 1922: 2.
Craw, Evelyn. "Canadian Girls in Training: Canada's Mixing Bowl." *Pleasant Hours: A Paper for Canadian Girls* 26 Nov. 1927: 190.
– "The Teen-Age Girl in Canada." *The Canadian Girl* 8 June 1935: 178–9.
Creighton, Mrs. "To the Girls of the Empire: The Call to Service." *The Empire Annual for Girls* (1911): 39–44. *Internet Archive.* Web. 1 Feb. 2016. <https://archive.org/details/theempireannualf18661gut>.
"'Critics Miss Point' Is Old-Timer's Reply." *Toronto Daily Star* 30 Apr. 1921: 13.
Cupples, Ann Jane. *The Redfords: An Emigrant Story.* London: Blackie & Son, [1886].
Davison, Frank Dalby. *Children of the Dark People.* Sydney: Angus & Robertson, 1936.
"Dog Toby." "The Antipodean Girl." *Auckland Star* 4 Sept. 1909: 11.
Dwyer, Vera G. *With Beating Wings: An Australian Story.* London: Ward, Lock & Co., 1913.
"Eaton's Daily Store News." *The Globe* 9 Dec. 1911: 32.
Embree, Beatrice. *The Girls of Miss Clevelands'.* Toronto: Musson Book Co., 1920.

"Empire Day." *School Journal* (June 1916): 138–46.
Garrard, Phillis. *Doings of Hilda.* London: Blackie & Son, 1932.
– *Hilda at School: A New Zealand Story.* London: Blackie & Son, [1929].
"Gift-Books: Stories for Girls." *The Spectator* 9 Dec. 1916: 737–8.
"Girls at Play." *The Young New Zealander and Schools' Gazette* 11 Sept. 1924: 33.
"The Girls of New Zealand." *Otago Witness* 25 Nov. 1887: 33.
Glen, Esther. *Robin of Maoriland.* Auckland: Whitcombe & Tombs, 1929.
– *Six Little New Zealanders.* London: Cassell & Co., 1917.
Gourlay, Reginald. "The Canadian Girl." *The Canadian Magazine* 7.6 (1896): 506–10.
"Grafton, Garth" [Sara Jeannette Duncan]. "Woman's World." Rev. of *An Algonquin Maiden* by G. Mercer Adam and A. Ethelwyn Wetherald. *The Globe* 13 Jan. 1887: 6.
"Grey Owl" [Archibald Stansfeld Belaney]. *The Adventures of Sajo and Her Beaver People.* London: Lovat Dickson & Thompson, 1935.
Gunn, Mrs Aeneas. *The Little Black Princess of the Never-Never.* 1905. Sydney: Angus & Robertson, 1962.
Hanray, Lawrence. "The British Empire Girl." Music by J. Clifton Solomon. London: Phillips and Page, 1907.
Harcus, Edna. "The Young Canada Club." *Grain Growers' Guide* 14 June 1916: 28.
Haverfield, E.L. *Queensland Cousins.* London: Thomas Nelson and Sons, 1908.
"Here and There." *Victoria Daily Colonist* 9 Sept. 1909: 8.
"H.M.S. 'New Zealand' at the Battle of Jutland." *School Journal* (Aug. 1916): 217–21.
"H.M.S. 'New Zealand' in the North Sea Fight." *School Journal* (June 1915): 158–9.
"Humming Bee" [Lucy Gullett]. "A Parcel of Girls' Books." *The Australasian* 21 Feb. 1885: 343.
Inter-Imperial Relations Committee. *Balfour Declaration.* London: Imperial Conference, 1926.
"James Adams & Co." *The Young New Zealander and Schools' Gazette* 11 Sept. 1924: 42.
Jamieson, Molly E. *Ruby: A Story of the Australian Bush.* London: Society for Promoting Christian Knowledge, 1898.
Kenyon, Edith C. *A Girl from Canada.* London: Religious Tract Society, 1911.
Kingston, W.H.G. *Milicent Courtenay's Diary; or The Experiences of a Young Lady at Home and Abroad.* London: Gall & Inglis, 1873.
– *Waihoura, the Maori Girl.* London: Gall & Inglis, 1872.
"The Letter Box." *Daily Herald* 31 Dec. 1921: 3.
"Literature: Notes on New Books." *Examiner* 18 Oct. 1913: 8.
"Literature: Publications Received." *The Queenslander* 12 Dec. 1903: 59.

Loch, Henry. "Education in the Colonies." *Progress in Women's Education in the British Empire: Being the Report of the Education Section, Victorian Era Exhibition, 1897*. Ed. Frances Evelyn Warwick. London: Longmans, Green and Co., 1898. 285–8.

Lorne, Lord (John Campbell). "Education in Canada." *Progress in Women's Education in the British Empire: Being the Report of the Education Section, Victorian Era Exhibition, 1897*. Ed. Frances Evelyn Warwick. London: Longmans, Green and Co., 1898. 288–95.

"Louise Mack: Death of Australian Novelist and Poetess." *Western Mail* 23 Jan. 1936: 35.

Low, Florence B. "The Reading of the Modern Girl." *Nineteenth Century and After* 59 (Feb. 1906): 278–87.

L.S.B. "A Maori Princess: Te Rangi Pai." *The Girls' Empire* 1 (1902): 89–90.

Mack, Louise. *Teens: A Story of Australian Schoolgirls*. Sydney: Angus & Robertson, 1897.

Mackness, Constance. *Di-Double-Di*. Sydney: Cornstalk Publishing, 1929.

"Maclellan and Co." *The Age* 12 Dec. 1919: 5.

Marchant, Bessie. *A Countess from Canada: A Story of Life in the Backwoods*. London: Blackie & Son, 1911.

– *The Ferry House Girls*. London: Blackie & Son, 1912.

– *A Girl of the Fortunate Isles*. London: Blackie & Son, 1906.

– *A Heroine of the Sea*. London: Blackie & Son, [1904].

– *Sally Makes Good*. London: Blackie & Son, 1920.

McClung, Nellie. *Purple Springs*. Toronto: Thomas Allen, 1921.

– *The Second Chance*. Toronto: William Briggs, 1910.

– *Sowing Seeds in Danny*. Toronto: William Briggs, 1908.

Meyer, Olga P. *The Four of Us: New Zealand School-Girls' Story*. Auckland: Unity Press, 1935.

"Miss Modern Girl Answers Old-Timer." *Toronto Daily Star* 25 Apr. 1921: 10.

"Modern Girl." *The Brisbane Telegraph* 17 July 1919: 3.

"The Modern Girl." *The Horsham Times* 29 Apr. 1910: 7.

"The Modern Girl." *West Gippsland Gazette* 6 June 1911: 6.

"The Modern Girl: Manifestations of Feminine Independence." *Marlborough Express* 26 Jan. 1910: 3.

Montgomery, L.M. *Anne of Green Gables*. 1908. Ed. Cecily Devereux. Peterborough, ON: Broadview Press, 2004.

– *Emily Climbs*. New York: Frederick A. Stokes Company, 1925.

– *Emily of New Moon*. New York: Frederick A. Stokes Company, 1923.

– *Emily's Quest*. London: Hodder & Stoughton, [1927?].

– *Further Chronicles of Avonlea*. Boston: The Page Company, 1920.

– "How I Became a Writer." *Manitoba Free Press* 3 Dec. 1921: 3.
– *Rilla of Ingleside.* New York: A.L. Burt, 1921.
Moule, Handley C.G. "To My Friends the Readers." *The Empire Annual for Australian Girls* 3 (1910): 9–12.
Rev. of *My Friend Phil,* by Isabel Maud Peacocke. *Gippsland Mercury* 24 Sept. 1915: 6.
"My Post Bag." *Catholic Press* 4 Mar. 1915: 42–3.
"Myra." "The Social Sphere." *Observer* 22 Feb. 1919: 8.
"New Books and Publications." *The Press* 16 Dec. 1911: 7.
"New Fiction." Rev. of *Captain Cub* by Ethel Turner. *Sydney Morning Herald* 20 Oct. 1917: 8.
"New Items in Christmas Books." *Victoria Daily Colonist* 2 Dec. 1909: 18.
"New Novels." *The Advertiser* 31 Oct. 1913: 13.
"A New Writer." *The Register* 11 Oct. 1913: 4.
"New Zealand Children's Motor Ambulances at the Front." *School Journal,* Part II (June 1916): 207–15.
"New Zealand Writers." *Evening Post* 24 Dec. 1927: 21.
"Old-Timer Denounces Slangy Modern Girl." *Toronto Daily Star* 20 Apr. 1921: 10.
"Other Novels." *The Queenslander* 14 Jan. 1922: 3.
"Our Australian Cousin." *Punch; or The London Charivari* 25 Jan. 1868: 44.
"Our Mail Bag." *Pleasant Hours: A Paper for Canadian Girls* 24 Apr. 1915: 67.
"Over the Tea-Cups." *Auckland Star* 30 Apr. 1910: 16.
"Paperknife." "Books and Authors." *Hearth and Home* 14 May 1896: 30.
Peacocke, Isabel Maud. *The Adopted Family.* London and Melbourne: Ward, Lock & Co., 1923.
– *Brenda and the Babes.* London: Ward, Lock & Co., 1927.
– *Robin of the Round House.* London: Ward, Lock & Co., 1918.
Pedley, Ethel. *Dot and the Kangaroo.* 1899. London: Thomas Burleigh, 1900.
"Playmate." "Children's Columns for Boys and Girls Who Read the 'Catholic Press.'" *Catholic Press* 18 Feb. 1915: 42.
Praed, Rosa Campbell. "The Australian Girl." *The Girl's Realm* 1 (1899): 249–53.
"Prefers 'Half Loaf' to No Reform At All." *Toronto Daily Star* 15 Apr. 1921: 12.
"The Publishers' Syndicate." *Bookseller and Stationer* 17.1 (Jan. 1901): 9.
"Recent Novels." *The Times* 4 Aug. 1896: 5.
Reeves, W.P. "Education in New Zealand." *Progress in Women's Education in the British Empire: Being the Report of the Education Section, Victorian Era Exhibition, 1897.* Ed. Frances Evelyn Warwick. London: Longmans, Green and Co., 1898. 307–20.
"Reviews: Christmas Prize Books." *The Mercury* 30 Nov. 1903: 2.
Richardson, Henry Handel [Ethel Florence Lindesay Richardson]. *The Getting of Wisdom.* 1910. Camberwell: Penguin, 2009.

Robertson, Margaret Murray. *Shenac's Work at Home: A Story of Canadian Life.* London: Religious Tract Society, 1866.

Salmon, Edward. "What Girls Read." *The Nineteenth Century* 20.116 (1886): 515–29.

Sanford, Mary Bourchier. *The Young Gordons in Canada.* London: Religious Tract Society, 1913.

Sclater, J.R.P. "The Dew on the Grass." *The Canadian Girl* 4 Jan. 1930: 4.

– "He Shall Have Dominion Also from Sea to Sea." *Pleasant Hours: A Paper for Canadian Girls* 30 June 1928: n.p.

Shannon, William, ed. *The United Empire Minstrel: A Selection of the Best National, Constitutional and Loyal Orange Songs and Poems.* Toronto: Henry Rowsell, 1852.

Skelton, Henrietta. *Grace Morton.* Toronto: A.S. Irving, 1873.

Stuart, Esmé. *Harum Scarum: A Poor Relation.* 1896. London: Jarrold & Sons, 1898.

"Tasma." "Tasma's Letter." *Clarence and Richmond Examiner* 18 Mar. 1899: 4.

Tate, Frank. "Our Debt to Our Soldiers: An Open Letter to the Children of Victoria from the Director of Education (20 March 1916)." *School Paper* April 1916: 1–4.

"Testimony to the Judgment and Diligence of Australian Soldiers." *School Paper* Nov. 1916: 157–8.

Thompson, Dora Olive. *Adele in Search of a Home.* London: The "Girl's Own Paper" Office, 1920.

Tracy, Mona. *Piriki's Princess and Other Stories of New Zealand.* Auckland: Whitcombe & Tombs, [1925].

Traill, Catharine Parr. *Canadian Crusoes: A Tale of the Rice Lake Plains.* London: Arthur Hall, Virtue & Co., 1852.

Turner, Ethel. *Brigid and the Cub.* London: Ward, Lock & Co., 1919.

– *Captain Cub.* London: Ward, Lock & Co., 1917.

– *The Cub.* London: Ward, Lock & Co., 1915.

– *Mother's Little Girl.* London: Ward, Lock & Co., 1904.

– *Seven Little Australians.* London: Ward, Lock & Bowden, 1894.

Turner, Lilian. *Paradise and the Perrys.* London: Ward, Lock & Co., 1908.

"The Undomesticated Modern Girl." *Telegraph* 23 Aug. 1912: 2.

"A Wandering Briton." "In Praise of Canada." *The Empire Annual for Australian Girls* 3 (1910): 333–6.

"War Notes." *School Journal* 8, no. 8 (Sept. 1914): 250–6.

Warwick, Countess of (Frances Evelyn Greville), ed. *Progress in Women's Education in the British Empire: Being the Report of the Education Section, Victorian Era Exhibition, 1897.* London: Longmans, Green, and Co., 1898.

"What a Girl May Do." *Barrier Miner* 26 Apr. 1913: 7.

"What Colonial Girls Read." *The Age* 5 Jan. 1907: 18.

– *Evening Post* 12 Jan. 1907: 4.
– *Otago Witness* 13 Feb. 1907: 74.
Wilde, Oscar. "New Novels." *Pall Mall Gazette* 28 Oct. 1886: 4.
Williams, Henry. "The Most Beautiful City in the Empire: Which Is It?" *The Empire Annual for Australian Girls* 3 (1910): 194–201.
"With Beating Wings." *Daily Herald* 6 Mar. 1913: 4.
"The Wohelo Group of Canadian Girls in Training." *Pleasant Hours: A Paper for Canadian Girls* 30 June 1928: n.p.
"Woman's Interests: Books for Girls." *West Australian* 16 Dec. 1927: 8.
"Women in War." *School Journal* (Mar. 1916): 34–41.
"The Young Canada Club." *Grain Growers' Guide* 19 July 1916: 28.
"The Young Folk." *The Australasian* 2 Aug. 1919: 248.
"The Young Folk: Answers and Letters." *The Australasian* 5 Oct. 1918: 688.
"The Young Folk: Answers and Letters." *The Australasian* 10 Mar. 1923: 512.

Secondary Texts

Alexander, Kristine. "An Honour and a Burden: Canadian Girls and the Great War." *A Sisterhood of Suffering and Service: Women and Girls of Canada and Newfoundland during the First World War.* Ed. Sarah Glassford and Amy J. Shaw. Vancouver: University of British Columbia Press, 2012. 173–94.
Allen, Ann Taylor. "Lost in Translation? Women's History in Transnational and Comparative Perspective." *Comparative Women's History: New Approaches.* Ed. Anne Cova. Boulder, CO: Social Science Monographs, 2006. 87–115.
Alston, Annette. *The Family in English Children's Literature.* New York: Routledge, 2008.
Anderson, Benedict. *Imagined Communities: Reflections on the Origin and Spread of Nationalism.* 2nd ed. London: Verso, 2006.
Anderson, Kristine J. "Children's Literature in English Translation." *Encyclopedia of Literary Translation into English: A–L.* Ed. Olive Class. London: Fitzroy Dearborn, 2000. 276–8.
Appadurai, Arjun. *Modernity at Large: Cultural Dimensions of Globalization.* Minneapolis: University of Minnesota Press, 1996.
Archibald, Diana. *Domesticity, Imperialism, and Emigration in the Victorian Novel.* Columbia and London: University of Missouri Press, 2002.
Ashcroft, Bill. "Beyond the Nation: Australian Literature as World Literature." *Scenes of Reading: Is Australian Literature a World Literature?* Ed. Robert Dixon and Brigid Rooney. Melbourne: Australian Scholarly Publishing, 2013. 34–46.
Ashcroft, Bill, Gareth Griffiths, and Helen Tiffin. *Post-Colonial Studies: The Key Concepts.* London: Routledge, 1998.

Atwood, Margaret. *Survival: A Thematic Guide to Canadian Literature.* Toronto: House of Anansi Press, 1972.

Axelrod, Paul. *The Promise of Schooling: Education in Canada, 1800–1914.* Toronto: University of Toronto Press, 1994.

Bal, Mieke. *Narratology: Introduction to the Theory of Narrative.* 3rd ed. Toronto: University of Toronto Press, 2009.

Beaumont, Joan. "Australian Citizenship and the Two World Wars." *Australian Journal of Politics and History* 53.2 (2007): 171–82.

Beetham, Margaret. *A Magazine of Her Own? Domesticity and Desire in the Woman's Magazine, 1800–1914.* London: Routledge, 1996.

Behlmer, George J. *Friends of the Family: The English Home and Its Guardians, 1850–1940.* Stanford, CA: University of Stanford Press, 1998.

Bhabha, Homi. "Of Mimicry and Man: The Ambivalence of Colonial Discourse." *October* 28 (1984): 125–33.

Bode, Katherine. *Reading by Numbers: Recalibrating the Literary Field.* London: Anthem, 2012.

Bones, Helen. "'A book is a book, all the world over': New Zealand and the Colonial Writing World 1890–1945." *Journal of Imperial and Commonwealth History* 43.5 (2015): 861–81.

Bradford, Clare. "Children's Literature in a Global Age: Transnational and Local Identities." *Nordic Journal of ChildLit Aesthetics* 2 (2011): 20–34.

– "'My blarsted greenstone throne!': Māori Princesses and Nationhood in New Zealand Fiction for Girls." *Colonial Girlhood in Literature, Culture and History, 1840–1950.* Ed. Kristine Moruzi and Michelle J. Smith. Houndmills, UK: Palgrave Macmillan, 2014. 95–109.

– *Unsettling Narratives: Postcolonial Readings of Children's Literature.* Waterloo, ON: Wilfrid Laurier University Press, 2007.

Bratton, J.S. "Of England, Home and Duty: The Image of England in Victorian and Edwardian Juvenile Fiction." *Imperialism and Popular Culture.* Ed. John M. Mackenzie. Manchester: Manchester University Press, 1986. 73–93.

Buckner, Phillip. "Introduction: Canada and the British Empire." *Canada and the British Empire.* Ed. Phillip Buckner. *Oxford Scholarship Online,* 2011. Web. 17 June 2016.

Burton, Antoinette. *Burdens of History: British Feminists, Indian Women, and Imperial Culture, 1865–1915.* Chapel Hill, NC: University of North Carolina Press, 1994.

– "Contesting the Zenana: The Mission to Make 'Lady Doctors for India,' 1874–1885." *The Journal of British Studies* 35.3 (1996): 368–97.

– "Introduction: The Unfinished Business of Colonial Modernities." *Gender, Sexuality and Colonial Modernities.* Ed. Antoinette Burton. London: Routledge, 1999. 1–16.

Butler, Judith. *Gender Trouble: Feminism and the Subversion of Identity*. New York: Routledge, 2006.

Cadogan, Mary, and Patricia Craig. *Women and Children First: The Fiction of Two World Wars*. London: Victor Gollancz Ltd., 1978.

Canada's Early Women Writers. SFU Library Digital Collections. Burnaby, BC: Simon Fraser University, 1980–2014. Web. 15 Nov. 2015. <http://digital.lib.sfu.ca/ceww-collection>.

"Censuses of Canada 1665 to 1871: Estimated population of Canada, 1605 to present." Statistics Canada, 2013. Web. 18 Nov. 2015. <http://www.statcan.gc.ca/pub/98-187-x/4151287-eng.htm>.

Clarke, Patricia. *Pen Portraits: Women Writers and Journalists in Nineteenth-Century Australia*. North Sydney: Allen & Unwin, 1988.

Coates, Donna. "Guns 'n' Roses: Australian Women Writers' Bold-and-Not-So-Bold Journeys into the Great War." *Journal of the Association for the Study of Australian Literature* (1994): 120–6.

Connelly, M.P. "Women in the Labour Force." *The Canadian Encyclopedia*. Toronto: Historica Canada, 2006. Web. 6 Aug 2016.

Cooper, Ronda. "Landscape." *The Oxford Companion to New Zealand Literature*. Ed. Roger Robsinson and Nelson Wattie. Oxford: Oxford University Press, 1998. Online 2006.

Dacorum Heritage Trust Ltd. "Colonal Francis Brereton." *The Dacorum Heritage Trust: The History of Berkhamsted, Hemel Hempstead, Kings Langley and Tring*. Web. 25 June 2014. <www.dacorumheritage.org.uk>.

Davey, Ian E. "The Rhythm of Work and the Rhythm of School." *Histories of Canadian Children and Youth*. Ed. Nancy Janovicek and Joy Parr. Toronto: Oxford University Press, 2003. 108–21.

Devereux, Cecily. "Fashioning the Colonial Girl: 'Made in Britain' Femininity in the Imperial Archive." *Colonial Girlhood in Literature, Culture and History, 1840–1950*. Ed. Kristine Moruzi and Michelle J. Smith. Houndmills, UK: Palgrave Macmillan, 2014. 30–44.

– *Growing a Race: Nellie McClung and the Fiction of Eugenic Feminism*. Montréal and Kingston: McGill-Queen's University Press, 2005.

– "New Woman, New World: Maternal Feminism and the New Imperialism in the White Settler Colonies." *Women's Studies International Forum* 22.2 (1999): 175–84.

– "A Note on the Text." *Anne of Green Gables*. By L.M. Montgomery. Ed. Cecily Devereux. Peterborough, ON: Broadview Press, 2004. 42–50.

Distad, Merrill. "Newspapers and Magazines." *History of the Book in Canada, Vol. 2: 1840–1918*. Ed. Yvan Lamonde, Patricia Lockhart Fleming, and Fiona A. Black. Toronto: University of Toronto Press, 2005. 293–303.

Donaldson, Laura E. *Decolonizing Feminisms: Race, Gender, and Empire-Building.* Chapel Hill, NC: University of North Carolina Press, 1992.

Dunlap, Thomas R. *Nature and the English Diaspora: Environment and History in the United States, Canada, Australia, and New Zealand.* Cambridge: Cambridge University Press, 1999.

Eddy, John, and Deryck Schreuder. "Introduction: Colonies into 'New Nations.'" *The Rise of Colonial Nationalism: Australia, New Zealand, Canada and South Africa First Assert Their Nationalities, 1880–1914.* Ed. John Eddy and Deryck Schreuder. Sydney: Allen & Unwin, 1988. 1–16.

Edwards, Gail, and Judith Saltman. *Picturing Canada: A History of Canadian Children's Illustrated Books and Publishing.* Toronto: University of Toronto Press, 2010.

Edwards, Owen Dudley, and Jennifer H. Litster. "The End of Canadian Innocence: L.M. Montgomery and the First World War." *L.M. Montgomery and Canadian Culture.* Ed. Irene Gammel and Elizabeth Epperly. Toronto: University of Toronto Press, 1999. 31–46.

Epperly, Elizabeth Rollins. *The Fragrance of Sweet-Grass: L.M. Montgomery's Heroines and the Pursuit of Romance.* Toronto: University of Toronto Press, 1992.

Fabian, Johannes. *Time and the Other: How Anthropology Makes Its Object.* New York: Columbia University Press, 1983.

Felski, Rita. *The Gender of Modernity.* Cambridge, MA: Harvard University Press, 1995.

Fisher, Susan R. *Boys and Girls in No Man's Land: English-Canadian Children and the First World War.* Toronto: University of Toronto Press, 2011.

Flint, Kate. *The Woman Reader, 1837–1914.* Oxford: Clarendon Press, 1993.

Foucault, Michel. *Discipline and Punish: The Birth of the Prison.* Trans. Alan Sheridan. New York: Vintage, 1977.

– *Power/Knowledge: Selected Interviews and Other Writings, 1972–1977.* Ed. Colin Gordon. New York: Pantheon, 1980.

Francis, Daniel. *The Imaginary Indian: The Image of the Indian in Canadian Culture.* Vancouver: Arsenal Pulp Press, 1997.

Freeman, Victoria. "Attitudes Toward 'Miscegenation' in Canada, the United States, New Zealand, and Australia, 1860–1914." *Native Studies Review* 16.1 (2005): 41–69.

Friedman, Susan Stanford. "Locational Feminism: Gender, Cultural Geographies, and Geopolitical Literary." *Feminist Locations: Global and Local, Theory and Practice.* New Brunswick, NJ: Rutgers University Press, 2001. 13–36.

Frye, Northrop. "Conclusion to a *Literary History of Canada.*" *The Bush Garden: Essays on the Canadian Imagination.* Concord, ON: House of Anansi Press, 1995. 215–53.

Galway, Elizabeth. *From Nursery Rhymes to Nationhood: Children's Literature and the Constructions of Canadian Identity.* New York: Routledge, 2008.

Gelder, Ken, and Rachael Weaver. "Colonial Australian Romance Fiction." *The Anthology of Colonial Australian Romance Fiction.* Carlton, VIC: Melbourne University Publishing, 2010. 1–11.

Gerson, Carole. *Canadian Women in Print, 1750–1918.* Waterloo, ON: Wilfred Laurier University Press, 2010.

– "'Dragged at Anne's Chariot Wheels': L.M. Montgomery and the Sequels to *Anne of Green Gables.*" *Papers of the Bibliographical Society of Canada* 35.2 (1997): 143–59.

– "Literature of Settlement." *The Cambridge History of Canadian Literature.* Ed. Coral Ann Howells and Eva-Marie Kröller. Cambridge: Cambridge University Press, 2009. 87–103.

Gilderdale, Betty. "Children's Literature." *The Oxford History of New Zealand Literature in English.* 2nd ed. Ed. Terry Sturm. Auckland: Oxford University Press, 1998. 525–74.

– "Colonial and Postcolonial Children's Literature: New Zealand." *Children's Literature: An Illustrated History.* Ed. Peter Hunt. Oxford: Oxford University Press, 1995. 343–51.

– *A Sea Change: 145 Years of New Zealand Junior Fiction.* Auckland: Longman Paul, 1982.

Giles, Paul. "Transnationalism and National Literatures: The Case of Australia." *Journal of the Association for the Study of Australian Literature* 15.3 (2016): 1–7.

Goldie, Terry. *Fear and Temptation: The Image of the Indigene in Canadian, Australian and New Zealand Literatures.* Montréal and Kingston: McGill-Queen's University Press, 1989.

Grant, Kevin, Philippa Levine, and Frank Trentmann. "Introduction." *Beyond Sovereignty: Britain, Empire and Transnationalism, c. 1880–1950.* Ed. Kevin Grant, Philippa Levine, and Frank Trentmann. Houndmills, UK: Palgrave Macmillan, 2007. 1–15.

Grimshaw, Patricia. "Women and the Legacy of Britain's Imperial 'Civilising Mission' in New Zealand, 1894–1914." *Britishness Abroad: Transnational Movements and Imperial Cultures.* Ed. Kate Darian-Smith, Patricia Grimshaw, and Stuart Macintyre. Carlton, VIC: Melbourne University Press, 2007. 169–86.

– *Women's Suffrage in New Zealand.* 2nd edition. Auckland: Auckland University Press, 1987.

Griswold, Jerry. *The Classic American Children's Story: Novels of the Golden Age.* New York: Penguin, 1996.

Haebich, Anna. "Forgetting Indigenous Histories: Cases from the History of Australia's Stolen Generations." *Journal of Social History* 44.4 (2011): 1033–46.

Haggis, Jane. "White Women and Colonialism: Towards a Non-Recuperative History." *Gender and Imperialism.* Ed. Clare Midgley. Manchester: Manchester University Press, 1998. 45–75.

Hall, Catherine. "Culture and Identity in Imperial Britain." *The British Empire: Themes and Perspectives.* Ed. Sarah Stockwell. Malden, MA: Blackwell Publishing, 2009. 199–217.

Hassam, Andrew. *Through Australian Eyes: Colonial Perceptions of Imperial Britain.* Carlton, VIC: Melbourne University Press, 2000.

Hendley, Matthew C. *Organized Patriotism and the Crucible of War: Popular Imperialism in Britain, 1914–1932.* Montréal and Kingston: McGill-Queen's University Press, 2012.

Howells, Coral Ann, and Eva-Marie Kröller. "Introduction." *The Cambridge History of Canadian Literature.* Ed. Coral Ann Howells and Eva-Marie Kröller. Cambridge: Cambridge University Press, 2009. 1–6.

Huggan, Graham. *Australian Literature: Postcolonialism, Racism, Transnationalism.* Oxford: Oxford University Press, 2007.

Hunt, Peter. "Retreatism and Advance (1914–45)." *Children's Literature: An Illustrated History.* Ed. Peter Hunt. Oxford: Oxford University Press, 1995. 192–224.

Jacklin, Michael. "The Transnational Turn in Australian Literary Studies." *Journal of the Association for the Study of Australian Literature.* Special Issue: Australian Literature in a Global World (2009): 1–14.

Jay, Paul. *Global Matters: The Transnational Turn in Literary Studies.* Ithaca and London: Cornell University Press, 2010.

Jenkins, Elwyn. *South Africa in English-Language Children's Literature, 1814–1912.* Jefferson, NC: McFarland, 2002.

Johnson, Deirdre. *Edward Stratemeyer and the Stratemeyer Syndicate.* New York: Twayne Publishers, 1993.

Kaufmann, Eric. "'Naturalizing the Nation': The Rise of Naturalistic Nationalism in the United States and Canada." *Comparative Studies in Society and History* 40.4 (1998): 666–95.

Kennedy, Rosie. *The Children's War: Britain, 1914–1918.* Houndmills, UK: Palgrave Macmillan, 2014.

Kingsbury, Celia Malone. *For Home and Country: World War I Propaganda on the Home Front.* Lincoln, NE: University of Nebraska Press, 2010.

Lake, Marilyn. *Getting Equal: The History of Australian Feminism.* St Leonards, NSW: Allen & Unwin, 1999.

Lake, Marilyn, and Henry Reynolds. *Drawing the Global Colour Line: White Men's Countries and the International Challenge of Racial Equality.* Cambridge: Cambridge University Press, 2008.

Lamond, Julieanne. "Zones of Connection: Common Reading in a Regional Australian Library." *Print Culture Histories beyond the Metropolis*. Ed. James J. Connolly, Patrick Collier, Frank Felsenstein, Kenneth R. Hall, and Robert G. Hall. Toronto: University of Toronto Press, 2016. 355–74.

Lemon, Barbara. "Women Journalists in Australian History." *The Women's Pages: Australian Women and Journalism since 1850*. Web. 15 July 2016.

Levine, Philippa, ed. *Gender and Empire*. Oxford: Oxford University Press, 2004.

Lewis, Norah. *"I want to join your club": Letters from Rural Children, 1900–1920*. Ed. Norah Lewis. Waterloo, ON: Wilfred Laurier University Press, 1996.

Locher-Scholten, Elsbeth. "Gender." *The Ashgate Research Companion to Modern Imperial Histories*. Ed. Philippa Levine and John Marriott. Farnham, UK: Ashgate, 2012. 449–70.

Lyons, Martyn. "Introduction." *A History of the Book in Australia, 1891–1945: A National Culture in a Colonised Market*. Ed. Martyn Lyons and John Arnold. St Lucia, QLD: University of Queensland Press, 2001. xiii–xix.

Mackay, Jane, and Pat Thane. "The Englishwoman." *Englishness: Politics and Culture 1880–1920*. Ed. Robert Colls and Philip Dodd. London: Croom Helm, 1986. 191–229.

Magarey, Susan. *Passions of the First Wave Feminists*. Sydney: University of New South Wales Press, 2001.

McCallum, Janet. "Barnicoat, Constance Alice." *Te Ara: The Encyclopedia of New Zealand*. 30 Oct. 2012. Web. 17 June 2014. <https://TeAra.govt.nz/en/biographies/3b10/barnicoat-constance-alice>.

McClintock, Anne. *Imperial Leather: Race, Gender and Sexuality in the Colonial Contest*. New York: Routledge, 1995.

McGrath, Leslie. "Print for Young Readers." *History of the Book in Canada, Vol. 2: 1840–1918*. Toronto: University of Toronto Press, 2005. 401–8.

McGregor, Russell. "Degrees of Fatalism: Discourses on Racial Extinction in Australia and New Zealand." *Collisions of Cultures and Identities: Settlers and Indigenous Peoples*. Ed. Patricia Grimshaw and Russell McGregor. Parkville, VIC: History Department, University of Melbourne, 2006. 194–208.

– *Imagined Destinies: Aboriginal Australians and the Doomed Race Theory, 1880–1939*. Carlton, VIC: Melbourne University Press, 1997.

McKenzie, Andrea. "A 'Revolutionary' War: Girls Writing Girls in America's *St Nicholas Magazine*." *Children's Literature and Culture of the First World War*. Ed. Lissa Paul, Rosemary R. Johnston, and Emma Short. New York and London: Routledge, 2016. 60–76.

Mitchell, Sally. *The New Girl: Girls' Culture in Victorian England, 1880–1915*. New York: Columbia University Press, 1995.

Morton, Peter. *Lusting for London: Australian Expatriate Writers at the Hub of Empire, 1870–1950*. New York: Palgrave Macmillan, 2011.

Moruzi, Kristine. "'The freedom suits me': Encouraging Girls to Settle in the Colonies." *Relocating Victorian Settler Narratives: Transatlantic and Transpacific Views in the Long Nineteenth Century*. Ed. Tamara Wagner. London: Pickering & Chatto, 2011. 177–92.

Mount, Nick. *When Canadian Literature Moved to New York*. Toronto: University of Toronto Press, 2005.

Myers, Janet C. *Antipodal England: Emigration and Portable Domesticity in the Victorian Imagination*. New York: State University of New York Press, 2009.

Nelson, Claudia. *Little Strangers: Portrayals of Adoption and Foster Care in America, 1850–1929*. Bloomington and Indianapolis: Indian University Press, 2003.

New, W.H. *A History of Canadian Literature*. Montréal and Kingston: McGill-Queen's University Press, 2003.

Newbolt, Peter. "Henty, George Alfred (1832–1902)." *Oxford Dictionary of National Biography*. Oxford: Oxford University Press, 2004. Online ed., May 2006. Web. 25 June 2014. <http://www.oxforddnb.com/index/33/101033827>.

Niall, Brenda. *Australia through the Looking-Glass: Children's Fiction, 1830–1980*. Carlton, VIC: Melbourne University Press, 1984.

Nile, Richard, and David Walker. "The Paternoster Row Machine and the Australian Book Trade, 1890–1945." *A History of the Book in Australia, 1891–1945: A National Culture in a Colonised Market*. Ed. Martyn Lyons and John Arnold. St Lucia, QLD: University of Queensland Press, 2001. 3–18.

Nolan, Melanie. "Putting the State in Its Place: The Domestic Education Debate in New Zealand." *History of Education* 30.1 (2001): 13–33.

O'Malley, Andrew. "Island Homemaking: Catharine Parr Traill's *Canadian Crusoes* and the Robinsonade Tradition." *Home Words: Discourses of Children's Literature in Canada*. Ed. Mavis Reimer. Waterloo, ON: Wilfrid Laurier University Press, 2008. 67–86.

Paisley, Fiona. "Childhood and Race: Growing Up in the Empire." *Gender and Empire*. Ed. Phillipa Levine. Oxford: Oxford University Press, 2004. 240–59.

Paris, Michael. *Over the Top: The Great War and Juvenile Literature in Britain*. Westport, CT: Praeger, 2004.

Parkins, Wendy. *Mobility and Modernity in Women's Novels, 1850s–1930s: Women Moving Dangerously*. Houndmills, UK: Palgrave Macmillan, 2009.

Peters, Laura. *Orphan Texts: Victorian Orphans, Culture and Empire*. Manchester and New York: Manchester University Press, 2000.

Phillips, Richard. *Mapping Men and Empire: A Geography of Adventure.* London: Routledge, 1997.

Pickles, Katie. *Female Imperialism and National Identity: The Imperial Order Daughters of the Empire.* Manchester: Manchester University Press, 2002.

Pierce, Peter. *The Country of Lost Children: An Australian Anxiety.* Cambridge: Cambridge University Press, 1999.

Pierson, Ruth Roach. "Girlhood, Education and the Teenage Years." *No Easy Road: Women in Canada 1920s to 1960s.* Ed. Beth Light and Ruth Roach Pierson. Toronto: New Hogtown Press, 1990. 21–31.

Potter, Jane. *Boys in Khaki, Girls in Print: Women's Literary Responses to the Great War.* Oxford: Clarendon Press, 2005.

Potter, Simon J. "Communication and Integration: The British and Dominions Press and the British World, *c.*1876–1914." *The British World: Diaspora, Culture and Identity.* Ed. Carl Bridge and Kent Fedorowich. London: Frank Cass, 2003. 190–206.

– "Webs, Networks, and Systems: Globalization and the Mass Media in the Nineteenth- and Twentieth-Century British Empire." *The Journal of British Studies* 46.3 (2007): 621–46.

Potvin, Claude. *Le Canada français et sa littérature de jeunesse.* Moncton: Éditions CRP, 1981.

Pratt, Catherine. "Fictions of Development: Henry Handel Richardson's *The Getting of Wisdom.*" *Antipodes* 9.1 (1995): 3–9.

Price, Hugh. "Educational publishing." *Book and Print in New Zealand: A Guide to Print Culture in Aotearoa.* Ed. Penny Griffith, Ross Harvey, and Keith Maslen. Wellington: Victoria University Press, 1997. 144–6.

Probyn, Clive, and Bruce Steele. "Introduction." *The Getting of Wisdom.* Ed. Clive Probyn and Bruce Steele. St Lucia, QLD: University of Queensland Press, 2001. xxi–lv.

Pykett, Lyn. "Reading the Periodical Press: Text and Context." *Victorian Periodicals Review* 22.3 (1989): 100–8.

Reynolds, Kimberley. "Changing Families in Children's Fiction." *Cambridge Companion to Children's Literature.* Ed. M.O. Grenby and Andrea Immel. Cambridge: Cambridge University Press, 2009. 193–208.

– "'A Prostitution Alike of Matter and Spirit': Anti-War Discourses in Children's Literature and Childhood Culture before and during World War I." *Children's Literature in Education* 44 (2013): 120–39.

Richards, Jeffrey. *Imperialism and Juvenile Literature.* Manchester: Manchester University Press, 1989.

Richards, Thomas. *The Imperial Archive: Knowledge and the Fantasy of Empire.* London: Verso, 1993.

Rossiter, Richard. "The Return of Judy: Repression in Ethel Turner's Fiction." *Writing the Australian Child: Texts and Contexts in Fictions for Children.* Ed. Clare Bradford. Nedlands, WA: University of Western Australia Press, 1996. 55–75.

Rowbotham, Judith. *Good Girls Make Good Wives: Guidance for Girls in Victorian Fiction.* Oxford: Blackwell Publishing, 1989.

Rowse, Tim. "'Rooted in Demographic Reality': The Contribution of New World Censuses to Indigenous Survival." *History and Anthropology* 25.2 (2014): 246–62.

Rukavina, Alison. *The Development of the International Book Trade, 1870–1895: Tangled Networks.* New York: Palgrave Macmillan, 2010.

Sanders, Joe Sutliff. *Disciplining Girls: Understanding the Origins of the Classic Orphan Girl Story.* Baltimore: Johns Hopkins University Press, 2011.

Scutter, Heather. "Children's Literature." *A History of the Book in Australia, 1891–1945: A National Culture in a Colonised Market.* Ed. Martyn Lyons and John Arnold. St Lucia, QLD: University of Queensland Press, 2001. 298–309.

Sharpe, Jenny. *Allegories of Empire: The Figure of Woman in the Colonial Text.* Minneapolis: University of Minnesota Press, 1993.

Shepard, Paul. *English Reaction to the New Zealand Landscape before 1850.* Wellington: Department of Geography, Victoria University of Wellington, 1969.

Singley, Carol J. *Adopting America: Childhood, Kinship, and National Identity in Literature.* Oxford: Oxford University Press, 2011.

Smith, Michelle J. *Empire in British Girls' Literature and Culture: Imperial Girls, 1880–1915.* Houndmills, UK: Palgrave Macmillan, 2011.

Søland, Birgitte. *Becoming Modern: Young Women and the Reconstruction of Womanhood in the 1920s.* Princeton: Princeton University Press, 2000.

Stafford, Jane, and Mark Williams. "Fashioned Intimacies: Maoriland and Colonial Modernity." *The Journal of Commonwealth Literature* 37.1 (2002): 31–48.

Stephenson, Maxine. "Learning about Empire and the Imperial Education Conferences in the Early Twentieth Century: Creating Cohesion or Demonstrating Difference?" *History of Education Review* 39.2 (2010): 24–35.

Stoler, Ann Laura. *Carnal Knowledge and Imperial Power: Race and the Intimate in Colonial Rule.* Berkeley: University of California Press, 2002.

Stone, Michael. "Colonial and Post-Colonial Children's Literature: Australia." *Children's Literature: An Illustrated History.* Ed. Peter Hunt. Oxford and New York: Oxford University Press, 1995. 322–33.

Sutherland, Neil. "Popular Media in the Culture of English-Canadian Children in the Twentieth Century." *Historical Studies in Education* 14.1 (Spring 2002): 1–33.

Sykes, Gillian, "The New Woman in the New World: Evelyn Dickinson and a New Type of Australian Heroine." *Australian Studies* 16.1 (2001): 1–22.

Thiel, Elizabeth. *The Fantasy of Family: Nineteenth-Century Children's Literature and the Myth of the Domestic Ideal.* New York: Routledge, 2007.

Torney, Kim. *Babes in the Bush: The Making of an Australian Image.* Fremantle, WA: Curtin University Books, 2005.

Trainor, Luke. "Colonial Editions." *Books & Print in New Zealand: A Guide to Print Culture in Aotearoa.* Ed. Penny Griffith, Ross Harvey, and Keith Maslen. Wellington: Victoria University Press, 1997. 113–17.

Treagus, Mandy. *Empire Girls: The Colonial Heroine Comes of Age.* Adelaide: University of Adelaide Press, 2014.

Turner, Graeme. *National Fictions: Literature, Film and the Construction of Australian Narrative.* Sydney: Allen & Unwin, 1986.

Union List of Serials in New Zealand Libraries. Wellington: National Library Service, 1953.

Vance, Jonathan F. *Death So Noble: Memory, Meaning and the First World War.* Vancouver: University of British Columbia Press, 1997.

Walsh, Patrick. "Education and the 'Universalist' Idiom of Empire: Irish National School Books in Ireland and Ontario." *History of Education* 37.5 (2008): 645–60.

Wanhalla, Angela. "To 'Better the Breed of Men': Women and Eugenics in New Zealand, 1900–1935." *Women's History Review* 16.2 (2007): 163–82.

Ward, Stuart. "Imperial Identities Abroad." *The British Empire: Themes and Perspectives.* Ed. Sarah Stockwell. Malden, MA: Blackwell Publishing, 2009. 219–43.

Ware, Vron. *Beyond the Pale: White Women, Racism and History.* London: Verso, 1992.

Waterston, Elizabeth. *Children's Literature in Canada.* New York: Twayne Publishers, 1992.

– *Rapt in Plaid: Canadian Literature and Scottish Tradition.* Toronto: University of Toronto Press, 2001.

Weaver-Hightower, Rebecca. *Empire Islands: Castaways, Cannibals and Fantasies of Conquest.* Minneapolis: University of Minnesota Press, 2007.

Weinbaum, Alys Eve, Lynn M. Thomas, Priti Ramamurthy, Uta G. Poiger, Madeleine Yue Dong, and Tani E. Barlow. "The Modern Girl as Heuristic Device: Collaboration, Connective Comparison, Multidirectional Citation." *Modern Girl around the World: Consumption, Modernity, and Globalization.* Ed. Alys Eve Weinbaum et al. Durham, NC: Duke University Press, 2008. 1–24.

White, Richard, and Hsu-Ming Teo. "Popular Culture." *Australia's Empire.* Ed. Deryck Schreuder and Stuart Ward. Oxford: Oxford University Press, 2008. 336–62.

Wighton, Rosemary. *Early Australian Children's Literature.* Melbourne: Lansdowne Press, 1963.

Williams, Raymond. *The Country and the City.* New York: Oxford University Press, 1975.

Woollacott, Angela. *Gender and Empire.* Houndmills, UK: Palgrave Macmillan, 2006.

– *To Try Her Fortune in London: Australian Women, Colonialism and Modernity.* Oxford: Oxford University Press, 2001.

– "White Colonialism and Sexual Modernity: Australian Women in the Early Twentieth Century Metropolis." *Gender, Sexuality and Colonial Modernities.* Ed. Antoinette Burton. London: Routledge, 1999. 49–62.

Young, Robert J.C. *Colonial Desire: Hybridity in Theory, Culture and Race.* London: Routledge, 1995.

Index

www.ingramcontent.com/pod-product-compliance
Lightning Source LLC
LaVergne TN
LVHW040151080826
844660LV00014B/914/J

* 9 7 8 1 4 8 7 5 0 3 0 9 3 *